Convent Life in Colonial Mexico

UNIVERSITY PRESS OF FLORIDA

Florida A&M University, Tallahassee
Florida Atlantic University, Boca Raton
Florida Gulf Coast University, Ft. Myers
Florida International University, Miami
Florida State University, Tallahassee
New College of Florida, Sarasota
University of Central Florida, Orlando
University of Florida, Gainesville
University of North Florida, Jacksonville
University of South Florida, Tampa
University of West Florida, Pensacola

Convent Life in Colonial Mexico

A Tale of Two Communities

Stephanie L. Kirk

University Press of Florida
Gainesville Tallahassee Tampa Boca Raton
Pensacola Orlando Miami Jacksonville Ft. Myers Sarasota

Copyright 2007 by Stephanie L. Kirk
Printed in the United States of America on acid-free paper
All rights reserved

First cloth printing, 2007
First paperback printing, 2018

23 22 21 20 19 18   6 5 4 3 2 1

The publication of this book is made possible in part by a grant from the Program for Cultural Cooperation between Spain's Ministry of Education and Culture and United States Universities.

Library of Congress Cataloging-in-Publication Data
Kirk, Stephanie L.
Convent life in colonial Mexico : a tale of two communities / Stephanie L. Kirk.
p. cm.
Includes bibliographical references and index.
ISBN 978-0-8130-3030-2 (cloth: alk. paper)
ISBN 978-0-8130-6493-2 (pbk.)
1. Monastic and religious life of women—Mexico—History—17th century.
2. Mexico—Church history—17th century. 3. Monastic and religious life of women—Mexico—History—18th century. 4. Mexico—Church history—18th century. I. Title.
BX4220.M4K57 2007
271'.9007209032—DC22   2006023028

A version of chapter 3 appeared in *Latin American Literary Review* 33, no. 66 (July–December 2005).

The University Press of Florida is the scholarly publishing agency for the State University System of Florida, comprising Florida A&M University, Florida Atlantic University, Florida Gulf Coast University, Florida International University, Florida State University, New College of Florida, University of Central Florida, University of Florida, University of North Florida, University of South Florida, and University of West Florida.

University Press of Florida
15 Northwest 15th Street
Gainesville, FL 32611-2079
http://upress.ufl.edu

Contents

Preface vii

Acknowledgments ix

1. Introduction: A Tale of Two Communities 1

2. Death and the Maiden: Buried Alive in the New World Cloister 17

3. The Community of Lovers: *Mala amistad* in the Convent 51

4. Mobilizing Community: The Fight against *vida común* 81

5. Sor Juana, Serafina de Cristo, and the Nuns of the Casa del Placer: Intellectual Alliance and Learned Community 127

Conclusion 176

Appendix 181

Notes 189

Bibliography 223

Index 235

Preface

Convent Life in Colonial Mexico: A Tale of Two Communities analyzes how women formed and configured alliances, friendships, and communities within the colonial Mexican convent in defiance of the mechanisms employed by the Church to contain and control them. Foregrounding little-known texts, while drawing on a rich and diverse corpus that ranges from religious tracts and didactic manuals on convent behavior to historical artifacts (Inquisition documents, letters, sermons, official decrees) and literary texts (poetry and inspirational religious biographies of exemplary nuns), this book reconstructs in scrupulous but lively fashion the cultural and intellectual dynamics of female communities and alliances in the colonial Mexican convent in the seventeenth and eighteenth centuries. In counterpoint, the book examines the motivations that drove the Church's desire to regulate all aspects of convent life, as well as the discursive structures it employed to do so.

Close textual readings balance fresh theoretical perspectives from gender studies to address such important questions as the relationship between power and gender, female colonial agency and authorship, early modern subjectivity, and conflicting gender ideologies. Taking an important methodological turn away from other studies on early modern convent life that represent the nun as either a secular or religious writer, this interdisciplinary study, through analytical juxtaposition of discourse and practice, focuses on the nun as historical agent, elucidating the intricacies of female colonial subjectivity.

This book will interest not only those working in colonial Latin American and early modern studies, but also scholars engaging the broader issues of gender, sexuality, religion, and theories of community, power, and authority.

Acknowledgments

I owe thanks to many people who have helped me as this book has passed through its several incarnations. First, I am incredibly grateful to my advisor at NYU, Kathleen Ross, for her mentoring and continued words of wisdom. Who knew writing a dissertation could actually be a pleasant experience? The members of my committee—Marta Peixoto and Gigi Dopico-Black—were wonderful readers and teachers. I would also like to thank my NYU professors Sylvia Molloy and Gabriela Basterra for their support and inspiration.

At Washington University, I benefitted greatly from the advice and encouragement of my senior colleagues, and I am indebted to them for that. Margaret Chowning and Kathryn McKnight read the manuscript, offering different perspectives and suggestions that have made this an infinitely better book. Thanks, too, to the great staff at the University Press of Florida for making this all go so smoothly.

My friends scattered in different places—Nathalie Bouzaglo, Lena Burgos-Lafuente, Daniel Chávez, María Cisterna, Kevin Donnelly, Lila Heymann, Amy Kaufman, María Fernanda Lander, Tabea Linhard, Michael Maloy, and Margarita Muñoz—have been an amazing source of support.

Thanks to my family—my parents Max Carr and Marny Carr, and my brother Michael Carr—who are always close by despite the geographical distances.

Finally, I dedicate this book with all my love to Tony—you put up with a lot!

I

Introduction

A Tale of Two Communities

La mujer huyo a la soledad donde tenía un lugar preparado por Dios.
(The woman fled into solitude in the desert, where she had a place prepared for her by God.)

Revelation 12:6

On a trip to Mexico City several years ago, I came across a plaque tucked away in a dark corner of the Catedral Metropolitana. The plaque bore the above-cited epigram, which comes from the Book of Revelation. It refers to a woman who, after having done battle in heaven with a great red dragon with seven crowned heads and ten horns, gives birth to a male child. God then takes the child and places him on a throne, sending the woman away into the desert, to a site of solitude he has prepared for her. I am obviously glossing over a great deal of the context in which this quotation appears in the Book of Revelation. However, I am simply echoing the lack of context in which this exact phrase first came to my attention. The plaque, appearing as it does on the wall of the supreme symbol of the power of the Church in Mexico built at the height of its powers in the baroque period,[1] highlights the historical attitude of the Catholic Church toward women throughout the many centuries of its existence. It also perfectly exemplifies the attitude of the colonial Mexican Church to the nuns who were supposed to live by its rules in seventeenth- and eighteenth-century Mexico.

In this book, I argue that for the Mexican ecclesiastical authorities, the convent in the seventeenth and eighteenth centuries functioned as the special place, the ideal place, of solitude prepared by God for women. I have chosen to focus on these two centuries in particular because of the rich reserves of both printed matter and archival material I was able to uncover from this time period. Moreover, the seventeenth century with its still lingering post-Tridentine fervor was a time when the Church tightened its control of all aspects of religious life. The convents and their inhabitants came under intense scrutiny and vigilance as the ecclesiastical authorities worried about the implications of religious women's singularity. The eighteenth century is a contradictory time for the convents. Against a backdrop of political reform and Enlightenment ideals, the convents became places where some members of the Church hoped to perpetuate—often, ironically, in the name of reform—the misogynist ideals of Trent laid down two centuries before.

The Mexican colonial context derives, of course, from the Western Christian tradition, from which it inherited a complex series of gender ideologies and prejudices honed over the centuries since the very first years of the Early Church.[2] The idea of a place of solitude cut off from society had informed the initial desires to cloister female religious in the first few centuries of Christianity.[3] Cloister, initially adopted as "a means to an end" (Makowski 126) to protect all-female communities from marauding invaders, eventually developed in the Middle Ages into "an end in itself" (126). Enclosure became something gender based—and biased—that strove to protect society from women's carnality and, in turn, to protect weak-willed women from compromising their own virtue. Peter of Abelard (1079–1142) summed up the ideal of solitude in a letter to the Abbess Heloise: "Solitude [...] is all the more necessary for your woman's frailty, inasmuch as for our [men's] part we are less attacked by the conflicts of carnal temptations and less likely to stray toward bodily things through the senses" (qtd. in Makowski 31). In theory, the convent space provided the Church with the perfect site from which to keep women in solitude. This they believed served their purpose well: many women could be simultaneously withdrawn from society, as a result making vigilance more feasible.

Tracing the trajectory of the politics of cloister inherited by the Mexican convents, we see that until the thirteenth century, the enclosure of female communities had been a rather patchy and haphazard affair, entrusted to each specific order for enforcement. People entered and left the cloister freely. Many communities did not observe enclosure and were thus able to administer their own affairs and be involved in matters that required women to travel outside the convent. Despite the vigilance of the Church authorities, scholars of female monasticism agree that female houses enjoyed a period of relative autonomy up until the twelfth century (see Johnson; McNamara; Makowski). This was the period of the so-called double monastery in which female abbesses, wielding considerable power, often ruled over male houses as well. Obviously, we should not regard the early medieval period as fostering a proto-feminist utopia, but instead should view it in the context of the Church's embrace of a relative spiritual commonality (Johnson 3–5). However, dissenting voices warning against the dangers of women and power were always present, and by the middle years of the twelfth century, as Penelope Johnson points out, "a hostile backlash slammed the door on female monastic equality" (5). Many factors contributed to this change in climate for women in monastic orders beginning in this period. With the closure of the double monasteries, the exclusion of women from many male orders, the growth of the friar's movement in which men freely wandered the lands preaching, and the university clerical education to which only men had access, by the twelfth century the Church had begun to definitively marginalize women religious.

The Church worked hard to generate an ideology that would justify and sustain this subordination of women. They relied on what McNamara calls "complex myths of fragility, vulnerability, and incompetence" that would serve to disguise what she terms "the structural realities denying women self-sufficiency" (*Sisters* 261). One of the watershed moments in this generation and institutionalization of misogynistic mythmaking came in 1298 with the promulgation of the decree known as *Periculoso* by Pope Boniface VIII. *Periculoso*, so called after the first word in the Latin text, laid the cornerstone for the Church's suppression of relative female autonomy. The Pope found the notion of female religious who strayed from the convent walls, engaging in wandering or preaching, to be especially egregious. Obviously, it was more difficult to control and discipline women once flexibility of movement was permitted. *Periculoso* claimed to protect women from ill-intentioned men, but more significantly, from themselves. One has only to look at the first lines of the edict to realize the true impetus behind the decree: "Wishing to provide for the dangerous and abominable situation of certain nuns, who casting off the reins of respectability and impudently abandoning nunnish modesty and the natural bashfulness of their sex, sometimes rove about outside of their monasteries, to the injury of that to which by free choice they vowed their chastity, to the disgrace and dishonor of the religious life and the temptation of many ..." (qtd. in Makowski 133–35).[4]

The decree marked the beginning of the official establishment of gender differences between monks and nuns, with its mandate of cloister for women based solely on the weaknesses associated with their gender.[5] No similar legislation was enacted for the male houses (Makowski 3). Moreover, this gender bias stood in sharp contrast to Boniface's claim, and those of *Periculoso*'s subsequent commentators, of monastic spiritual equality between the sexes (125). This has been called the "paradox of *Periculoso*" (56). Church authorities were able to justify this enormous inconsistency by citing the singular relationship between women and chastity, what one could almost call an obsession with female sexual purity (127), that would extend far beyond *Periculoso* into the era of the Council of Trent, and into the post-Tridentine context of the colonial Mexican Church.

Scholars of female monasticism have noted, however, that chastity has often been a source of empowerment for nuns (Perry; McNamara). Since the very beginnings of the Christian Church, women in particular had been attracted by the freedom celibacy accorded them (McNamara, *Sisters* 47). However, as the institutionalization of the Church progressed throughout the centuries, men in power in the Church attempted to co-opt the concept of chastity, using it as a tool to enhance their own dominance while simultaneously controlling and subduing the authority of women. Moreover, men could abdicate from personal responsibility for chastity by projecting the female body as the site of purity and thus "the vessels of their [own] redemption" (49). As the influence of women waned in the Church, the symbolic value of their chastity took on more and more importance. The symbolism attached to female chastity became a mainstay of the Church's outlook. It was still firmly in existence in the periods of the seventeenth and eighteenth centuries in Mexico, where it became even more pressing in the New World context, as I shall go on to explore later in this book.

Beginning in the Middle Ages, the emblematic importance society attributed to chastity rendered it an inherently misogynist ideal that intended to essentialize the female body and cast it as the locus of society's redemption from sin.[6] Virginity under these terms could not be viewed in any way as liberating, as it effectively functioned as a "device for the virtual immobilization of women" (McNamara, *Sisters* 323). Enclosure, conceived of principally to protect women's chastity, was also a misogynist act as it denied women agency in the care and control of their own physical movements, thus necessitating the handing over of other responsibilities, among them economic, to men.[7] Women were not encouraged to cultivate manly qualities, but were instead redefined as the guardians of purity (321–22). The burden of the role of "guardian of purity" was a heavy one, and women in particular were doomed to failure from the outset. The Christian tradition, as the Mexican case I examine in this book will bear out, considered women to be the very incarnation of sin, while at the same time investing them with all the symbolism of purity in order to wipe away the sins of others (Glantz, "El cuerpo" 179–80; Burns 24). Woman's identity was based on her corporeality (Ibsen, "The Hiding Places" 261)—an ambivalent referent at best and one prone to conflictive interpretations. Thus, the idealization of women had its counterpart in the mistrust and denigration of women, as the

Church constantly struggled to make them fit into an unrealistic ideal of the Church's own making.

Boniface's decree created the "bedrock" (Makowski 127) of female religious enclosure, upon which the Church would build and obsessively rebuild. The Church constantly struggled to effectively enforce enclosure, as well as to control just how women lived their lives once shut away in the cloister. Formal enclosure, begun with *Periculoso*, was stringently revisited at the Council of Trent, where it was ratified in the final session on December 3, 1568. Female orders were to observe strict universal enclosure, both passive and active,[8] upon pain of punishment, according to the mandates laid out in Boniface XVIII's *Periculoso*:

> The holy council [. . .] commands all bishops that [. . .] they make it their special care that in all monasteries subject to them by their own authority and in others by the authority of the Apostolic See, the enclosure of nuns be restored wherever it has been violated and that it be preserved where it has not been violated: restraining with ecclesiastical censures and other penalties, every appeal being set aside, the disobedient and gainsayers, even summoning for this purpose, if need be, the aid of the secular arm. (qtd. in Schroeder, 220–21)

Women were forbidden to go out of their convent unless they had first gained episcopal permission. For McNamara, this ratification of what she calls the "hostile sentiments of fourteenth century popes" was a blow to any female autonomy gained through "bitter struggles" in the intervening centuries between *Periculoso* and its commentators,[9] and the ratification at Trent.[10]

The Council of Trent ushered in a period of masculinist reform of a Catholic Church under threat from the onslaught of Protestantism. The Church, on the offensive, became the Church militant, an organization in which there was to be no active role for women. The mandate of enclosure sums up the attitude to women that prevailed. They were both troublesome and not equipped to take on the mantle of this active and combative Church. The Counter-Reformation Church aimed to control the faithful and strengthened the male ecclesiastical hierarchy in order to do so. The primacy of the sacraments was to be the centerpiece of the Church's onslaught, and thus women were ruled out of active participation in consolidating the Catholic faith. Male religious orders formed during the Counter-Reformation—including the Jesuits, Oratorians, and Theatines—deliberately made ordination a requirement for admission, thus excluding women from their Christianizing projects (McNamara, *Sisters* 490). Male clergy often scorned women who wished to actively participate in the battle, condemning their devotion as "hysteria or even fraud" (490). Manifestations of ardent or militant religiosity were not to be valued unless sanctioned first by the ecclesiastical authorities, who took a poor view of anything that fell outside of their purview.

The Mexican convents, whose foundations coincided with the galvanization of the Counter-Reformation,[11] inherited the complex and prohibitive gender ideologies developed in the Western Christian tradition. These ideologies were then shaped and influenced by the cultural specificities of the New World context. The New World's first female convent—Nuestra Señora de la Concepción—was founded in Mexico City in 1540. By the 1580s, four new convents had been established in the viceregal capital. Of twenty-one convents to be founded in Mexico in the colonial period, eleven were founded between 1540 and 1601 (Holler 5). Scholars have commented on the symbolic importance held by convents of cloistered female religious in the colonization project of New Spain. For Elisa Sampson Vera Tudela, communities of enclosed elite white women represented proof of the "resounding civility of a society that could regulate its own reproduction so successfully that many of its women could be reserved in marriage for the Deity" (41). Moreover, prestige was at stake as the Mexican Church attempted to establish its position—not without a certain sense of urgency—in the "long-held tradition of female monasticism" (Holler 7). The New World context fed this desire to establish prestige. While its mission—vast territories populated by heathens ripe for conversion—gave it energy and dynamism, it also challenged the maintenance of long-held religious traditions. The establishment and population of the convents represented "a precocious patriotic desire to defend New Spain from all charges of inferiority by intervening in the issue of the New World's difference and the modes of infusing its representation with authority" (Sampson Vera Tudela 11).

These hostile circumstances and cultural exigencies put pressure on the authorities to ensure the control of the New World convent community. More than ever, the ecclesiastical authorities were faced with the desire to ensure the production and maintenance of female docile bodies in the special space of solitude God had prepared for women.[12] The gender bias traditionally displayed by the Church in its treatment of male and female monastics was heightened in the New World context. The relegation of women to a contemplative role (while many men were charged with an active mission), begun in the Middle Ages and heightened in the militant years of the Counter-Reformation, was carried over and intensified in colonial New Spain. The regular orders—initially the Franciscans, Augustinians, and Dominicans—were charged with the evangelization of the Indians in New Spain. The seventeenth and eighteenth centuries brought them as well the responsibilities of the education of the rising criollo population (and, of course, we see the rise to prominence of the Jesuits in this period). The "in the world" activity (Holler 20) of the male orders threw even more into relief the cloistering of women who were to be dead to the world.[13] Women were important to the colonial project, but it was an importance predicated on their stasis and immobilization.

Taking a *longue durée* look at the gender ideologies inherited by the Mexican convents, we find that the enclosure of female communities had never ceased to cause difficulties for the Church throughout its history. The results of its obsessive will to contain and control caused their own set of problems as enclosure brought together multiple female bodies without the normalizing and stabilizing effects of the male presence. The flip side of this fear was the eroticization of the convent space. The same isolation and separateness the Church needed to fulfill its wish to control and contain inspired a fascination and titillation in those who contemplated the phenomenon of the cloistered convent of women. Kate Chedgzoy has written: "Historically, the Catholic Church has been a place that empowers women in ways unavailable to them elsewhere in the culture, but which is at the same time profoundly invested in a nexus of problematic sexual ideologies" (64). The overarching emphasis on the control of the female body in didactic texts and conduct manuals that appear throughout the history of enclosed female monasticism foregrounded female corporeality, highlighting the dangerous sexual overtones that have always attended it. Moreover, as abundant examples from history attest, the border separating the body of the prostitute from the body of the nun was a traditionally unstable one. McNamara quotes the Carolingian convent reformers of the eleventh century who described many convents as *lupanaria* or brothels. As she says, these types of comments say more about the "male imagination" than they actually do about female behavior, with the enclosed nature of the convent space—like that of the brothel—provoking "thoughts of mysterious and forbidden women" on the part of the vivid imaginations of "enterprising men" (*Sisters* 372).

This fear of female community has been described as a fear of "contagion" (Auerbach 14). This disease imagery epitomizes the distrust the Church felt toward these communities of women. At the turn of the first century, Clement of Rome criticized female virgins who chose to come together in communal religious activities, dismissing these pious endeavors as "masks for idleness and unwarranted curiosity" (qtd. in McNamara, *Sisters* 41). In his text on female spirituality, *De virginibus*, Ambrose, Bishop of Milan and Doctor of the Church

(340–97), proclaimed that "women were not of the sex that lives in common" (qtd. in McNamara, *Sisters* 54). It was sentiments such as these that had inspired the Church to co-opt the female community in order to better control it, culminating in *Periculoso*. Yet, the Church never entirely succeeded in converting the enclosed convent community into its own creature. The convent continued to exist as an entity that constantly threatened to escape from its handlers. To this end, endless examples of recommendations and legislation aimed at better controlling how women actually lived their lives in convent communities populated the landscape of ecclesiastical history, both before and after Trent. This great quantity of prescriptive texts notwithstanding, there was a great deal of slippage between the *de jure* ideal community desired by the authorities and the *de facto* convent community as experienced and created by the women who inhabited it. The Church attempted to control every aspect of convent life, in the most excruciatingly minute detail. This same excruciating detail, however, coupled with the vast quantity of texts of this kind, serves only to reveal the anxiety brought about by the knowledge that, in effect, the female community always lay beyond the control of the authorities.

It is through this disjuncture between the idealized community of the authorities and the reality of the lived community of the convent inhabitants that I propose to show how Mexican nuns challenged the prescriptions the male ecclesiastic authorities laid down. By examining these acts of subversion, we can elucidate further the status of female religious in seventeenth- and eighteenth-century Mexico, simultaneously exposing weaknesses and anxieties in an ecclesiastical power structure that was deemed to be monolithic and all-encompassing. Reading archival material side by side with published literary works, I propose to uncover the lived experiences of women that belie the rigid controls male clerics mandated in their prescriptive texts. In her study of nuns in medieval France, Penelope Johnson has underscored the importance of just such a technique in order to elucidate the world as it was and not as it should be (7). She draws a distinction between what she calls "documents of practice," which indicate the lived reality of women in the convent, and "documents of theory," which she classifies as the array of prescriptive treatises and theological tracts that "reveal what church leaders thought the world should be, in contrast to what it was" (7).

Despite this important distinction, it is essential to remember that even documents of practice do not always give us complete access to how women experienced the world. A complexity of registers and polyphony of voices often mediated and characterized even these types of documents. One must weigh the overreaching discursive power of men in positions of authority against the silencing of women, who had no access to the authority that conferred this kind of discursive power (Perry 9–11). In order to get at the lived reality of women, one must often read between the lines—not only of the official reports and treatises, but also of those texts that are written in their own words. It is imperative to read all texts with the knowledge that they have most always been "filtered through the reporting of those at the center of power" (9). It cannot be assumed that, although women may have spoken the words on the page or even written them with their own hand, other, more powerful voices have not intruded into the text.[14]

We must always value the importance of the subtext when reading historical documents concerning women's history. I believe we can decode this subtext through a careful reading that involves the recognition of the historical context, together with the employment of a gender critique that elaborates a different reading strategy that will call into question issues of agency. I use a gender studies critique to question the "transparency of facts" (Scott 1066), opening up the possibility for human agency and disproving the position that these texts were written in a vacuum in which negation, resistance, and reinterpretation played no part (1066). This gendered critique cannot be carried out successfully, however, without a close reading of texts that also display the motivations of men as they attempt to control women's behavior. An elucidation of patriarchal discourses aimed at women as subjects of control will help us go beyond "truncating binary paradigms" (Powers 19) in which women are often posited as victims and men as the perpetrators of their oppression.

Despite this unequal balance of power, the enclosed convent did possess value for women. Many scholars of female monasticism (see, for example, McNamara; Perry; Arenal and Schlau) have highlighted the ways that cloistering could empower its inhabitants. McNamara cites the case of Teresa of Ávila, who envisioned the cloistered convent space as the perfect "staging ground" for her missionary vocation:

> The more strictly her nuns could fortify themselves behind their walls, the more effectively they could send their spirits soaring to heaven or out across the globe. Enclosure and silence, discipline and mental prayer were intended to train the nun as a militant participant in the Christianizing mission. (*Sisters* 515)

These same critics have also cited the greater opportunities women had for education in the convent, both in the Hispanic tradition and elsewhere, although as I have shown, the Church had severely curtailed these by the Middle Ages. These greater opportunities notwithstanding, it is not my intention to portray the convent as a utopian feminist space where nuns lived side by side in perfect harmony. First of all, the idea of a feminist consciousness as it is understood in our twenty-first-century context would, of course, be completely anachronistic. While not completely discounting any of these claims, I argue that it was the existence of a community that women reconfigured on their terms that gave these nuns the opportunities these critics outline. It is my contention that women in convents mobilized themselves into alliances and communities, formed on their own terms, to engage with patriarchal controls and thus reshape their experience of community in a multitude of ways.

Another caveat is essential here. We must be wary of the tendency to both essentialize and idealize female communities of the historical past, remaining cognizant of the exclusionary tactics often practiced in these communities (D'Monté and Pohl 6). Scholars must resist the temptation to "strongly and blindly believe in the viability and political rectitude of all-female space" (6). Archival work has shown that communities of female religious did not always live peaceably; tales of discord, factionalism, and even violence have emerged through historical investigation. Convent communities in colonial seventeenth- and eighteenth-century Mexico were highly hierarchical and stratified in terms of race and class.[15] The issues of race and class operational within the convent walls could often mirror those in the *siglo*—the outside world. Nuns of the black veil, the highest rank one could attain, were almost always elite white women. Moreover, white women in the cloister had servants who were most often not white and not of their class, and in addition they often possessed slaves. Discord and disparity existed at all levels. However, one must consider this discord in the context in which it took place and in which it has been reported. Community disharmony was not exclusive to the female gender, an oft-portrayed stereotype. Male religious were as prone to conflict and internecine strife as were their female counterparts. As Penelope Johnson has written, the structure of monastic life was based on the family model, and so, as in many families, conflict was inevitable in both male and female communities:

> The erosion of family community occurred in houses of both religious men and religious women, so quarreling and violence do not seem to have been specifically gender linked. Rather, people who lived close together in the cloister might care a great deal about other members of the community, but also nurse resentments exaggerated by lack of privacy. Fam-

ily members resent and compete with each other as well as loving one another. (250)

The way these instances of discord among female religious have captured the popular imagination throughout history, as well as the critics' pens, shows again a clear prejudice against women. This image of conflict in the convent community belongs to a more general gender bias that casts alliance between women as something impossible due to their conflictive natures and their desire to win the approval of masculine society at the expense of other women. Compared to a vast corpus of scholarship on male friendship and alliance, almost nothing exists on similar relationships between women, and where we find such information, it is often cast in the light of aberration or exception to the rule:

> Men's alliances, formalized in such institutions as the guild, government, law, church and university, left behind records, architecture, and literature that have invited generations of scholars to codify them. As a result, entire libraries are filled with books analyzing men's connections. The relations among women [. . .] have proved not only less visible but also more difficult to reconstruct, often because women did not formally record their activities or seek memorialization in material structures. (Frye and Robertson 3)

Moreover, men—who controlled access to official discourses—were not all that keen to acknowledge female alliances and other manifestations of community, let alone memorialize them in formal written records.

Silencing tactics were used to control the writing of autobiography and hagiography by and about nuns. These life writings of "exemplary" women emphasize the virtue of solitude and often depict the subject as the victim of ill-treatment at the hands of other members of the community, who are never individualized but rather appear as an "anonymous mass of persecutors" (Ibsen, *Women's Spiritual Autobiography* 72). The intrinsic worth of solitude is further emphasized by the fact that hagiographers often choose to define the worth of their subject based on the mortification to which she would submit her body (73). Ibsen highlights what she calls the "specific historical context of documents written in Colonial Spanish America" to understand why these ecclesiastical biographers "emphasize the lives of women more attuned to bodily mortification than political authority in the convent" (74). Women were only to achieve political authority under the strict supervision of the (male) Church hierarchy. True, abbesses did wield power over the members of their communities, but in their historical period and sociocultural context that power, more symbolic than real, favored the authorities over the convent community of whom the abbess was "mother."[16] Even so, if we read beyond the official discourse, which sought to promote conflict and circumscribe agency, we can find examples of female alliance and positive representations of female community that challenge the view of community the Church authorities constructed. There is, then, what I call a "double discourse" of community. In this book I analyze this double discourse as manifested in the discursive strategies the Church employed to control community. In counterpoint, I study the acts by and between women that go against that imposition of community and strive to redefine it.

An important point to discuss before I go any further is what the word "community" actually means. We always use it to refer to the group of nuns who inhabited a particular convent. Yet, what are we really saying when we use "community" in this context? There are indeed many variables and contexts at play in the definition of the word (D'Monté and Pohl 3–4). Community carries with it the connotation of a safe haven, a place to which one can retreat voluntarily—in times of trouble, perhaps (Bauman 32). However, we also use the word to refer to those groups who are constrained and disciplined in the way they live their common lives, such as schools and prisons. Indeed, the convent space has always borne striking similarities to the prison space, and the Mexican cloistered communities of the seventeenth and eighteenth centuries were no exception. Although membership was in most cases (but not always) voluntary, those external to the community mediated and controlled life within it. The Church authorities operated a panoptic regime over the female houses (if not architecturally, most definitely symbolically), with a network of confessors and priests all conducting surveillance and reporting their findings to the relevant authorities—a perfect example of Foucault's theorizing of the capillaries of power.

In what sense can we consider a coerced community, such as the one I have outlined above, to be a "community"? Once again I come back to the question of what do we mean when we use this term; what are we trying to articulate? I believe a coerced community—such as that which the Church authorities attempted to impose—is not a community at all, as it lacks the element of voluntariness. We cannot consider the "communal life" the Church authorities desired as a true community, since it was legislated from outside, by those who were not its members. The ecclesiastic authorities desired a community in which sameness and a shared (non)identity were operational. In her theorizing of community, Shane Phelan has described this type of fixing of identity as a "form of oppression" (245), in which identities are consolidated and reified, thus allowing no room for agency on the part of a community's members. Phelan has drawn the distinction between what she calls "a voluntarist conception of community and a use of that conception to distinguish stigmatized, externally imposed identities from valorized, self-fashioned ones" (237). The "externally imposed community" attempts to insert its members into a "reified concept that pre-exists its members" (239). Yet this cannot be considered as a community, for community is by definition dynamic and changing, its identity constituted by those who inhabit it and not vice versa. Although community does give its members a sense of mutuality and shared bonds (236) it does not erase individuality or essentialize identities. Phelan cites Jean-Luc Nancy's definition of "being-in-common" (as developed in his *The Inoperative Community*), and it is useful here for the definition of community I propose. For Nancy, this concept signals a group of individuals who, while they may share certain commonalities, still remain singular beings. He writes: "Being in common means that singular beings are present themselves and appear only to the extent they compear (*comparaissent*), to the extent that they are exposed, presented, or offered to one another" (Nancy 58).[17]

It is this definition of community that women in the convent ascribed to as they formed bonds, alliances, friendships, and micro- and macro-communities of different kinds that stood in opposition to the controlled community that the Church authorities attempted to impose from outside. Theoretically, this outwardly imposed community, with its all-encompassing panoptic gaze, negated the need for agency and action on the part of nuns and other women in the convent. As prescriptive and didactic texts of the period claimed, these women were "muertas al mundo" (dead to the world) and ideally—as this book will show—dead to each other, their only sanctioned relationships being with their divine husband and his earthly intermediary, the confessor. In furtherance of this goal, these women were not to be individuals, were not to display any singularity in their behavior; instead they were to be an amorphous mass of docile bodies who lived according to the strict rules the ecclesiastical hierarchy laid down.

Women challenged the autonomy of the ecclesiastic authorities by forming counter-communities in acts of solidarity that allied individuals. Hannah Arendt's theorizing of the attainment of power through collective action sheds light on the construction of female solidarity. Community is not attained through a fixed shared identity, but instead is realized through collective action. In her analysis of Arendt's theory, Amy Allen writes:

> Hannah Arendt provides feminists with the resources necessary for reformulating solidarity as a kind of power that emerges out of concerted action—as something that is achieved through action in concert, rather than as the sister-feeling that automatically results from the sharing of a pre-given, fixed, and hence repressive, identity. (104)

Allen here reads Arendt's work in order to analyze conceptions of power through the lens of feminist theory. Her ultimate goal is to overturn the "multiple axes of stratification affecting women in contemporary Western societies" (2). Her argument, I believe, can also be used to elucidate the situation of colonial Mexican nuns. Joan Scott's insistence on the importance of using gender theory to study historical uses of power supports my point. She advocates the use of theory as a way to dismantle and challenge what she calls "the fixed and permanent quality of the binary opposition" and calls for "a genuine historicization and deconstruction of the terms of sexual difference" (1065).

Both Allen and Scott challenge the traditional view of the monolithic nature of patriarchal power in which the existence of female agency was always obscured or denied. Scott claims: "We need to replace the notion that social power is unified, coherent and centralized with something like Foucault's conception of power as dispersed constellations of unequal relationships discursively constructed in social 'fields of force'" (1067). By seeing power as constructed in these social fields of force, writes Scott, we can also see the possibility of human agency challenging and dislocating this discourse of power. She describes this seizure of agency as "the attempt [. . .] to construct an identity, a life, a set of relationships, a society with certain limits and with language—that at once sets boundaries and contains the possibility for negation, resistance, reinterpretation, the play of metaphoric invention and imagination" (1067).

In this book, I analyze both the "certain limits" and the language "that sets boundaries" alongside these possibilities for "negation" and "resistance." I scrutinize the discursive structures the Church utilized to contrive their fields of force and to contain and control convent communities. In counterpoint to this, I also examine how women in the convent constructed communities, alliances, and friendships within these fields of force to both challenge them and reformulate them. It is my belief that the two opposing views exist in mutual tension, each one constructing itself in response to the other. While many studies of convent culture in the colonial period have focused on individuals or nuns as writers of spiritual *vidas* (lives, or autobiographies), here I analyze how women form alliances, friendships, and communities within the convent, engaging with and subverting the view of community the authorities held, in which they desired its inhabitants to be "muertas al mundo."

In chapter 2, "Death and the Maiden: Buried Alive in the New World Cloister," I consider two texts written by Antonio Núñez de Miranda, the Mexican Jesuit priest and erstwhile confessor of Sor Juana Inés de la Cruz. He was exceptionally interested in the control of the convent space, and in two of his tracts—the *Plática doctrinal que hizo el Padre Núñez de la Compañía de Jesús en la Profesión de una Religiosa del Monasterio de San Lorenzo* (printed in 1697) and the *Cartilla de la doctrina religiosa dispuesta por uno de la Compañía de Jesús para dos niñas hijas espirituales suyas, que se crían para monjas y desean serlo con toda perfección* (printed in 1698)—he specifies the exact nature of convent living.[18] The two texts are very different in tone, using different registers and strategies to accomplish the same ambition: the discursive control and choreography of every aspect of a nun's life in the convent. Through a close reading of these didactic treatises, I trace the elements of the colonial Mexican Church's construction of the ideal convent community, examining its methods and motivations.

Chapter 3, "The Community of Lovers: *Mala amistad* in the Convent," examines a case from the eighteenth-century Mexican Inquisition of a nun accused of a *mala amistad* (an illicit relationship) with a servant girl. In this chapter, I explore literary and didactic materials concerning "particular" (a euphemism for aberrant) friendships between women in the convent. Through this analysis, I show how a double discourse hides the fear of homoerotic contact between women behind prohibitions against factionalism and lack of rigor in religious observance. The chapter also examines how the Inquisition forged a connection between illness and female homoerotic relationships, using this somatic correlation to further discredit the nun. I also study the importance of the role of the confessor in this process of censure. It is, of course, the perspective of the ecclesiastic authorities that emerges owing to its control of information via record keeping. Yet, reading through the rhetoric of disapproval and manipulation, one can trace the vestiges of a relationship between the two women, grounded in a passionate attachment that challenged the carefully controlled community the authorities wished to impose.

In chapter 4, "Mobilizing Community: The Fight against *vida común*," I also study historical documents from eighteenth-century Mexico, in which I analyze the ecclesiastical and secular authorities' attempts to reconfigure convent communities to better fit the paradigms of male control through the imposition of the so-called *vida común*—the Church's imposition of communal life on convents that had hitherto enjoyed private living conditions. Using documents from the same period, I also study the political mobilization of communities and micro-communities of nuns in protest against this reconfiguration of their communities. This case study affords me the opportunity to analyze the different perceptions of community that existed across the gender divide.

Chapter 5, "Sor Juana, Serafina, and the Nuns of the Casa del Placer: Intellectual Alliance and Learned Community," looks at how women formed intellectual alliances and communities in the convent in defiance of the Church's proscription of this kind of activity. The chapter takes Sor Juana as its protagonist, discussing her participation in two different female alliances. This is a reading that goes against the popularly held critical belief in her intense solitude. I examine the seventeenth-century *Carta de Serafina de Cristo* (*Letter of Serafina de Cristo*) to show how women wielded the pen in support of each other and the *Enigmas ofrecidos a la Casa del Placer* (*Enigmas Offered to the House of Pleasure*) to explore the creation of a virtual community by Sor Juana and a group of Portuguese nuns, from which the women wrote safely for and to each other.

These conflicting views of community expose a double discourse in which solidarity among women, in its varying forms, is pitted against the concept of indistinguishable docile bodies living in communal solitude. Through these acts of community, alliance, and friendship, nuns challenged the desires of the Church to control every aspect of their convent lives. Though not always ultimately successful, they did force the ecclesiastical authorities into a defensive position in which their anxiety regarding the control of the convent communities clearly emerges. It is, I believe, important to draw attention to this slippage between the intent of gendered processes of control and the reality of women's responses to them. An examination of these subversions and dislocations of patriarchal control encourages us to look beyond the historically and socially created vulnerabilities of women in the convent in seventeenth- and eighteenth-century Mexico to elucidate their role in both their communities and in the social order as historical actors and protagonists in colonial Mexican society.

2

Death and the Maiden
Buried Alive in the New World Cloister

As the Church moved into the New World, it brought along its centuries-old patriarchal and misogynist philosophy. The convent, moreover, took on an added importance for the Church in this new environment, intensifying the ecclesiastical authorities' desire to enclose and control its inhabitants. Asunción Lavrin describes the function of the New World cloister in the following terms:

> Un convento era un lugar de refugio y protección para mujeres cuyo nacimiento en la elite colonial no había sido acompañado de suficiente riqueza familiar para protegerla de un matrimonio desigual. La mujer, representada en todos los textos pedagógicos y forenses como un ser débil y sujeto a toda clase de peligros, necesitaba "recogerse" si no en su propio hogar, en una institución dedicada a ese fin. ("La celda" 143)[1]

Convents became sources of civic pride—the ultimate in enclosed spaces—as the New World Church strove to compete with its counterpart in the metropolis (Lavrin, "La celda" 153). Elisa Sampson Vera Tudela has described the New World convent as "a fortress for [white, Spanish] cultural values" (40). It also served another symbolic purpose: a community of virgins wiped away both past and future sins of those that lived *extramuros* (outside the walls) at least in the male imagination. This symbolism held no power for women and was as much an essentializing gesture as the depiction of them as creatures of unstable morality. Margo Glantz has written:

> El convento opera como un mecanismo de sustitución: las religiosas, seres débiles, inocentes, practicantes de las virtudes teologales—son caritativas y humildes, obedientes, castas, abnegadas—ejercen en su contra un suplicio corporal para ayudar a borrar los pecados del mundo. ("El cuerpo" 178)[2]

These women were to be offered up, devoid of agency, like the virgins of old in order to satiate a God angry at the sins of those who were allowed to sin, safe in the knowledge that someone else would pay the price. Glantz refers to the nuns as "chivos expiatorios" (scapegoats) ("El cuerpo" 179). Female religious were thus deemed not to be in possession of their own bodies, because society wanted them for a different purpose. This appropriation was, however, an enterprise fraught with danger owing to the corruptible nature of the flesh of she who was to be the vessel of purification. There existed a tremendous irony in the fact that the very image of sin was to be the upholder of purity.

For the ecclesiastical and civic authorities, the perfect community was one in which they controlled and regulated each member's every movement, gesture, and word (Moraña, *Mujer y cultura* 7–8). The convent space resembled a highly symbolic labyrinth in which women had to negotiate a complex web of discourse and discipline that governed their behavior. In such a rigidly controlled atmosphere, the Church viewed women as transgressive from the outset; only by strict adherence to the rules could they meet the standard of acceptable female behavior. Regulatory texts such as convent *costumbreros* (handbooks)—of which men were always the authors—dictated a model of female behavior in which women were to obey the ideals of obedience, chastity, humility, poverty, and enclosure, denying the body at the expense of the spirit. To this end, the authorities subjected the body of the nun to myriad forms of manipulation and control mechanisms that they "textually codified in confession manuals and the rules and constitutions of each religious order" (Ibsen, "The Hiding Places" 251). While male orders were of course subject to control, with the regulations for each laid down in their governing institutions, their situation was a very different one. As I discussed in the previous chapter, men's mission in the New World was an active, apostolic one. Male religious did have responsibilities in their monastery—study, choir, and prayer, for example—but they also had something women did not have: freedom to leave the monastery. Many positions outside the monastery were open to male religious—both ecclesiastic and academic. All these positions entailed them moving around the city or town where they lived. Many of these jobs also brought with them exoneration from the more contemplative and monastery-bound aspects of their vocation (Rubial, "Varones en comunidad" 170). Moreover, the monasteries were open to visitors—both religious and secular (except, of course, women)—and were often the scene of lively secular activities such as banquets, theatrical productions, *tertulias* (social or literary gatherings), and card games. Free time was seemingly ample—an excess of personnel led to what Antonio Rubial terms "poca labor ministerial," or few ministerial responsibilities (173). Outside the monastery, some monks would engage in unbecoming activities such as visiting prostitutes, gambling, and walking armed around the city (175). Prohibitions, of course, existed against such activities, but the fact that they were even possible underscores the enormous gulf between life in community for religious men and for religious women. There was so much more at stake in the regulation of the overdetermined, enclosed female space of the convent than in the male monastery.

It stands to reason, then, that so many more prescriptive texts existed for women than for men. The control of discourse belonged squarely in the masculine purview, and religious rhetoric was no exception. Women figured in the discursive realm only in the abstract—either as essentialized visions of purity in the usually male-authored hagiographies or as objects for instruction, discipline, and control (Ibsen, *Women's Spiritual Autobiography* 12). Mabel Moraña describes the ecclesiastical authorities' strategy in the following terms:

> La sumisión del cuerpo al espíritu es constantemente enfatizada y simbolizada a través de la gestualidad individual y de las actividades prescritas a todos los que integran la familia conventual. El papel del confesor, el régimen de castigos y de penitencias, así como la consistente obligación de negar el yo sometiéndolo por medios de la represión doctrinaria y la autocensura son aspectos insoslayables de la vida religiosa, que contribuyen a explicar los términos en los que va formalizándose el imaginario eclesiástico-letrado en la Colonia como expresión y trasgresión de una subalternidad planificada hasta en sus más mínimos detalles en beneficio del Poder. (*Mujer y cultura* 13)[3]

The Church wanted to create a controlled community of female religious in which they could erase the female body—along with any attendant singularity—as far as possible. In its place, they envisioned a body without agency that would carry out a series of highly-controlled movements. They intended to transform the convent space into a disciplinary institution inhabited by a community of docile bodies. Moraña refers to this vision of the convent space as "un recinto panóptico controlado por el dogma y la autoridad masculina" (a panoptic enclosure controlled by dogma and male authority) (*Mujer y cultura* 14). Sherrill Cohen has studied the creation and function of women's asylums since 1500. She writes that Western patriarchal society itself has historically functioned as a "panoptic regime" in which females are "watched, measured, judged and corrected when they deviate from prescriptions" (6). The New World cloister represents an ideal exemplum of this model, in which the Church discursively accounted for and controlled every aspect of the nuns' behavior.

One of the most renowned, prolific, and fervently obsessed of these ecclesiastical writers was the Jesuit priest Antonio Núñez de Miranda. He is best known today as Sor Juana Inés de la Cruz's confessor, with whom she enjoyed an antagonistic relationship. In his day he was a powerful member of the Church, head of the influential Congregación de la Purísima, *calificador* (inspector) of the Inquisition, and distinguished even among the ranks of the Jesuits as a great intellect and scholar (Muriel 72). He authored twenty-nine works between the years 1664 and 1712, of which he addressed eleven directly or indirectly to nuns (74). Octavio Paz glibly claims "su especialidad eran las monjas" (nuns were his specialty) (148). Josefina Muriel describes the purpose behind the large number of texts Núñez dedicated to this one subject:

> Sus obras tienen como propósito moverlas a vivir la vida religiosa que habían profesado de acuerdo con el contenido de los votos, haciendo hincapié en lo que le constaba que era violado con más frecuencia y que producían relajación en la vida conventual en perjuicio aun de las monjas más observantes. (74)[4]

In my view, Muriel underestimates the purpose and tone of these texts. A close reading reveals them as highly structured discourses of power that attempt to intimidate the nuns into observing a communal life that fits with the wishes of the Church, one in which docile bodies live side by side, ostensibly living and working in community but ordered to prize solitude as the ultimate manifestation of righteousness.

Núñez writes with what has been termed "el gusto barroco por el tremendismo" (the baroque taste for the shocking) (Bravo, "La excepción" 264) as he attempts to manipulate and control the behavior of the nuns who constitute his audience. In this chapter, I analyze two of Núñez's texts: the *Cartilla de la doctrina religiosa dispuesta por uno de la Compañía de Jesús para dos niñas hijas espirituales suyas, que se crían para monjas y desean serlo con toda perfección* (printed in 1698) and the *Plática doctrinal que hizo el Padre Núñez de la Compañía de Jesús en la Profesión de una Religiosa del Monasterio de San Lorenzo* (printed in 1697).[5] Because the texts vary sharply in both genre and tone, they make an excellent comparative study of the author's range and abilities. These particular texts also expose the anxiety provoked by the convent space, as we see the lengths to which the writer is prepared to go to find the expressive model that best conveys his message of dominance. However, despite the differences, Núñez's purpose is the same in both texts: to manipulate and control the behavior of the nuns, who are literally a captive audience, and to ensure that the life of the community conforms to the exact specifications of the Church.

The *Cartilla de la doctrina religiosa*

In the first of Núñez de Miranda's texts that I explore in this chapter, he assumes the benevolently exasperated tone of a paterfamilias gently nudging his daughters onto the right path in order to help them better fulfill their religious vocations. He structures the *Cartilla* in the form of an imaginary dialogue between himself, in his role as spiritual advisor and confessor, and two novices of an unnamed convent who have purportedly spent their young lives there being educated by the nuns. Now they themselves want to take the veil. The text assumes the form of an always supercilious, occasionally playful dialogue between the priest and his two spiritual daughters. Núñez divides it into various sections; with each one, he takes the opportunity to expound in great detail on the responsibility of a cloistered nun, clearly establishing his and the Church's vision of community in which a clear-cut gendered binary of power appears. Núñez's pseudodialogue leaves nothing to chance, nor any room for interpretation. He dedicates the first section of the text to what exactly it means to be a nun. Thereafter, he explains the four vows a nun must take to profess: poverty, chastity, obedience, and enclosure. Subsequently, he touches on various topics, including which acts may lead to "pecado mortal," how to adhere exactly to the timetable of prayer during each day, how to vote correctly in the elections of the convent *preladas* (female superiors), as well as how to best obey one's confessor. Núñez finishes the *Cartilla* expounding on how to become the perfect bride of Christ, repeating and embellishing many of the points he has already made in previous sections so as to remove any possible ambiguity from what he has communicated to his "interlocutors."

Núñez's textual assumption of the voices of the young novices is an integral tool in his war of words. It affords him the opportunity to engage in a power play in which he, as official representative of the Church, emerges as the voice of reason and knowledge guiding the formless, ignorant minds of the novices. This gendered act of ventriloquized speech mediates the responses of the others. It creates the ideal nun, the docile body par excellence—one who responds perfectly to the requirements of the Church authorities because she has no will of her own. By fashioning the voices of the novices in the dialogue, Núñez inscribes them into a binary that highlights the power of the male voice and its superior discursive position (Parker and Willhardt 202). Núñez's hagiographer, Juan de Oviedo, praises him for the way he expresses his ideas in this text:

> Dio a la estampa un cuadernillo con título de *Cartilla de la doctrina religiosa*, en que por modo de diálogo de preguntas, y respuestas, allana con admirable método, claridad y brevedad, quántos tropiezos de dificultad se les pueden ofrecer a las Religiosas [. . .] sin el embarazo de sentencias y de citas y con grande claridad y suavidad en el estilo. (qtd. in Alatorre, "La carta de Sor Juana" 612)[6]

Employing and repeating words and expressions such as "claridad," "brevedad," and "suavidad en el estilo," Oviedo presents the dialogue as a transparent vehicle for the communication of simple information for neophyte nuns on how to avoid the possible pitfalls of convent life. However, there is nothing natural or transparent about the invention of the fictitious interlocutors of whom Núñez avails himself in the creation of his fake dialogue. Elizabeth Harvey has analyzed similar discursive maneuvers—male appropriations of the feminine voice—in English texts of the early modern period. She terms this tactic "transvestite ventriloquism" (1). The male-authored texts she studies in her book *Ventriloquized Voices: Feminist Theory and English Renaissance Texts* all employ a female voice—often, in the process, erasing the gender of the author, at least superficially (1). Even though Núñez in no way erases his gender in the *Cartilla*, the analysis that Harvey brings to these texts is most definitely applicable to the use of transvestite ventriloquism he employs in his invention of the young female interlocutors.

The Jesuit organizes the conversation along gender lines and in turn structures these along power lines, with the male voice—his voice—unequivocally occupying the seat of power. The ventriloquized voices of the novices function as a springboard from which Núñez launches his power play. He establishes a subordinate locus of enunciation for the novices in relation to his own, thus underscoring the Church's construction of gender roles as being at opposite ends of the spectrum in terms of power and agency (Harvey 32). As a dialogue, Núñez's text is particularly effective in displaying these unequal power relations. In the very first few lines, he clearly sets out the rules: he is in charge; he is the keeper and dispenser of knowledge. The "novices," in turn, embody the very blankest of blank slates—lacking even their own desires—upon which he will project his vision of convent life and convent community. The novices ask him in the opening lines of the *Cartilla*: "Padre amantísimo [. . .] dínos ahora las obligaciones de su altísimo estado, y enséñanos el modo de cumplirlas, suave y eficazmente; y en primer lugar muéstranos ¿para qué fin, y con qué intención, *hemos de desear y procurar ser monjas?*" (1, emphasis mine).⁷ These first lines establish the tone of this text in which the young women must appeal to Núñez's wisdom to even understand their own wishes. The personalities, or lack thereof, of the novices (dis)embody the perfect nun who seeks information and accepts answers. Continuing in this vein, the interlocutors are not identifiable as individuals. They always speak in chorus, and we have no idea of their names (Núñez refers to them only as "hijas mías") (my daughters). The textual reproduction of femininity that occurs in the *Cartilla* firmly establishes the goals of the ecclesiastical authorities for the convent communities. They want to create and maintain a gender-based hierarchy, as well as foster a lack of both personality and singularity on the part of the inhabitants of the convents, which in turn would lead to an unquestioning acceptance of all rules the Church laid down.

While there is no doubt that Núñez's act of cross-gendering perpetuates an inequity with its mediation of women's speech (Parker and Willhardt 194), this very act also serves to expose the fear the specter of uncontrolled female utterances provokes, underscoring the patriarchal establishment's anxiety about the stability of gender roles. Harvey explains: "In male appropriations of feminine voices we can see what is most desired and most feared about women and why male authors might have wished to occupy that cultural space, however contingently and provisionally" (32). Moreover, as I go on to examine, this assumption of the female voice and creation of a female (non)personality illustrates the "separation between male representation and female experience" (Trill 35). In the chapters to follow, I show how women's lives in convent communities did not conform to the rigid standards clergy such as Núñez de Miranda laid down in their didactic texts.

After seeking information about what they should desire, the novices then ask Núñez how to achieve it: "¿Y qué entenderémos por ser monjas, o qué es serlo?" (And what should we understand by being nuns, or what does it mean to be one?) (2), thus offering Núñez a tabula rasa from which he can begin his ideological warfare. The principal element of Núñez's ideology, a distinguishing feature of both of the texts I analyze in this chapter, is the importance of the complete denial of self, mind, and body, which he refers to as "holocausto"—the offering of the body in sacrifice. In his list of what they must sacrifice to God in this holy immolation, Núñez leaves nothing to the imagination. The nun must basically obliterate her very being in order to give herself freely to God. When the novices ask for clarification, he responds, making use of a fire-and-brimstone rhetoric popular in the baroque Church: "Que es un sacrificarse a Dios toda entera una virgen, con todo su cuerpo, alma, potencias, sentidos, haberes y quereres, sin reservar cosa alguna de sí para sí, ni para el mundo, ni carne ni sangre; sino que todas las sacrifica a Dios en el fuego sagrado de su caridad" (3).[8]

Margo Glantz offers the following analysis of the concept of *holocausto* and its relation to the trope of the sacrifice of the female body in early modern Mexico:

> Son vírgenes ofrecidas en holocausto, como en la Antigüedad, semejantes a las víctimas sacrificiales inmoladas por un sacerdote durante una ceremonia ritual. Es más, su cuerpo mismo se transforma en un espacio sagrado, cuando al suplicarse se constituyen de manera simultánea en altar, víctimas y sacerdotes, es decir concentran en su corporeidad todos los elementos del sacrificio y de la víctima propiciatoria. ("El cuerpo" 178–79)[9]

When the novices inquire just how they can achieve *holocausto*, Núñez gives them the four basic tenets that form the framework of his argument: "Por medio de la profesión solemne de los cuatros votos, de pobreza, castidad, obediencia, y clausura con las reglas y constituciones del orden, y santas costumbres de su convento" (3).[10] Before tackling a detailed description of each vow, he responds to a question from the novices regarding exactly what such a promise entails: "Déjala obligada [la promesa] a cumplir lo prometido al pie de la letra" ([The promise] obliges her to carry out what she promised to the letter of the law) (4). He thus leaves the young women in no doubt: the word of the Church authorities is to be final.

"Profanidad y exorbitancia" (Profanity and exorbitance): The Vow of Poverty

With blind obedience as his backdrop, Núñez responds in detail to the question posed about the first vow: "¿A qué obliga el voto de pobreza?" (What does the vow of poverty entail?) (6). He responds succinctly: "A no dar, no recibir, ni prestar, ni gastar, ni disponer en manera alguna de cosa de valor, sin licencia general o particular, formal o interpretativa del superior legítimo" (7).[11] Women in the convent shall not exchange objects of any value either with each other or with outsiders without the permission of the authorities. The Church greatly frowned upon the exchange of gifts between women in the convent. Teresa of Ávila mentions this prohibition in chapter 5 of *Camino de perfección*, "Declara la primera de estas tres cosas, qué es amor de próximo; y lo que dañan amistades particulares" (In which she outlines the first of three things, which is love of our neighbour; and the harm particular friendships cause) (42). Teresa dedicates this chapter to an exposition of the perils of particular friendships, which often manifest themselves in the exchange of gifts. Teresa writes: "Y hace otros daños para la comunidad muy notorios; porque de aquí viene el no amar tanto a todas, el sentir el agravio que se hace aquélla, *el deseo tener para regalarla*, el buscar tiempo para hablar" (44, emphasis mine).[12]

Núñez echoes this anti-gift-giving sentiment in his text. When his interlocutors press him for a specific example of the dangers of such an activity (7), he recites the story of "una gran señora" who comes one day to the convent, whereupon an object belonging to one of the nuns strikes her fancy ("agradada de una alhajuela de una religiosa") (7). The lady requests the object, and because she is a personage of such importance ("por ser de tanta autoridad") (7), the nun gives it to her. This action, however, as Núñez tells his avid "listeners," the authorities do not permit without first granting a special license. The ecclesiastical authorities' prohibition on gifts goes beyond merely not wishing the nuns to own "worldly goods," but rather speaks to the powerful connection between the giving of gifts and friendships. Ronald Sharp dedicates an entire chapter of his book *Friendship and Literature* to the importance of gift exchange in relationships. He writes: "The language of exchange, particularly of gift exchange, seems to be the appropriate language for describing friendships" (87–88). He describes the richness of gift-giving as a metaphor for friendship, explaining how the gift joins people together with its symbolic attributes of love and attachment (85). Most importantly for Sharp, the gift strengthens friendship, inspiring a circular movement that becomes perpetual: "When the gift moves in a circle its motion is beyond the control of the personal ego, and so each bearer must be a part of the group and each donation is an act of faith" (97).

Clerics such as Núñez reacted with great hostility to such acts, fearing the power of gift-giving to solidify the bonds of friendship. In response to a question about the degree of sin involved in such activities, Núñez speaks very emphatically:

> Siempre que se da o recibe, presta o enajena cualquier cosa, sin verdadera licencia del legítimo superior, se quebranta el voto de la pobreza con culpa de propiedad, la cual si la material es grave, será pecado mortal, y si es leve se queda en venial por parvedad o pequeñez de la material. (8, emphasis mine)[13]

In a related topic, Núñez expounds in an absolutist fashion on the possession of personal and decorative adornments. He believes that both undermine the vow of poverty and contravene the Church's idea of the perfect community by highlighting a woman's singularity. His language, overflowing with baroque hyperbole, leaves the listener in no doubt of the dangers he perceives in such distinguishing objects:

> En todas las cosas, alhajas, vestuario interior y exterior, comida, gasto, celda y criadas &c.; porque todas deben ser modestas y templadas como de pobres religiosas y si en las rejas, convites o regalos, hicieseis gasto superfluo o exorbitante, o en la celda o persona usaseis alhajas tan preciosas y costosas que parezcan o huelan a profanidad secular, o ajena disformamente de la pobreza y modestia religiosa; yo al menos no alcanzo como se pueda excusar de culpa grave, conforme a la medida o desmedida de su profanidad u exorbitancia. (12–13)[14]

Núñez's profuse and bombastic baroque rhetoric surpasses itself as he has his two young novice interlocutors ask of him: "Y ¿cuáles y cuántas son estas, para que podamos huir de ellas y evitarlas con horror muy de lejos?" (And what and how many are these, so we can flee from them, and avoid them with horror from afar?) (13). Feigning exasperation at their ignorance and perpetual questions ("¡O, válgame Dios, y qué impertinentes y preguntonas estáis!" [O Lord give me strength, what impertinent and inquisitive girls you are!]) (13), Núñez refuses to name these evils lest the mere mention corrupt their innocence ("que aun nombradas empañan su decencia" [to even name them would tarnish your decency]) (13). He does, however, take the opportunity to rail against what he considers to be the excesses and sins of the *siglo* (the world outside the convent), blasting the evils of its "confusa babilonia de ropa, vestuarios, joyas, adornos [...] y otras doscientas mil baratijas" (Babylonian confusion of clothing, costumes, jewels, adornments and two hundred thousand other cheap trinkets) (13). He does not use the word "babilonia" in the dialogue accidentally. Here he clearly refers to that disorderly female par excellence—the Whore of Babylon—who appears in the Book of Revelation, richly adorned and drinking the blood of saints:

> The woman was dressed in purple and scarlet color and richly glittering with gold, precious stones and pearls, her hand holding a golden cup full of abominations and filthiness of her fornication: And on her forehead a name was written, a mystery: Babylon the Great, the mother of prostitutes and the abomination of the earth. (Revelation 17:1–6)

The luxury problem was not confined to the *siglo*. The authorities protested constantly against the use of adornments the nuns affected in the more liberal convents. Asunción Lavrin writes of the *calzada* (calced, literally "shod") convents: "By the end of the seventeenth century, for example, they had adopted the use of such fine materials and such fashionable lace and adornments in their habits that they ran into the stern condemnation of a devoted archbishop and several other minor clerical authorities" ("Value and Meaning" 375–76). Octavio Paz refers to the inhabitants of the Convent of Jesús María, who at the end of the seventeenth century were apparently sporting "pulseras de azabache, anillos y plisados el escapulario y las tocas" (jet bracelets, rings and pleated scapular and wimple) (162).

These adornments notwithstanding, it is an awfully big leap from jet bracelets to the Whore of Babylon. This image, however, reflects the historical associations made between the nun and the prostitute. The fact that Núñez invokes the image of the Whore of Babylon to describe the clothing—and by extension, the moral climate of the *siglo*—speaks to the patriarchal authorities' dread of the innate corruptibility and sinfulness of women. Moreover, in the former's eyes only a very flimsy border separated the body of the nun from that of the prostitute. The border between these two archetypes of femininity easily collapsed, quickly turning the virgin into the harlot (although not, of course, the other way around). Janice Raymond refers to the "age-old hetero-relational tactic of transmogrifying the virgin—she who is untouched by men—into the prostitute—she who is despoiled and constantly handled by men" (74). In early modern Seville, for example, there existed a spillover in terminology referring to both brothels and convents, with the madam of a convent often referred to as "abbess" (Perry 46). The prostitute also wielded a symbolic significance in society: "Regarded as vessels to collect the filth of the flesh, prostitutes were seen as a necessary evil to prevent the worse sins of homosexuality, incest, rape, and seductions of honorable women" (47). Just as nuns expiated the sins of society through their immaculate behavior, at the other end of the spectrum the prostitute fulfilled the same function. The symbols of Eve and Mary were thus two sides of the same coin, and at times the distinction was not clear.

Here, in this discussion of the importance of strict adherence to the vow of poverty, runs an undercurrent of sex and sensuality as Núñez, with his Babylonian imagery, hints at the intimacy between these two emblematic figures of womanhood. He will make this sexual threat more explicit in the next section of the *Cartilla*, in which he tackles the importance of the vow of chastity.

Empty Vessels: The Vow of Chastity

Núñez has his novices ingenuously ask of him: "Y el voto de castidad, ¿qué es o en qué consiste?" (What is the vow of chastity, or of what does it consist?) (18), once again providing him with a completely blank canvas onto which he can project his moralizing. He describes the chaste body of the nun:

> Así el alma pura, y casto cuerpo de las religiosas esposas de Cristo son vasos purísimos, consagrados por sus votos al culto divino y servicio de Dios; y permitirlos, o consentirlos a cualquier humano amor o profano divertimiento, pareciera profanar los vasos sagrados en abusos indignos y culpables. (19)[15]

Opening the discussion on chastity, Núñez highlights the responsibility of the nun to be better than all other women: "Yo juzgo eleva tanta la dignidad de su persona a la esposa de Cristo, y las obligaciones de su sagrado, que puede representar en prudente estimación culpa grave en una religiosa, la que en una secular se pudiera juzgar muy leve" (19).[16] He mentions this by way of an introduction to the abhorrent topic of "las devociones de las señoras religiosas" (20), which, he explains, constitute a mortal sin and must be avoided at all costs.

The very strictures of the vow of chastity and the intensity of the symbolism society invested in it projected a complex web of erotic ideologies onto this chaste body that offered a flip side to the promotion of the nun as the site of purity. The idea of a chaste woman locked up in a convent with only other women for company inspired in men—both secular and religious—the practice of *devociones*, the cult of admiration of female religious. Octavio Paz compares these *devociones* with modern-day society's cult of celebrity: "Una curiosa y extendida costumbre: así como hay los aficionados a las cómicas, las cantantes, las bailarinas o las campeonas de tenis, había los que cortejaban a las monjas" (164–65).[17] Paz, I imagine, makes this comparison based on the same level of inaccessibility and mystery that surrounds both the celebrity and the cloistered nun. The comparison, although amusing, is superficial. It is important to investigate the specificity of the situation of the nun in colonial Mexico to understand what set of circumstances led her to become the subject of these ardent *devociones*.

Men gained access to the objects of their affection through visits to the convent's *locutorio* (visiting room), although the ecclesiastical authorities constantly proscribed this activity.[18] According to Paz, at times the nuns received their visitors with their faces scandalously uncovered and did not always remain, as they should, behind the wooden *rejas* (grill) (164). Paz's description of the nuns' role in these relationships or *devociones* implicitly places the nun in the role of seducer, with her uncovered face and lack of modesty. He echoes here the attitudes of the time, as exemplified in tracts and treatises written by male clergy such as Núñez de Miranda, which held that women—in essence—threatened male virtue and honor (McNamara, *Sisters* 492). The unveiled nun emerging from behind the safety (for whom, one might ask) of the *reja* tempts otherwise virtuous men to commit sinful acts.

Still, the Church was its own worst enemy in this battle to keep the dangerous female body free from sin. The more symbolism it attached to the nun as the vessel of purity, the more fascinated and drawn to her men became because of her inaccessibility. The convent walls provided the perfect space for the projection of all kinds of perversities, which were often manifested in satirical literature. Despite the differences in both genre and purpose, these satirical texts exist in a continuum with regulatory texts such as those authored by Núñez de Miranda, and their examination sheds light on the complex web of gender ideologies that engendered fears such as those displayed by our Jesuit.

Manuel Ferrer Chivite has studied what he calls "burlerías monjiles" (nunnish satires) in Spain in the sixteenth and seventeenth centuries. He first addresses those works that depict the misery of a woman confined to a convent, one who ostensibly would be far happier married. Implicit in the texts of both the poets and Ferrer Chivite who studies them is the idea that any man would be better than none:

> Ante esa tesitura de convento o himeneo, sin duda que un porcentaje máximo de dichas españolas tendería a optar por lo segundo. Pero desgraciadamente [...] uno piensa el bayo otro el que lo ensilla, y aunque todo este supuesto máximo porcentaje prefiriera el matrimonio, siendo los padres los que ensillaban el bayo bien se entiende que muchas de esas doncellas —y aun más de una que ya no lo debía ser tanto—se vieron obligadas a aceptar la otra posibilidad, lo que no quiere decir en absoluto, claro está, que para las mismas fuera ésa la solución más envidiable. (38)[19]

Obviously there were women who entered the convent against their will. However, the evidence Ferrer Chivite offers here is not particularly convincing, based as it is on satirical poems written by men.

Ferrer Chivite formulates his argument around the popular trope of the "manless woman" as somehow lacking or wanting. The celibate nun, living in an all-female community, lacks male company, and thus her erotic wants and needs—women are nothing if not carnal, after all—are not met. As women, the nuns necessarily seek the attentions of longed-for men, these *galanes de monjas* or nuns' gallants. The nunnish satires thus validate the centuries-old claim that enclosure protects society from women and their fleshly desires.[20] Ferrer Chivite quotes from Quevedo's *El buscón*, in which the poet suggests both the nuns' depravity and their dominion over their suitor. Quevedo, ever the enthusiastic misogynist, writes that to be the nun's gallant is to be the Antichrist's suitor ("pretendiente de Antecristo, [que] es lo mismo que galán de monjas") (61).

Back across the Atlantic in Mexico, we find another text similar in spirit to the "burlerías monjiles." A poem attributed to "el bachiller Pedro Muñoz de Castro, dominico" (the graduate Pedro Muñoz de Castro, Dominican monk),[21] probably written around the early eighteenth century,[22] is the New World's version of the satire men had for centuries directed against the eroticized body of the nun.

> Vivo tan cobijado de monjillas
> dice Don Juan con todas sus agallas
> que no de estar contento hasta acabarlas
> no me mate el Señor hasta extinguirlas.
>
> Los padres, quiero yo, que en volandillas
> a las hijas dispongan el casarlas,
> y si no, menos daño que enmonjarlas
> será se acomoden a putillas.
>
> Alcanzar con la mano las estrellas
> Será más fácil que encerrar las pollas
> sin gallo en el corral oh, Jaramillas!
>
> Ya sé que aunque decís que sois doncellas,
> más queréis galas, telas y bambollas,
> maridos o galanes, que cogullas.[23]

The poem expresses in cruder language the subtext of Núñez de Miranda's extravagant baroque rhetoric on chastity. While Núñez tries, unsuccessfully, to erase the body of the nun, the anonymous author of this poem foregrounds it, holding it up as the root of all sin and corruption. Both impulses, the repressive and the erotic, are two sides of the same coin of a male fantasy that struggles with concurrent feelings of repulsion and attraction.

The author wastes no time in sexualizing the body of the nun. In the first stanza, he establishes the link between *monja* (nun) and Don Juan, leaving the reader in no doubt of his opinion of female religious. In fact, it is Don Juan himself who speaks in this poem, which is voiced almost entirely in the first person.[24] In the first line, the poet depicts the nun as a sexual predator. It is not Don Juan—the world's greatest seducer of women—who seeks to corrupt the innocent nun, but rather the "monjillas" who pursue and throw themselves at him, literally covering or perhaps smothering him ("cobijar") with their lustful bodies. He, in turn, will happily have his way with all of them and appeals to God for strength to be able to meet the challenge: "no me mate el Señor hasta extinguirlas." The use of the words "acabar" and "extinguir" here have a double meaning that introduces a violent tone to the poet's sexualization of the nun's body. Don Juan wants to have his way with them—to finish them off, in the sexual sense—but perhaps he also wants to kill them.

In the second stanza, the poet echoes the popular trope of the convent as a poor substitute for marriage. The first two lines of the stanza depict Don Juan in philanthropic and seemingly moral mode, desiring that parents quickly marry off their daughters rather than send them to the convent. However, in the last two lines, the sexual vocabulary returns as he seizes on another familiar trope: the very fine line separating the brothel from the convent. It would be, he declares, less harmful for them to be "putillas" than "monjillas." In the third stanza he explains his belief: it is impossible for women to live together in community without the male presence. This statement can be read on two levels: on the first that a woman needs the normalizing presence of the man to live morally and well and on the second that the nun, closely connected to the prostitute, is so lascivious that she cannot live without a man to fulfill her voracious needs. Although the poet connects these two concepts, in the final stanza he highlights the second one. Nuns are not pious brides of Christ, obeying the vows of poverty and chastity, but have more in common with Núñez's invocation of the Whore of Babylon with her sinful trappings of luxury. The poet juxtaposes the clothing the nun should wear, "cogullas,"[25] with what she desires: "galas, telas y bambollas." Don Juan connects extravagance in dress to licentious behavior as he adds "maridos o galanes" to the list of things desired by the nuns who claim to be "doncellas" but are patently anything but.

This brief textual detour away from Núñez's text shows us that despite the moral rectitude of the Jesuit's discourse, his work has points in common with more salaciously oriented texts in its representation of the fragile border between the nun and the prostitute. As we return to Núñez, we find him bringing the section on chastity to a close, summing up his argument by repeating his warnings against *devociones* both in and out of the convent. He advises the novices to be vigilant of their senses, especially "ojos, oídos y lengua" (eyes, ears and tongue), precisely those that open her up to contact with other people. He finishes with a dramatic exhortation to humility and chastity: "¡O cuántas al fin cayeron, y cuán torpemente, sólo porque vanamente aseguradas pensaron que no podían caer! Sed muy humildes hijas mías, y Dios os conserverá muy castas" (22).[26]

"Al pie de la letra": The Vow of Obedience

In the *Cartilla*, Núñez also presents his views on the vow of obedience. Here he establishes a gendered hierarchy of power that places the nun at several removes from a direct connection with God. Moreover, the existence of this hierarchy and the control mechanisms in place that sustain it point explicitly to a coerced community that undercuts any voluntary action on the part of its members. When the novices ask Núñez to explain the elements that make up the vow of obedience, he replies: "En sujetar a los prelados y preladas toda su persona y acciones, con un mismo juicio y voluntad, que es la primera y principal sujeción" (22–23).[27] The Church does not require members of the "community" to have agency, as blind and unquestioning obedience is owed to the prelates. Núñez declares that they owe this obedience to both *prelados* and *preladas*. At times this female intermediary stood in solidarity with her daughters, but the masculine power structure of the Church co-opted her position and used her as their instrument to the detriment of the nuns to whom she was supposedly mother. María Dolores Bravo describes the subordinate role of the abbess:

> Al igual que en la vida laica, la figura masculina detenta la autoridad última que rige cada una de las conciencias que le están subordinadas. Esto es la configuración de una sociedad patriarcal. La madre sólo juega un rol subalterno de mediadora, vicaria auténtica entre el irrebatible verbo patriarcal y los hijos. En un convento femenino sucede lo mismo, y aunque la Abadesa o Superiora detenta un mando indiscutible dentro del limitado ámbito del claustro, la jurisdicción espiritual última la ejerce el Prelado o Visitador de la orden masculina correspondiente. ("El costumbrero" 161–62)[28]

A far more powerful figure in the life of a community of female religious was the confessor. When the novices ask how they should obey their confessor, Núñez is absolutely unequivocal on the subject: "Al pie de la letra, inviolablemente, sin duda, interpretación, ni dilación. Y si en este artículo no os vencéis con heroica resolución, siempre estará sobresaltado y peligrado vuestro espíritu"

(25).²⁹ The relationship between nun and confessor was, in theory, the only close relationship the Church sanctioned for the cloistered nun. Kristine Ibsen sees this relationship, and its pivotal role in the observance of the vow of obedience, as linked to what I have identified as the coerced community with its abomination of manifestations of individuality:

> Because of women's inherent vulnerability towards sin, the precept of obedience was specifically fostered by Church doctrine as a means of containing dangerous manifestations of individuality in general and feminine singularity in particular. Emphasizing pride as an element that could lead to condemnation of the soul, this doctrine, channeled through the direct influence of the confessor, ensured the male authority upon which ecclesiastical hierarchy depended. The confessor's authority lay in his position as an instrument of Christ's power in the world, the intercessor between God and Man. ("The Hiding Places" 265n.5)

The importance of this intercessor between earth and heaven was even more crucial when the earthbound individual was a woman. As we can see from Núñez de Miranda's vehemence regarding the level of obedience owed the confessor, the nun was supposed to give herself over, body and soul, to her spiritual director.

Control and Containment: The Vow of Enclosure

Finally, the *Cartilla* addresses the last vow, that of enclosure. As usual, Núñez's comments mix intense baroque rhetoric as he thunderously warns of mortal sin and prosaic details as he delineates the directives the nuns should blindly obey. Firstly, he claims that no one must be allowed in or out of the convent without special permission from the prelate. The person specified as "el legítimo prelado" (the legitimate prelate) may only be the "señor arzobispo o obispo" (the reverend archbishop or bishop) as the jurisdiction of the abbess "no alcanza esta línea" (does not extend this far) (25–26). This is a prime example of how the virtual panopticon functioned in the female convent space. By controlling movement in and out of the convent to create both passive and active enclosure, the ecclesiastical authorities hoped to maintain the immutability of the "community" they had planned.

This issue of ingress and egress proved most slippery, inciting constant anxieties that manifested themselves in proclamations and prohibitions. One of these anxieties centered on the visits of the vicereine, who as the representative of the Queen had the right to enter at will the convents of female religious in New Spain (Lavrin, "Value and Meaning" 378). This liberty of entrance greatly disturbed the authorities. It is not difficult to see why. As the wife of the viceroy, the vicereine embodied a dangerous female power that threatened to undermine the influence of the Church, if that power were put to the service of female alliance and friendship. A celebrated example of just this kind of influence can be found in the case of Sor Juana, who enjoyed the protection of the Condesa de Paredes from 1680 to 1686 when she was in Mexico—a protection that afforded the nun liberty to write and enjoy intellectual pursuits, albeit for a limited time. In 1690 a *cédula* (official document) was issued that restricted the number of times a vicereine and her entourage could enter a convent in New Spain (378).

Beyond the Vows: Mortal Sins

Núñez dedicates over half the *Cartilla* to his vehement replies to the novices' questions on other aspects of convent life, attempting to ensure he has left no room for improvisation in his choreography of convent life. Having exhausted the structure of the vows, he frames his proscriptions around questions regarding what other behaviors—besides the breaking of the vows—could lead to mortal sin (27). His first recommendation concerns the use of the *oficio divino*,[30] that is, how the nuns are to conduct their daily worship of God. The detail Núñez brings to his guidelines on observing, without distraction, the rites of the *oficio divino*, speaks to the ecclesiastical authorities' desire to leave no space for any activity that may jeopardize the community of women living in shared solitude. Nothing, he emphasizes, should be allowed to interrupt the adherence to the timetable of the Divine Office:

> Maitines se pueden ya por costumbre rezar desde las cuatro de la tarde antecedente, o poco antes, hasta las doce de la noche del día siguiente. Pasadas estas horas no se pueden rezar los maitines del día antecedente, porque ya pasó todo su tiempo: antes de las cuatro, media hora se puede empezar, porque ya las empieza a reconocer, y aun con causa justa se podrán rezar a las tres. (32)[31]

If the nuns feel a pressing need to alter anything, they should do so only in the extreme case of "raro y gravísimo embarazo" (unusual and most serious impediment) (32) and then only after consulting the works of the Church Fathers (32) through the offices of a "buen varón, como el confesor o el padre espiritual" (a worthy man, such as the confessor or spiritual father) (35). This last comment indicates the gender bias Núñez holds with regard to religious practice and adherence to doctrine. Even though there was no explicit gendering of the *oficio divino*—it was to be practiced by all—Núñez believes women need special guidance.

The novices ask him if there is any difference between male and female religious in the dispensations that the ecclesiastic authorities may give to not always thoroughly observe the Divine Office. He does not mince words in explaining why he believes women less capable of the rigors of this activity:

> Yo juzgo que sí la hay [una razón], y la razón acumulada de muchas; porque la debilidad del seso, la flaqueza del sujeto, la peregrinidad ignorada de la lengua latina, la dificultad y embarazo de las lecciones y rúbricas, con lo menos constante de la obligación [...] y parece abren puerta a la diferencia y facilitan la excusa en las religiosas de esta obligación con menor causa que en los varones eclesiásticos, cuyo título y precepto es indubitable; la fuerza mayor, la facilidad y la expedición en la latinidad y rezo, mucha: y así podrá prudentemente juzgarse por bastante excusa en una religiosa, la que no parecería bastante para excusar a un religioso o clérigo; pero siempre y en todo caso de duda, debéis consultar al prudente confesor y estar a su parecer. (39–40)³²

With this answer, Núñez exemplifies the belief the Church held for centuries concerning commonality of observance between the sexes. Here he highlights the judgment that women had inferior brainpower, thus accentuating the power of the confessor and other male prelates in supposedly determining the functioning of life in the all-female convent space. The claim is self-serving and circular, as the New World cloister provided no real educational opportunities for women and certainly did not encourage or facilitate the studying of Latin.

When the novices ask him to mention another obligation, the incorrect fulfillment of which could also lead to mortal sin, Núñez mentions the issue of voting in convent elections. According to him, "se puede con grande facilidad pecar" (it is very easy to sin) (47) by not behaving correctly on these occasions. This part of Núñez's text blatantly reveals the coerced community that the Church wished to impose on the convent space. In the instructions that follow, Núñez sweeps away the need for agency on the part of any woman in the community, including the abbess, as he tries to put in place mechanisms that would rigidly monitor and manipulate the convent space. Obviously, the ideal abbess is one who is the pawn of the authorities. According to Núñez, one can "pecar gravemente" (gravely sin) during the process of elections by choosing "la indigna" (the unworthy woman). Núñez cites the long list of abuses that the "indigna" may commit, the most egregious of which is the formation of factions and the improper behavior this implies: "los empeños, agencias, bandos, parcialidades, medios ilícitos, que no se pueden aplicar a fines torcidos con las discordias, odios, murmuraciones, quejas, sentimientos, baldones, testimonios, publicación de defectos graves, injurias e inquietudes" (48).[33]

Núñez's extraordinarily detailed and repetitive list of types of relationships and their attendant behaviors reveals the fear the Church experienced when it considered the possibility of empowerment such relationships presented. Obviously, factionalism had its negative and unpleasant side for women in the convent, but the positive side of such relationships was the strength women gained through alliance and communal action. The Church feared anything that threatened the coerced community of docile bodies, and this explains Núñez's articulation ad nauseam of every possible synonym for factions and the dangers to which they give rise. Indeed, he instructs that in the choosing of an abbess the novices must first purge themselves of "todo afecto terreno y respeto humano" (all earthly affection and human respect), something the Church would like to see operational at all times. However, if they have any doubts, they must never discuss the matter with their sisters, "huyendo no sólo de juntas y conferencias en común; pero aun de pláticas particulares" (fleeing from not only communal gatherings[,] but also from private chats) (49). They must turn instead to the confessor, chaplain, spiritual father, or seemingly any man on hand (49).

Concluding the Conversation

Núñez's text loses structure toward the end, as if he were trying to ensure he has closed off the possibility for agency by addressing every minute detail of convent life. The questions and answers come rapidly and range from specific queries, "Y ¿es necesaria disposición para comulgar, el confesarse antes?" (And is it necessary to confess before taking communion?) (58)—the answer here being yes—to more general and wide-ranging questions, "¿Cómo seremos muy santas?" (How may we be especially saintly?), which is answered with "Queriendo con heroica resolución, y amor fuerte y verdadero" (By wanting it with heroic resolution and stong and steadfast love) (66). He gets himself back on track, however, with his final recommendation, which functions as the perfect conclusion, symbolizing as it does the complete conformity with all he has demanded of the novices during the *Cartilla*. The initial question reads: "¿Cuál es la principal obligación de una religiosa, en cuanto esposa de Cristo?" (What is a nun's primary obligation in her capacity as bride of Christ?) (64).

Núñez's reply encapsulates the central theme of his argument: "Amar únicamente a su Esposo de todo su corazón, sobre todo las cosas criadas, queriendo antes perderlas todas que ofenderle en nada" (To love only her Husband with all her heart, forsaking all created things, wishing to free herself from everything rather than offend Him in any way). The "cosas criadas," he makes clear in subsequent statements, refer to the other members of the convent. Núñez constantly invokes the importance of the *comunidad*, stressing that the novices must render complete obedience to it: "Acudir indefectiblemente a la comunidad. ¡O que virtud ésta!" (To bow unfailingly to the wishes of the community. O what virtue is that!) (65). However, he juxtaposes this with what he believes life in community to entail:

> El estaros retiradas, dejadas y calladas en vuestra rincón, mientras la precisa obligación no os compeliere a salir. Cuidar de sí: descuidar de las otras: no saber, no ver, no oír, no gustar ni tocar, ni aun oler de lejos nada [. . .] la suprema independencia, y santo desprecio de toda cosa y persona criada. ¿Una esposa verdadera de Cristo se ha de dejar prendar ni aun pender, ni aun imaginar de cosa o persona criada? ¡O que indignidad tan digna de abominarse aun soñada! Ya no habéis de tratar sino con ángeles del cielo, y vuestro Esposo, de criaturas como si no las hubiera en el mundo para vosotras. Dios y vosotras. Dios y vosotras, y no más en todo el mundo. (68–72)[34]

What, then, is this community that Núñez envisions? It is certainly not one in which alliances and friendships are forged, but rather a community of collective solitude. As at many other times in the text, Núñez moves quickly from high-flown rhetoric, such as that in the passage above, to simple and straightforward information, as if he didn't quite trust his audience to understand him. Querying Núñez' statements, the novices seek clarification: "Pues ¿no hemos de tener nuestras amigas, dependencias, visitas y rejas algunas decentes y lícitas?" (So we must not receive friends, dependents, and visitors at the grill even if they are decent and permitted?) (73). This issue has proved itself to be the pivotal one throughout the *Cartilla*, as Núñez himself underscores, saying: "Esa no es preguntar para acabar la cartilla, sino para empezar un tratado entero" (This is not a question with which to begin this primer, but rather to begin a whole new treatise) (73). To be a perfect bride of Christ, one needs to be not only dead to the world but also dead to the so-called community.

The *Plática Doctrinal*

The concept of the living death enjoyed by the perfect bride of Christ forms the core of the *Plática doctrinal que hizo el Padre Antonio Núñez de la Compañia de Jesús en la profesión de una señora religiosa del convento de San Lorenzo*. Images of death permeate this text, as the author describes not only the ceremony of profession itself but also the responsibilities inherent once the novice becomes a true bride of Christ. Here, the Jesuit's tone picks up on those moments in the *Cartilla* when he leaves aside his benevolent and didactic manner and instead embraces a sinister baroque rhetoric that paints macabre images of death, *vanitas*, and the devil. Again, as in the *Cartilla*, Núñez's text exposes the dichotomy of society's fear and fascination with the female body: the lustful female is despised for her incarnation of sin, but at the same time her body becomes the site of a tangled web of perverse projections of desire. In the *Plática*, Núñez takes these obsessions to an extreme degree, concocting a complicated and contradictory rhetoric predicated on images of death and immobility. The purpose behind this rhetoric is to stress that the only intimate relationship the nun may have is with Christ. In the *Plática*, Núñez returns time and time again to the theme of necessary solitude and the prohibition against human relationships of any kind (barring that of spiritual father and daughter, which is a relationship the Church believed it could control). However, such is the fervor of the author to indoctrinate his listeners with this idea that he overdetermines the intimate bonds between the nun and her divine husband, rendering it the site of erotic connection.

Núñez begins his sermon with a citation from the *Song of Songs*, a text in which the sensual bodies of the lovers loom large: "Ven del líbano, esposa mía; ven del líbano: bajo a coronarte reina desde la empinada cabeza, desde la coronada cumbre y volada frente de los encumbrados montes Amaná, Sanir y Hermon. Sal de las peligradas madrigueras de los leones, y de las peñascosas grutas de los pardos" (77).[35] Núñez describes this citation as the "Amorosa vocación; y nupcial convite del Esposo a su virgina esposa, en el cap. 4 al V. 8 de su castísmo epitalámio" (Loving vocation; and the Husband's nuptial invitation to his virginal bride, in chapter 4, verse 8 of his chaste epithalamium) (77). As always the Jesuit priest speaks with great authority, but here he passes over the fact that the *Song of Songs* could not really be considered "castísimo," and that perhaps the Beloved in this text is not the most appropriate role model he could have chosen for the perfect bride of Christ.

The *Song of Songs* was a controversial text in the early modern Hispanic world, causing problems for such Church luminaries as Fray Luis de León, Teresa de Ávila, and Juan de la Cruz. According to Francis Landy, interpreting the *Song* has always been a challenge, given that its metaphors are "wonderfully perplexing, sometimes surreal in their juxtaposition of extreme incongruities, their baroque development, their cultivation of disproportion" (310). In the text, a series of "intricate connections between the beauty of the Lover or the Beloved and the world" foregrounds the preeminence of the physical beauty of both Lover and Beloved, male and female (309). These descriptions are highly evocative of sensory qualities and accentuate the physicality of the love between the two.

Moreover, the Beloved is depicted as both sexually aggressive and adventurous. Landy writes:

> The dominance and initiative of the Beloved are the poem's most astonishing characteristics. Metaphorically aligned with a feminine aspect of divinity, associated with the celestial bodies, the land, and fertility, the Beloved reverses the predominately patriarchal power of the Bible. Male political power is enthralled to her [in the figure of the Lover who is also a King]. (317)

However, the Beloved's power does not last forever. She suffers the fate of sexually adventurous women in a patriarchal society and pays the price for her daring: her family casts her out, shepherds despise her, and watchmen beat her (317). Yet, despite her sexual transgressions, she is still reunited with the Lover.[36]

Why did Núñez choose this sexually charged text to begin his sermon? It is an unusual option for a sermon that seeks to outlaw and erase corporeality and sensuality. Perhaps he was responding to the trope of the sexually adventurous woman whom society punishes for her sins? This is possible, as time and time again he compares the sins of Lebanon—from where the Beloved comes—to the virtue of Jerusalem from where the Lover calls her. Núñez turns the barren and rocky Lebanon of the *Song* into the *siglo*; he refers to it further on in the sermon as "los peligrados bosques, infames montes y sangrientas fieras del siglo, temporalidades y vicios del mundo" (the dangerous forests, infamous mountains and bloodthirsty wild beasts of the outside world with its temporalities and worldly vices) (80) where women can only sin. And he transforms Jerusalem into the convent—"la Jerusalén pacífica y sagrada Sión de la religión" (the peaceful Jerusalem and sacred Zion of religion) (80)—where the woman can live in perfect probity with her divine husband. He threads the metaphor of the *Song* throughout the first half of the text, using it as a backdrop against which he places the perfect wife. The nun, like the Beloved, must give herself entirely to her husband, eschewing all worldly temptations. Subtly, but nonetheless distinctly, his text projects perversity on the nun's body, his use of the Song framing his sermon within a discourse of eroticism and corporeality, which is what he has precisely sought to obliterate.

Relinquishing the Body: The Lady Vanishes

After quoting from the Song, Núñez describes how it is important for the nun to surrender her body to God, a symbolic action that forms the core of the ceremony of profession. Before detailing the various rites involved in the ceremony, he wants to make sure his audience realizes the importance of what they are doing—that by handing their bodies over to God, these young women are offering up their greatest commodity. Their bodies may not be so special (indeed they are not, as he will make clear), but if they prize them, if they believe what they are offering to God is really valuable, the offering will then be transformed into something of value:

> Quien da un diamante de altísimo fondo y valor exquisito, pensando que sólo da un contentible vidrio, agravia con su vileza, como si de en realidad de verdad ofreciera solo éste; mas si suponiendo con error prudente que era un carbunclo imperial, ofreciese de hecho un ordinario vidrio, merece sin controversia en la aceptación grata del que recibe. (76)[37]

He continues in this vein, describing the relinquishing of the nun's body to God as "una dádiva tan magnífica" (a most magnificent gift) (76). It is his job in this sermon, he says, to make them aware of the precious gift they are giving to God. This text is a clear attempt at indoctrination, to make sure the nuns realize their bodies may no longer afford them any individuality or agency, and Núñez spells out ("breve y claro") exactly what the Church expects of them:

> Profesar una señora religiosa es, desposarse reina con Cristo; y desposarse reina es, entregarse toda por entero con todo su ser, cuerpo y alma, a la voluntad de su Esposo: es quedar toda de Cristo, con todas sus dependencias, quereres y haberes; y no en nada suya, ni aun en el albedrío; porque todo se ofrece en holocausto por virtud de la profesión. (80)[38]

Here, once again, his attempt to deemphasize the importance of the female body only serves to foreground it. Before initiating any action, the nun must ask herself: "¿Esto será del gusto de mi Esposo?" (Will this be to my husband's liking?) (82-83). His subtext here is very clear: will her actions also be pleasing to the male authorities that rule over the convent in their role as intermediaries between the wife and her divine husband—they to whom the nun owes "obediencia ciega y sincera" (unquestioning and genuine obedience) (93)?

Núñez wants to make it clear that once the nun's body belongs to God, it may no longer be the site of individualizing activities. For him, such manifestations of singularity can only be attributed to the devil. The Church will not sanction even those that may be considered approved acts ("calificadas") such as "la religión, penitencia, mortificación, oración, éxtasis y revelaciones" (piety, penitence, mortification, prayer, raptures and visions) (83) without prior approval from the "padre espiritual." The male ecclesiastical hierarchy encouraged extreme acts of religious observance such as self-mortification and penitence as long as they remained firmly within the control of the confessor. The body must at all times be monitored. Núñez, however, doesn't stop here: the body of the nun is a sacrificial object "como un vaso, ropa o res" (like a vessel, garment or beast) (97). The nun, then, has as much agency as these objects, and she exists only as an offering made to God: "se llama la profesión sacrificio, oblación y más propiamente holocausto" (the profession is a sacrifice, offering or, more accurately, holocaust) (97).

Núñez progressively takes agency away from the nun as his sermon continues. She starts off as the keeper of a precious body, but once she has given this gift to God, she becomes a docile body who only does His bidding (or really that of his earthly male intermediaries). Following this, he turns her into an object to be sacrificed—a chalice, an item of clothing, a sacred cow. These images are just the warm-up for Núñez's crowning image of the nun's reified body: that of the corpse.

Death and the Maiden: From Thanatos to Eros and Back Again

From here on in, Núñez's text focuses on the dead body of the nun. He structures his text around the ceremony of profession, describing each rite involved and the symbolism attached, as well as the responsibilities each implies. In order to set the scene, to create this macabre mood of death and renunciation, he details what awaits the nun who is about to undergo the ceremony of profession. The backdrop is reminiscent of a gothic horror novel, as he re-creates the funereal procession that accompanies the nun to the chapel. Núñez's scene uses elements of chiaroscuro that suggest the dualities of life and death. That darkness predominates in this crypt-like scene is no accident, as the nun is to go triumphantly to her death rejecting the light of the (evil) outside world:

> La primera ceremonia es, llevar toda la comunidad con luces en las manos a la profesa, como si la acompañaran de entierro muerta de amor, que se va por su pie a la sepultura hasta el coro bajo, donde de antes de llegar al comulgatorio que es el tálamo de sus bodas, prostrada a lo de difunta le dicen las letanías de agonizantes. (99)[39]

There is no escaping the images of death in Núñez's description of the ceremony. But the dead body is also an erotic body. The conflation of the nuptial bed with the deathbed does not erase the female body. Instead, the very image of the prostrate and immobile female body awaiting the attentions of her heavenly bridegroom becomes erotically charged in a way that fulfills male fantasies of the female body.

The dead woman was an even more perfect version of the patriarchal ideal of enclosed or contained woman in the baroque period. Georgina Dopico-Black has commented on the symbolism of the body of the dead wife in Calderon's *El médico de su honra* (*The Surgeon of his Honor*). She writes of the playwright's inscription of the wife's "perfection within the absolute stillness and total containment of death" (118), which she interprets as "the culminating moment of an escalating process throughout the play that seeks to enclose—and even encorpse—the female body, as a means to control her erotic agency and the male anxiety it provokes" (118). Here, Núñez also details the rites involved in the profession ceremony in the form of an escalation, the culmination of which is the burial of the "dead" body of the nun within the four walls of the convent.

This notion of a dead, contained body has much to do with the contradictory role of the body in Christianity. As Beth Ann Bassein writes:

> Christianity sets the soul so far out in front that when the body asserts itself it is beaten back with such vigor that, at some moments in history, it literally was totally destroyed. Ironically, harnessing the body is one important means to an end which Christianity seeks, and without the body to combat and become the source of sin, much of the whole edifice would crumble. (18)

This is exactly what occurs in Núñez's text, written in a time when the Church tried to erase the body—especially the female body. Núñez hangs the entire rationale of his sermon on the framework of the erased body, but in doing so must evoke it time and time again until the nun's body dominates the text. Treating the baroque period, Margo Glantz has spoken of the female body and its inevitable discursive presence ("presencia insoslayable en el discurso") (270). Núñez further underscores this trope, structuring his sermon as he does around the deadly nuptials of the *Sponsa Dei* and her holy bridegroom.

The death/desire relationship loomed large in the culture of the baroque in which Núñez lived and wrote (Dollimore, *Death, Desire, and Loss* xi), and his text is a superlative example of "la fusión antagónica de Eros y Thanatos" (Bravo, "Erotismo y represión" 133). Valerie Traub has written of the "eroticized yet chaste corpse" of the female body in Shakespeare, suggesting that it implies not only "the connection between sexuality and death [. . .] but also suggests that sexuality is finally safely engaged in only with the dead" (*Desire and Anxiety* 33). It is this trope that operates in Núñez's text. He eroticizes the dead, chaste body of the nun/bride, which is "fetishized to the extent that it is utterly devoid from the rest of her being" (33) and thus embodies "a masculine fantasy of a female essence wonderfully devoid of that which makes women so problematic: change, movement, inconstancy, unpredictability—in short, life" (32).

Núñez informs his audience that during the whole process of the novitiate, the neophyte nun has been slowly dying in preparation for her final demise: "todo el año del noviciado, está como agonizando con las ansias de dejar el mundo" (she spends the whole of the novitiate year as if dying of the desire to leave the world behind) (99). Not only is the novice going to die at the end of her novitiate but also she is anxious to do so—*dying* to do so—and so finally leave the evil and corrupt world behind her. What is more, not only will the nun leave the evil of the world behind her when she professes—she will be "muerta al mundo"—but she will be dead to all but her divine husband and his intermediaries. Thus, with this discursive maneuver, Núñez hopes to fulfill their ideal of the perfect convent community, the collective solitude for women the Church had always upheld as the ideal solution to the necessary containment of women. These women are not only dead to the world but also dead to each other:

> Profesar, es morir al mundo, y al amor propio y a todas las cosas criadas, para vivir sólo a su Esposo. Para todo ha de estar muerta y sepultada sin padres, parientes, amigas, dependencias, cumplimientos, visitas, y en una palabra a todo amor de criatura, respondiendo de todo: los muertos ni visitan ni son visitados; no saben de cortesanía ni de cumplimientos. ¿Quién regala a un muerto, o quiere que le regale? (100)[40]

Here Núñez returns, with a rather unsubtle touch of sarcasm, to his obsession with the liveliness of convent life. If these women are dead, how can they possibly have contact either with the outside world or with each other? They are the ultimate docile bodies—dead bodies—unable to contaminate and infect each other with their propensity to sin. Núñez doesn't stop here. Not only are these bodies to be docile, but also they are to be abject: they are to inspire repulsion in all those who look upon them. Only then can the ever-tempting female body, as Núñez claims, "apagar y resfriar los más ardientes bochornos de la concupiscencia" (extinguish and cool off that most burning shame of the lusts of the flesh) (100). The brides of Christ, declares the Jesuit, "no se contentan con no amar a hombres; sino que desean ser aborrecidas de todos, y que huyan de ellas como de un cuerpo muerto. A esta causa aborrecen su misma hermosura y prendas, de modo que desean ser muertas por verse afeadas, y tan horribles, que huyan de ellas todas" (101).[41] They are corpses, and as such must say goodbye to any worldly beauty they may enjoy.

The association of the body of the female religious with abjection loomed large in baroque New Spain and other Catholic countries. The rhetoric of men like Núñez was designed to penetrate the minds of nuns and other women—Bassein refers to fervor on the part of women to destroy their bodies by engaging in abject acts. She refers to the excesses of female saints, who were held up as role models, such as "drinking the water lepers have washed their feet in and cleaning up with the tongue the vomit and excrement belonging to the patient" (Bassein 32). Acts such as these show women as susceptible to a "life-denying kind of existence that in many instances presupposes a tropism toward death" (33). If women were indeed more susceptible to these acts, it was because men with power over women, such as Núñez, crafted a life-denying rhetoric with this end in mind.

The Church authorities actually encouraged extreme manifestations of penitence, such as these acts of self-mortification and abjection, as long as the confessor first granted permission. These acts exemplified two tenets of the Christian experience in the Hispanic baroque: pain and obedience (Ibsen, *Women's Spiritual Autobiography* 71).[42] The benefits for the clergy were numerous. Acts of extreme penitence, as described by some New World nuns, served to isolate the nun from other members of the community and thus fulfilled the Church's desire to keep the woman in solitude. Moreover, a confessor whose spiritual daughter committed acts of extreme self-mortification could gain reflected glory. These acts, when committed to writing at the instigation of the confessor, became celebrated in society. The mortification of the body appealed to baroque society's fascination with the grotesque, and the female body was an ideal site. As Ibsen writes: "The grotesque fascination of the reader for graphic descriptions of mutilated bodies further reveals the sadistic implications of commodification of the female body as narrations glory in the most gruesome details of aesthetic practice" (74). Nuns were taught to believe that this was the model to which they must aspire in hopes that "through this methodical manipulation of the body the ideological apparatus was inscribed on the individual subjectivity" with the effect that, with their energies engaged in self-monitoring and self-abuse, "control over their bodies—and their minds—was ensured at all times" (75).[43]

These images of abjection also reminded women that their physical charms were fleeting. In both the *Cartilla* and the *Plática*, Núñez condemns female adornments and vanity. In this section of the *Plática* in particular, he promotes a ghastly mixture of death and abjection, seizing on the popular *vanitas* trope or the triumph of death over beauty. Several artists of the baroque period explored the affinity between women and *vanitas* with their representations of "death and the maiden," which showed Death's conquest of female beauty. One such artist was Hans Baldung-Grien whose 1510 *Death and the Maiden* shows the decomposing, almost skeletal form of Death tugging at the long, flowing hair of a beautiful and naked young woman. The woman is oblivious to Death's presence as she gazes into her hand mirror, her attitude appearing to waver between modesty and seductiveness. The painter's moral warning emanates from this image where the vain maiden, gazing fondly at her own reflected beauty, remains unaware of the inexorable fate that awaits her: Beneath the pristine beauty of young womanhood lurks the rotting corpse of death. The artist's Death is clearly masculine, a seducer; but there is no doubt that the young woman is complicit in her own corruption. Núñez's text has many points in common with Baldung-Grien's painting: the pervasive evocation of death, the description of a grotesque, rotting body, the representation of vanity—female vanity—as immoral and sinful, with woman's propensity to incite lust in all who look upon her.

A useful weapon in the furtherance of this rhetorical style was the trope of the female virgin martyr. In the *Plática*, Núñez invokes Santa Inés, who, according to the Jesuit, on being led to her execution explained to those who were mourning the impending loss of her beauty: "Perezca y muera esta corporal hermosura que los hombres miran con ojos menos castos, que a cambio de que no me quieran así deseo ya verme muerta, despedazada y repodrida para causarles horror" (101).[44] The invocation of one of the female virgin martyrs strengthens the image of the female erotic body that emerges from the *Plática*, underscoring the duality conferred on the female body. Female sexual attraction is to be flaunted before it is destroyed. The female virgin martyrs of the early Christian tradition are described in hagiographic literature as young—usually just entering puberty—and endowed with a beauty that seduces all who look upon them. Their faith in the Christian God and their dedication to the consecrated life is often revealed when they refuse to marry pagan nobles (Petroff 68 n. 6). This negation of marriage unleashes what Elizabeth Petroff has described as the sexual sadism inherent in the virgin-martyr legends, in which beautiful young women are "publicly stripped naked, whipped, [and] exposed to various tortures at the hands of men" (63 n. 8).

This voyeuristic gaze that traps and objectifies the naked female body does not, as Martha Easton points out, figure in the legends of the male martyrs (57). Easton takes this notion of sexual sadism and voyeurism one step further, describing the treatment meted out to young women in these legends as a form of "sexual molestation" that renders a rather "mundane" literary account "visually prurient" (57). Núñez captures the prurience inherent in the tone and images of these legends with his representation of a passive female body prostrating herself before God. Purity is erotic, in other words.

"Retirada, cubierta, tapada" (Hidden away, covered, concealed): Christ's Slave

At the end of the ceremony of profession, the nun steps up to the *tálamo*—the area symbolizing the marriage bed—where she acknowledges the obligation of her vows and claims she does so of her own free will. Núñez is quite insistent on this point, and he cites the ruling of the Council of Trent that threatened excommunication to anyone who forcibly remitted a woman to the convent. There is, however, some irony present in this insistence on the nun entering under free will, since she is subsequently expected to relinquish it. Once she has said her vows, she must then answer three of her beloved's wishes ("vocaciones de su querido") (113). Núñez describes them as "grados y escalones por donde se sube al tálamo de su virginales bodas" (the steps and stairs by which she ascends to her virginal nuptial bed) (112). The wedding ceremony itself begins the trajectory of the nuns' death-in-life, in which they must consent to go on

> creciendo de virtud en virtud, como de hora en hora, hasta el último flamante medio día de coronación, correspondiendo con esta temporal fineza y perfección sucesiva, aquella instantánea adelantada providencia, con que abaeterno las escogió el Rey de los cielos por esposas. (113)[45]

In the first of these declarations, the nun promises to be vigilant of her body and thus circumspect in all her actions. Her body, as we have seen, no longer belongs to her. Secondly, she promises that she has renounced ("despreciado") the earthly kingdom and all that it entails. At the mention of this, Núñez cannot resist a digression, in the form of a tirade, into one of his pet topics—disgustingly immoral "galas profanas y atavíos peligrosos del mundo" (profane finery and pernicious worldly garb) (116). He even mentions how some of these adornments have been taken up in the convent and hectors his audience, asking: "¿Qué asco y enfado causará a Dios y a sus ángeles, ver que una reina del cielo, esposa de su Rey, así estime y pompee los asquerosos andrajos de los esclavos prisioneros de la tierra o del infierno?" (117).[46]

The nun makes the third and final declaration while she kneels with her eyes cast down and her arms crossed over her breast. She claims to be Christ's slave and promises to show her status in every aspect of her life in the convent. Once these three declarations have been made, she is finally given the object that will most identify her as a nun: "la insignia del velo negro" (the insignia of the black veil) (123). The veil symbolizes her being stripped of all the evil associated with the world—"los viciosos fueros del mundo, abusos y costumbres malas" (the dissolute laws, excesses and immoral practices) (123)—and her acceptance of her divine husband as her only lover. According to Núñez this is the most important aspect of the taking of the veil, and he stresses the importance of not only not loving anyone else but also of not being loved either. This, he claims, is of paramount importance—especially for women—as it goes against "la natural ambición de las mujeres, aun de las más honestas a lo humano, que no suele pesarles ser amadas y celebradas" (the natural desires of women who, even the most virtuous among them, like to be loved and admired) (124).

Just as the veil serves to identify the nun, it will conversely also serve to *dis*-identify her, erasing both her individuality and her body: "El cual se extiende al que cubre no sólo la cabeza y cuello sino el rostro todo y pecho, para que ninguno pueda verlo ni aficionársele. Por eso ha de vivir siempre, y toda encerrada dentro de su velo, donde retirada, cubierta y tapada, parece mejor al Esposo" (124–25).[47] Yet this dis-identification does not signify a shared experience with other brides of Christ. This is not a communal burial space but rather an individual and intimate tomb wherein she must only commune with her husband: "*Intra velum*: debajo de tu velo o lazos, dentro de tus tocas: allá, allá, a solas con tu Esposo" (*Intra velum*: underneath your veil, within your wimple: there, there alone with your Husband) (125).

The final element in the wedding ceremony is the ring "aquella partícula hilativa o conclusiva" (that binding or definitive component) (131). The ring is not merely a ring but also a crown: "y le llama corona, no sólo porque corona el dedo anular y por este el corazon, que se comunican por una arteria [...] sino porque haciéndola verdaderamente esposa del Rey del cielo la corona reina, pues desposarse con el rey es ser reina" (134).[48] According to Núñez, this great honor brings with it enormous responsibilities as well as a debt of gratitude:

> Aquí el agradecimiento debido a tanto beneficio: el decoro conveniente a tanta dignidad. [...] Ajena de todos, como quien se ve libre del fuego mundano y horno babilónico de sus abrasadas dependencias, da reconocidas las gracias al Padre de su Esposo y Señor Jesucristo, por cuyos méritos la libró de tan voraz incendio, y de su tizne y calor noscivo, y la sublimó al estado celeste de angélica pureza. (134)[49]

Once she has attained this state of angelic purity, the woman becomes untouchable, monumentalized. This discursive gesture has much in common with the other predominant trope in the *Plática*, the dead body of the nun. Both function as strategies of containment, and both help to quell masculine anxieties about female sexuality.

These tropes form a continuum that seeks to reify the woman's body so as to render her absent. All that remains is a chimerical vision of the nun that serves as a symbolic force of virtue in society. The vision can only be a chimera, however, for the reality represents disorder and sin and has therefore, supposedly, been erased.

As both the ceremony and Núñez's text reach their close, the priest officiating gives the nun a ring, along with with a palm leaf—"la palma de tu virginidad." The "imperial novia" recognizes the spiritual adornments she is receiving, while rejecting "la infame cadena de sus yerros en la obscura masmorra de la carne, como vil esclava de su apetito" (the ignoble bondage of her errors in the flesh's dark dungeon, appetite's vile slave) (138). Society can confer no greater honor, says Núñez, than that of the *Sponsa Dei*: "Virgen, esposa de Cristo, no hay más que decir, ni pedir, ni desear" (Virgin, Bride of Christ, there is nothing more to say or desire) (139). Finally, the *prelado*, as God's earthly intermediary, hands over the newlywed to the care of the *superiora* (Mother Superior), who must watch over her every move until the moment when her death-in-life, her convent life, is over and she is joined with her heavenly husband for eternity.

Núñez supposedly gave this sermon on the day of the profession of a nun in the Convent of San Lorenzo. His text was meant to be heard as well as read, and it is easy to imagine the terrible thrall in which Núñez held his audience with his macabre rhetoric of death and denial. Like any good fire-and-brimstone preacher, he brings his text to a hair-raising climax, designed to leave his audience convinced that no other road can be taken other than the one he lays out in his sermon. In the last section of his tract, he returns to a technique he employed in the *Cartilla*: assuming the first-person feminine voice of the Esposa and dramatically offering himself up devoid of all agency to God:

> Tomad allá mi corazón y mi voluntad; poseed mi cuerpo y mi alma; tomad mis potencias y sentidos; disponed de todo como en cosas propias; mandad, desmandad, haced y deshaced, que toda estoy a vuestra disposición y albedrío &c. ¡O y así sea! Y sea para siempre, sin fin ni interrupción. Amén. (145)[50]

In this case, his ventriloquism serves to make his words more immediate. He uses the dead body of the nun as a staging ground from which to launch his commandments. After all, she has no voice of her own. And so the *Plática* ends. The nun is left without free will, body, or soul, and finally, in the culminating gesture, without voice. Not only does the Church, here via Núñez, obliterate her body but also it feigns her own voice to do so. The transformation is complete, the tomb is sealed, and the maiden is dead.

In Conclusion: Back from the Dead

María Dolores Bravo has called the *Plática doctrinal* an "espléndido y terrible discurso de poder" (a splendid and terrible discourse of power) ("Erotismo" 126). The *Cartilla*, in a different way, is also a highly structured discourse of power. We cannot underestimate the discursive force texts such as Núñez's wielded over seventeenth-century colonial Mexican society.[51] Octavio Paz has characterized intellectual life in Mexico as a "cultura de púlpito y cátedra" (culture dominated by pulpit and university) (84). Núñez, the all-powerful learned Jesuit, would have been viewed as a leading intellectual figure of his time. However, the power of someone even as awe-inspiring as Antonio Núñez de Miranda was not monolithic. The texts themselves, with their desperate discourse of containment and control, belie the success of the Church's claim of community in which each woman, shrouded in her veil, should sit anonymously in her "rincón" (corner).

Speaking of early modern England, Valerie Traub has warned against allowing the "seemingly relentless power of [masculine] containment" ("Desire and Anxiety" 49) to take us in. She advises us to go beyond it to see "the possibility of female agency [that emerges] in excess of masculine control" ("Desire and Anxiety" 49). The following chapters will examine these "excesses" that challenge the control the Church authorities in colonial Mexico carefully and obsessively laid down, as Núñez de Miranda exemplifies here. Far from dead, the New World nun was alive and well, finding strength in acts of alliance and community that challenged the Church's proscriptions.

3

The Community of Lovers
Mala amistad in the Convent

> *El estar también en conocimiento de lo que es comunidad de mujeres,*
> *entre las cuales nunca falta quien con la luz se ciegue por gustar de sombras.*
> (The importance of knowing what a community of women is like—wherein there
> is always someone blinded by the light for too great a love of the shadows.)
>
> Carlos de Sigüenza y Góngora, *Paraíso Occidental*, Libro Tercero-XXII, 317

On an unspecified day in September 1792, an eighteen-year-old professed nun, Sor María Josefa Ildefonsa de San Juan Bautista of the *concepcionista* Convent of Jesús María in Mexico City, wrote a letter of denunciation to the Inquisition. The letter concerned the activities of one Tomás, whose last name she was unable to recall. In her denunciation, the young nun described how she had heard it said that Tomás was a sorcerer, "un mago." She had contacted him, she said, as she wanted to break her vows and abandon the convent, so as not to be separated from a servant girl who wanted to leave. She alleged that Tomás gave her a book, one whose pages were all blank, "no había letras ninguna" (there was no writing whatsoever) (f. 1). A series of extremely complicated instructions followed: if she needed to get in touch with him, she simply had to place any correspondence in the book, and magically he would receive it. He would also send correspondence to her in the same fashion. She must only read the papers at night, as during the day they would simply appear to be blank, and after reading them, she should immediately burn them. If she did not follow these rules exactly, "no habrá nada" (there will be nothing) (f. 1). Using this method, Tomás would inform her of when she was to leave the convent. He would arrange this so it would appear to the convent community that she was still physically present: "estaba [Tomás] pronto a sacarme sin que me vieran ni supieran nada pues podía ser que les pareciera a las de acá que estaba yo y no faltaba y yo estar a donde quisiera sin que me vieran ni conocieran" (f. 1).[1] According to the nun, although "siempre andaba confundida" (she was always confused) (f. 2), she was indeed able to receive correspondence this way. However, because Tomás never told her when to leave, she returned the book to him and resigned herself to stay in the convent.

The letter of denunciation, which the nun herself wrote in a small, childish script, is both extremely confused and confusing. Throughout the jumbled and repetitious narrative, we discover that she had wanted to leave the convent because she found herself "muy tentada del enemigo" (greatly tempted by the enemy) (f. 3), although at this point she offers no further details. We also discover what she knows of the background of Tomás: she believes him to be from Guanajuato and to have worked as a silversmith in a shop belonging to Don Eduardo Calderón. This is the first introduction we have to the specifics of this case, the testimony of the complaining witness, although her status as such will soon change. The chaotic nature of the narrative speaks to the fear the Inquisition inspired in an eighteen-year-old cloistered nun, a fear predicated on the fact that she knew she had contravened the rules of the convent by embroiling herself in a *mala amistad*.[2] It is a fear that proves to be well founded, as the documents that ensue attest.

The Church held up the paradoxical concept of collective solitude as the ideal modus vivendi for women living in the convent, frowning upon and attempting to prohibit intimate relationships of any kind between cloistered women. These types of intimacies challenged the Church's ideal of community in which "docile bodies," lacking in singularity and agency, lived side by side without contact or interaction. In his *Cartilla de la doctrina religiosa*, Antonio Núñez de Miranda counseled the nuns to purge themselves of "todo afecto terreno y respeto humano" (all earthly affection and human respect) (49). In the previous chapter, I showed how the Church strove to prevent the nun from having any other relationship than with her divine husband. In this chapter, I analyze a case in which a nun challenged the controlled community's insistence on isolation. I also address the psychosexual fears special friendships between women in the convent inspired in the ecclesiastic authorities. In this study, along with a discussion of the Inquisition documents that detail the relationship between the nun and the servant girl, I analyze texts that deal with prohibitions against these intimate relationships between women in the Hispanic convent. In these texts, I trace a discourse surrounding the phenomenon of *mala amistad* that reveals the Church's fear of the implications of these same-sex relationships, which they viewed as a threat to their vision of the controlled convent community.[3]

The strange case of Sor María Josefa Ildefonsa de San Juan emerges in a set of documents I unearthed in the files of the Mexican Inquisition at the Archivo General de la Nación in Mexico City.[4] The events I describe here take place at the end of the eighteenth century in Mexico City and touch on issues of sexuality, disease, and sorcery, as well as exposing the monolithic bureaucracy of the Inquisition as it entered its last few decades of existence. An interesting cast of characters will emerge from the pages of these documents: the nun herself, whose voice one must try to piece together from the words and control of others; a *mestizo*, Tomás, perhaps accused of sorcery; as well as a shadowy group of male clerics and Inquisition functionaries who marshal their not-inconsiderable power against a teenage nun. From the very first lines of the very first document in the collection, we learn that the nun stands accused of *mala amistad*, an illicit and particular relationship, with a servant girl in the convent. Although details of other issues will engage the time and the pens of the Inquisitors to a greater degree, it is this issue, in my opinion, that drives the investigation forward and colors the perception of the nun in the view of the Inquisition.

The Specifics of the Case: The First Investigation

After having read the nun's denunciation, the Inquisition officials write a report in which we learn more about Sor María Josefa. She is a professed nun, "de coro y velo negro" (f. 4), who took the habit before her fifteenth birthday.[5] We also find out that she denounced Tomás at the instigation of her confessor, Padre Patiño, a man who is to play a pivotal role in this story, one that will bear further examination. More details are revealed concerning the motive for her desire to leave the convent, as the Inquisitors themselves use the term *mala amistad* for the first time. In the initial interview, conducted by Padre Ignacio Pico of the Inquisition, it is reported that "con motivo de tener la que decía una mala amistad con una moza llamada María Gertrudis Rodríguez y haber determinado ésta salirse del convento quiso la declarante salir también por no separarse de ella" (f. 6).[6] Once Tomás facilitated their departure, he would give them shelter together—"tenía donde ponerla en compañia de la moza" (he had a place for her to stay with the servant girl)—on the condition that "estando en la calle, había de hacer lo que el Tomás le dijera" (once in the street, she had to do whatever Tomás told her) (f. 6).

In keeping with the slow speed the investigation was to take, the Inquisitors did not visit the nun until more than a year after they had received her original denunciation concerning Tomás's activities. The next interview takes place on December 12, 1793, and she is asked to read over her testimony and to make any additions or amendments. It is reported that "aunque ha procurado reflejar sobre los hechos que refiere, no se le ofrece cosa alguna que alterar porque como está todo escrito verdad" (although she has tried to think hard about what she says, she cannot think of anything to change because everything written down here is the truth) (f. 7). Her naiveté and youth are highlighted when she is asked to give her definition of what is a "mago." Her recorded reply is the following: "que entendió que los mágicos podían hacer todo lo que querían, y que esto quería decir mágico, y por tanto podía facilitarle el Tomás su salida" (she believed sorcerers could do anything they wanted, and that is what magic meant, and therefore Tomás could help her leave the convent) (f. 7). It was during this first visit that the Inquisitors began to question overtly her reliability as a witness. They ask Sor María Josefa if she can be sure the papers Tomás gave her were not, in fact, a figment of her imagination: "por efecto de alguna perturbación que en aquel tiempo padeciera su mente" (owing to the effect of some sort of disturbance that might have afflicted her mind at the time) (f. 8). Although she assures her questioners that this was not the case, they persist, their questions becoming more probing: "Preguntada si padece de Histérico o de lo que vulgarmente se llama Latido o si le da algún mal que por algún tiempo la perturbe, o padece hipocondría, u otra enfermedad?" (f. 8).[7] The nun admits to suffering from "latido," or hysteria and acknowledges that she has indeed had nervous episodes, which have lasted as long as twenty-four hours. She is adamant, however, that "los hechos que ha referido no han sido sólo imaginarios por efecto del mal, sino verdaderos, y que por tales los tiene" (she has not invented what she has said because of illness, but has instead told the truth as she believes it) (f. 8).

After this interview with Sor María Josefa, there follows a group of documents, dated January 15, 1794, which detail the efforts of the Inquisitors to discover the exact identity of this Tomás and to locate his whereabouts. After speaking to witnesses, they verify the information the nun gave them—the only discrepancy being that he is from Irapuato and not Guanajuato. His full name turns out to be Joseph Tomás Roberto Barreto, and it is reported that he is a young man known to be "lascivo en sus conversaciones" (f. 12). It is also stated that he has spent some time in the public prison for having caused a minor scandal with his attentions toward a young woman of the family with whom he was living, a young woman who subsequently became a nun. They do not know his present whereabouts; after leaving jail he returned to Irapuato, and there the trail comes to a dead end.

On October 3, 1794, the *Fiscal* issues a report, summing up the case to this point and deciding the direction the investigation is to take. The question is posed if Tomás is indeed "un hombre totalmente perdido" ("an utterly dissolute man") (f. 13) or if Sor María Josefa is suffering from an "enfermedad propia de su sexo" (an illness typical of her sex) (f. 13). The nun's illness seems to neutralize Tomás's bad reputation. Moreover, the authorities make their first connection between the charge of *mala amistad* and Sor María Josefa's illness, locating her behavior in "el engaño de una fantasía lastimada por enfermedad o por la misma vehemencia de los deseos que hubo de salir de la clausura para estar en la mala compañía de la moza con que hubo ilícito correspondencia" (f. 14).[8]

The report seems to focus more on the nun's problems and less on the sins of the missing Tomás. She is the only "criminal" available to them. With nowhere else to turn for the location of the accused and with a considerable amount of information that in the eyes of the Inquisitors undermines the credibility of the chief witness, perhaps they could refocus their investigation and still put all the man-hours and piles of paper to good use? After all, Sor María Josefa, the accuser, is standing on very shaky ground: a nun, who has broken the vow of chastity—in appearance at least—with this *mala amistad* so frowned upon. The odds do not favor a young woman of dubious sanity, prone to an illness peculiar to her inferior sex, and faced with a battery of educated, powerful male clerics. All she can offer in her defense is that "cree que los hechos denunciados son ciertos, y no imaginarios y por tales los tiene" (she believes the accusations to be true, and not figments of her imagination and she stands by her story) (f. 15).

Without completely closing the investigation against Tomás Barreto, an investigation of the accuser herself now takes priority, with the point of departure being the suspicion "que se había extraviado por la mala amistad a dejar la clausura para vivir con la amiga" (that she had been led astray by the illicit relationship, and had wanted to leave the cloister to live with her friend) (f. 16). They therefore decided to gather information on the nun herself and have the abbess of the convent monitor her behavior and report back to the Inquisition.

Before detailing the outcome of these bizarre events, it is necessary to examine the charge of *mala amistad* that colors this investigation, rendering Sor María Josefa Ildefonsa de San Juan Bautista an unreliable witness, vulnerable to accusation and manipulation by the Inquisitors.

Mala amistad in the Convent

In a keyword search using the terms *mala amistad* in the database of the Archivo General de la Nación, a small group of texts from the Inquisition collection emerge. All but two of these, the case I examine here and one other, concern accusations the authorities leveled at men for relationships with women.[9] In the wider context of those Inquisition cases involving charges of sodomy, none specify same-sex relationships between women. Moreover no other document details a same-sex relationship, of whatever kind, between women in the convent. This absence is curious because of the large amount of didactic and proscriptive material available that warns of this phenomenon among women in the convent. Why should there be a significant amount of material proscribing these relationships if so few cases are reported? Was the didactic material so effective as to curtail such relationships? There was, I believe, reluctance—one might almost say squeamishness—on the part of the ecclesiastic establishment to confront this issue and to deal with the sexual undertones implied in female relationships. Was this squeamishness perhaps informed by a refusal to believe that women, nuns, were capable of illicit sexual acts? This notion hardly seems plausible given the centuries over which patriarchal society has cast the female body as the site of all kinds of aberrant sexual behavior.

The body of the nun is no exception.[10] Judith Brown has described a "phallocentric" early modern sexual economy, one that held that "women might be attracted to men and men might be attracted to men but there was nothing in a woman that could long sustain the sexual desires of other women" (6). However, although this may have been the most widely articulated belief, there was a more implicitly held view—what could perhaps be termed a subliminal fear—that same-sex relationships were indeed possible and must be legislated or admonished to prevent their occurrence. With regard to such occurrences in the convents, Brown has charted prohibitions from as early as St. Augustine in 423 (8). She also cites laws passed at the Councils of Paris (1212) and Rouen (1214), which ruled that nuns were forbidden from sleeping together and that lamps must be kept burning in cells at all times. Brown claims that the reasons for these rules were, "of course," always implicit (36). There is, then, a definite contradiction at play here, a double discourse of fear and contempt.

In a study of the prosecution of sodomy, the so-called *pecado nefando*, by the Valencian Inquisition from the sixteenth to the eighteenth century, Rafael Carrasco shows how women who engaged in sexual relations with other women were often, but not always, theoretically considered as sodomites (34–35). Interpretations did vary as to whether they could be deemed guilty of such an act: "Todo dependía de la definición a priori que se podía dar al acto" (It all depended on what initial definition could be given to the act) (35). Most texts concurred on the issue of behaving "como un hombre" as being the decisive factor in establishing sin. As Carrasco writes, in order to behave as a man "se necesitaba la intervención de uno de esos objetos penetrantes de fino cuero que abundan en la literatura licenciosa" (the intervention of one of those fine leather objects so prevalent in licentious literature was necessary.) (35).[11] Valerie Traub points out that women's same-sex relationships were more visible if the authorities found evidence of "prosthetic uses of implements of penetration" ("(In)Significance" 66). Not only were these acts more visible, but perhaps they were also more threatening because they implied a world in which women could aim to supplant the role of the man.[12]

Critics of the history of lesbianism have debated the issue of how same-sex activity between women may have been recognized before it was actually "identified" as a manifestation of sexuality in the nineteenth century. In her influential essay "The (In)Significance of 'Lesbian' Desire," Valerie Traub analyzes the "historical obscurity of early modern women's erotic desires for one another" (64). She focuses on "the historical vacuum into which early modern women's desires for one another seem to fall" (64). Her context is early modern England and, as I have found with Mexico, she finds no evidence that women were prosecuted for sodomy. She challenges the widely held belief that "ipso facto no women practiced these behaviors" (64). As with my analysis of *mala amistad*, she cites the stumbling block that the discourses on same-sex female behavior are almost always, in this period, "highly mediated by the protocols of patriarchal control" (64). According to Traub, as "critics and historians" our job is to "crack the code organizing the conceptual categories of an earlier culture" (65) in order to understand better same-sex relationships between women as well as the ideological effects of such relationships or desires.[13]

Obviously, relationships between men in religious orders were also the subject of censure by the Church. Vern Bullough has noted that ecclesiastics throughout history have always been conscious of what he terms "the homoerotic drive" among monastics (2). However, he suggests that sodomy among priests was an issue "continually discussed in councils and widely ignored in practice" (2). There are instances in the history of the Spanish and New World Inquisitions of clerics who were burned for the "sin against nature," although as members of the clergy, discretion was imposed and they were not always identified as such (Gruzinski 269–70).[14] A case from the archives of the Inquisition in Brazil[15] suggests that the Church sometimes exiled repeat offenders to the colonies, often moving them from place to place.

The case with women, both in general terms of gender and more specifically in terms of their monastic role, is different. First, friendship between men had a venerable history, being idealized in works of great literature from Aristotle on

(Raymond 79; Faderman, *Surpassing* 65–68).[16] On the other hand, throughout history society usually considered female friendship of "little substance, watery imitations of male camaraderie, either shallow or morbid," and a poor substitute for erotic love with a man (Enright and Rawlinson 96). As for the specific milieu of monasticism, the primary difference lies in the mandate of enclosure for women. As I discussed in chapter 1, the origins of this gender divide date back to the thirteenth century, when Pope Boniface VIII published a decree that officially imposed enclosure on all female orders. This gender disparity was particularly acute in the context of New Spain, given the almost complete absence of cloistered male religious orders in New Spain (Holler 20).[17] The mandate of cloister for communities of female religious only served to provide a heightened scenario for male fears and fantasies of female aberrance in the convent through the creation of a separate female communal space unmediated by the "normalizing" male presence.

A phallocentric view of human sexual behavior led to a reluctance to accept the existence of women's same-sex activity. Yet such was the fear attached to the female body and her unruly sexual instincts that any type of aberrant behavior was deemed possible, and consequently prohibitions had to be composed to guard against it. For these contradictory reasons it is necessary, then, to read between the lines of didactic and proscriptive texts and to hunt down implicit warnings of female homoerotic contact so as to "crack the code" governing the prohibitions against *mala amistad*. In the following section, I examine four texts that address, in different ways and with varying degrees of explicitness, the issues of *mala amistad* in the Hispanic convent. The four authors—Teresa of Ávila, Carlos de Sigüenza y Góngora, Francisco Aguiar y Seijas, Archbishop of Mexico (1681–1698?), and the eighteenth-century Mexican cleric Andrés de Borda—use their texts to convey didactic and prescriptive messages concerning same-sex relationships between women in the convent. In no text do we find an outright acknowledgment of homoerotic content in the *malas amistades* or *amistades particulares* against which they so vehemently warn.[18] Instead, there are admonitions of a different kind. These include warnings of the dangers inherent in factionalism and in distraction from the worship of God, as well as nonspecific allusions to improper relationships between women in the convent. Embedded beneath the Church's reasons for mistrusting and fearing particular friendships is a discourse that exposes—through the Church's repression of it—a fear of female same-sex desire that actually implies the presence of illicit relationships in the convent.

In *Camino de perfección* (1562?), Teresa of Ávila confronts the topic of what she calls "amistad particular." She warns her sisters:

> Parece que lo demasiado entre nosotras no puede ser malo; y trae tantas imperfecciones consigo, que no creo lo creerá sino quien ha sido testigo de vista. Aquí hace el demonio muchos enredos, que en conciencias que tratan groseramente de contentar a Dios, se sienten poco y les parece virtud, y las que tratan de perfección, lo entienden mucho; porque poco a poco quita la fuerza a la voluntad para que del todo se emplee en amar a Dios. (29)[19]

Here, Teresa brings together two themes that echo throughout all the prohibitions against *mala amistad*: the high susceptibility of women to the lure of these diabolic relationships ("Y en mujeres creo debe ser esto aún más que en hombres" (And I think it is even worse in women than in men) (29) and the manner in which these relationships distract from the pursuit of perfection, which has as its true aim the love of God, forsaking all others. To make sure the nuns understand the severity of her prohibition, Teresa employs a vehement and almost vitriolic language: "Y guárdense, por amor de Dios, de estas particularidades, por santas que sean, que aun entre hermanas suele ser ponzoña y ningún provecho veo en ellas. Y si son deudos, muy peor; es pestilencia" (30).[20] It is not clear just why Teresa feels that an *amistad particular* between "deudos" or relatives is worse than one between nuns who do not share kinship bonds—perhaps she is alluding to the specter of incest. What is evident is the severity of her warnings, indicated by the terms "ponzoña" and "pestilencia," both of which are highly redolent of sickness and infection.

Teresa also details different manifestations of such relationships, warning against specific tendencies of one woman toward the other such as "el desear tener para regalarla, el buscar tiempo para hablarla—y muchas veces más para decirle lo que la quiere que lo que ama a Dios" (28).[21] She also cautions against the use of terms of endearment such as "'mi vida,' 'mi alma,' ni otras cosas de éstas que a las unas llaman uno y a las otras otro. Estas palabras regaladas déjenlas para con el Señor. [...] Es muy de mujeres, y no querría yo mis hermanas pareciesen en nada sino varones fuertes" (qtd. in Weber 84).[22]

According to Alison Weber, Teresa wrote *Camino de perfección* specifically for her female subordinates. It is, at least superficially, a "notebook of advice on convent life" (83), although Weber makes it clear that Teresa's writing was never free from the constant scrutiny of the ecclesiastic authorities. To this end,

Weber has identified a dual discourse in the text, which the author employs mindful of the vigilance of the Church, yet simultaneously eager to convey her ideas openly to her sisters (86). This strategy enables her to "engage in criticism and promote affiliation simultaneously" (86). One can see this borne out in the rhetoric of self-abasement with which she tackles the specific temptations confronting cloistered women (81). As Weber writes, "Hers is a book by a 'weak woman' for 'weak women'" (81). Teresa uses the "rhetoric of irony" to disguise her true aim, which is to write to her sisters using the "rhetoric of solidarity" (84). Weber surmises that Teresa assumed that her female audience would understand the true meaning of her words and that she did not intend to censure them but instead to warn against what might incite the wrath of the ecclesiastic authorities (89).

This dual rhetorical strategy is strikingly evident in Teresa's warnings against particular friendships. Weber believes that she employed this strategy to guard against the charges of factionalism that had dogged her at La Encarnación:

> Teresa was eager not only to transmit her knowledge of mental prayer to the nuns [in *Camino de perfección*] but to promote the tranquility they would need to practice contemplation. Her break with the Incarnation had incurred considerable ill-will among her Calced sisters. [. . .] The twelve nuns of San José, in spite of the Bishop's blessing, were still "impure" troublemakers in the eyes of many citizens of Avila. Consequently, during these early days of her reform Teresa was greatly concerned with avoiding factionalism within the convent. (84)

In establishing her new order, Teresa wanted to deflect criticism away from the nuns of San José. She sought to portray the nuns as women dedicated to the pursuit of perfection, undistracted by mundane relationships that might promote factionalism or divert attention away from the worship of God. There is also a subtext at work in Teresa's prohibitions, one that pays lip service to the view held by the Church authorities regarding the imperfection of the female body and its propensity for sin. Her vehement warnings against *amistades particulares* and her employment of a vocabulary associated with sickness speak to an acknowledgment of the aberrance that was projected onto these relationships, one predicated on some kind of awareness of the potential for illicit homoerotic content in an *amistad particular*.

In Carlos de Sigüenza y Góngora's *Paraíso Occidental* (1693), the subtext of a sinful female body, exposed to the dangers inherent in the convents, emerges more clearly, as do the vehement rhetoric and metaphors of aberrance and illness typical of the baroque era. Sigüenza y Góngora's history of the convent of Jesús María in Mexico City, written to commemorate its one-hundredth anniversary, is ostensibly a book written for women. In the "Prólogo al lector," Sigüenza identifies his aim in *Paraíso Occidental* as "el escribir historia de mujeres para mujeres" (to write a history about women for women) (45). The book does indeed portray the lives of many women, incorporating the *vidas* of various exemplary nuns and other figures associated with the convent to tell the stories of these women. However, although it may be a story *of* women, it is not necessarily only a story *for* women. Kathleen Ross warns not to "accept at face value Sigüenza's stated intention" (*The Baroque Narrative* 12) as expressed in the prologue, but instead advises an examination of "the different levels of discourse" on which the text operates (14). One of these levels of discourse constitutes a warning against what Ross calls "the dangers of female flesh and the need to securely control woman's desire" (11). Rethinking the importance of women in the baroque era, as Ross does, we begin to perceive their role as "central actors" in their historical moment (11), with this centrality often negatively predicated on their sexual behavior and how it was controlled. Reading *Paraíso Occidental* as an example of criollo historiography, Ross outlines the importance of "controlling the sexuality of European-blooded women, through marriage or the convent [which] would ensure the preservation of a criollo group that could continue to dominate the Indian, African, and increasingly mixed-race masses" (11). Sigüenza's exemplary tales can, then, be read in a new light: as regulatory examples of pious women designed to promote perfect behavior in the convent, necessary for its function as a redoubt against the dangers of miscegenation.

Like Teresa, Sigüenza y Góngora emphasizes the weakness of women and their mutual incitement to deviate from the path of perfection. Consequently, he highlights the dichotomy of the very institution of the convent, where women are separated from society to conserve their purity, yet are then susceptible to other dangers in the form of the bad influence of an all-female, weak-willed community. The convent is depicted as a place of "repressed sexuality" (Ross, *The Baroque Narrative* 11), where the danger of so many female bodies together in one place dictates the need to maintain "control" at all costs. As Sigüenza describes it in his history, special friendships between nuns lead to a relaxing of discipline ("introducen la relajación en los monasterios," 316) and divert attention away from the true purpose of the nuns' life: pursuit of perfection via the love of God. The issue of *amistad particular* appears in three of the descriptions of exemplary lives he recounts in his text.

Sigüenza dedicates the entire second book of *Paraíso Occidental* to the life of Madre Marina de la Cruz, as written by her confessor Pedro de la Mota. Sigüenza employs the trope of *escarmiento*, or chastising example, to convey the moral of his exemplary tale and show how its subject suffered for her faults to eventually emerge victorious on the path to religious perfection (Ross, *The Baroque Narrative*, 23). One of the chastising examples that Sigüenza offers is that of the excessive love Marina felt for her daughter, who accompanied her into the convent. As Sigüenza tells his readers, Marina's worldly love for her daughter interfered with her pursuit of spiritual perfection. In telling this tale, Sigüenza makes a link between the intimate mother-daughter bond and the excesses of particular friendship. He likens her offense to that of "cuantas religiosas" (however many nuns) who, "olvidándose de la fidelidad prometida a su esposo en su profesión, ocupan sus potencias y sentidos en la inquietud de los devaneos que, aun entre las que habitan el siglo, son execrables" (143).[23] He refers to such worldly attachments, filial or otherwise, as "el monstruo de la devoción mundana" (the monster of earthly love) (143) and goes on to describe the behaviors that characterize the human hostages of this "monster," as well as the punishment that awaits them: "Se les pasan muchos meses y aun muchos años en semejantes empleos, sin que sienten los rigores de su celoso esposo, ni siquiera les punce el estímulo de la conciencia, sino que viven como si no hubiera Dios, o como si fuera mentira la eternidad" (144).[24]

God metes out his wrath with severity to those who choose to ignore their "celoso esposo," as is the case with Marina, whose daughter is taken from her so that her mother can dedicate herself to the "primer ejercicio de su vida, que era el que sin duda necesitaba para conseguir en la eterna infinita gloria" (most important activity in her life, that which without doubt she needed in order to attain eternal glory) (144). Here, Sigüenza uses this event in Marina's life to tell an exemplary tale that warns of the pitfalls of particular friendship in the convent. As he tells the reader further on in the story, Madre Marina was able to use this experience to counsel other nuns on the dangers of "los terrenos afectos" (earthly affections) and their potential interference with the attainment of perfect union with God through prayer.

In Book III of his narrative, the short section XIV dedicated to the "Vida admirable de Petronila de la Concepción, india donada del Real Convento" ("Admirable life of Petronila de la Concepción, a lay Indian woman who lived in the Royal Convent"), Sigüenza spins another exemplary tale of sin and redemption in which the monster of "la devoción mundana" makes an appearance once more. Petronila arrives at the convent as a young girl to work as a servant. Once there, she becomes involved in a close relationship with a nun. In Sigüenza's words, "Había cobrado a una religiosa singular cariño" (She had become particularly attached to one of the nuns) (283). From such "detestables amistades particulares" (odious particular relationships) according to Sigüenza originate "las diversiones, pérdidas de tiempo, chismes y pesadumbres" (pastimes, pointless activities, gossip, and melancholy) (283). As in the case of Madre Marina, Sigüenza's main criticism stems from how these relationships distract the women from the worship of God. Petronila is not strong enough to resist the lure of this relationship: "Aunque todo se le alcanzaba a Petronila bastantemente, no se determinaba a dejar de comunicarla por parecerle imposible aun el emprenderlo" (283).[25] Mercifully ("misericordiosamente"), God came to her rescue, and as she gazed on a statue of Christ in the convent's church, it miraculously stretched out its arm and touched her heart. Such were the effects this miracle had on her that she became so full of divine love "sólo con él respiraba y en él vivía" (she breathed only for Him and lived in Him) (283). There, one must assume, the detestable particular friendship met its end, and Petronila was finally able to direct her energies to a more laudable end.

The final mention of *amistad particular* in *Paraíso Occidental* comes in Sigüenza's brief treatment in Book III of the life of María Antonia de Santo Domingo, to whom he dedicates sections XXI to XXIV. Hers is obviously a most exemplary life, as Sigüenza tells a story untouched by the trope of *escarmiento*. He describes Madre María Antonia's role as both director of novices and finally as abbess, elevating her as the perfect example for the nuns to emulate: "Donde más se vieron los primores de su fervor y los quilates de su virtud fue en el de la pedagoga y maestra de novicias que ejercitó once años" (315).[26] Who better than to espouse the dangers of those "detestables amistades particulares"? He reproduces the text of another nun who recorded the admonishments and guidelines Madre María Antonia gave to the novices under her care: "Su más ordinario consejo era que procurasen vivir retiradas del trato y conversaciones del mundo, de que se seguiría el que mutuamente se amasen en Dios, que es la más poderosa arma para oponerse a las parcialidades que son las que introducen la relajación en los monasterios" (316).[27] She led by shining example. Sigüenza describes her as a "clarísimo espejo" ("a sparkling mirror") for those who wished to lead a life of consummate perfection. Following the guidelines she gave her novices, she loved her sisters in a way that would please God and without falling into the distraction and demonic trap of "el monstruo de la devoción mundana" (appalling worldliness). Janice Raymond has written of the delicate balance between spiritual love for one's sisters and the prohibition against particular friendships that nuns have traditionally faced: "The coexistence of particular friendship and its prohibition was not an easy one, for the claims of the spiritual were very often pitted against the claims of the particular" (92). Seemingly, according to Sigüenza y Góngora, Madre María Antonia was able to resolve this thorny issue in an exemplary fashion.

Archbishop Francisco Aguiar y Seijas of Mexico City also jumped into this particular fray, affixing an edict in May 1693 to the doors of the "coros bajos" (lower choirs) of every convent in the Archdiocese of Mexico that called for the prohibition of these illicit relationships.[28] Aguiar y Seijas was an infamous misogynist whose hagiographer, José de Lezamis, tells of his inability to be in the presence of women: "Si supiera ha entrado una mujer en su casa, había de mandar arrancar los ladrillos que había pisado. [...] No quería que en casa suya pusiesen manos las mujeres ni que guisasen la comida ni oírlas cantar ni siquiera oírlas hablar quería" (qtd. in Octavio Paz 484).[29]

To this man was entrusted the control of the convents, and we see his suspicion of the all-female convent space and the potential for aberrant behavior in his particular edict:

> El Ilustrísimo señor doctor don Francisco de Aguiar y Seijas, arzobispo de México, ha recibido noticias que en los conventos de esta ciudad existe la práctica de las devociones, así de fuera como de dentro de la clausura, por lo que notifica a los prelados de dichos conventos y a las religiosas, se cuiden de tales desmanes e inquietudes de malas amistades con el título de devociones con personas de cualesquier estados. (Qtd. in Rubial, *Los libros* 417)[30]

The devotions he refers to as "fuera [...] de la clausura" are relationships nuns had with male admirers, who would come to the doors of the convent to pay court. However, the archbishop believed those relationships exclusively between convent women were even more dangerous:

> Sobre todo las [devociones] que más escándalo causan, que son las de dentro de dicha clausura que tienen las religiosas unas con otras, y éstas con niñas seculares y con mozas de servicio, y éstas unas con otras, por ser de gravísimo inconveniente y notable escándalo y ruina espiritual. Y para que cesasen dichas devociones y el perjuicio grave que con ellas se ocasiona, y para que en lo adelante se abstengan de ello por ser ofensas de Dios, Nuestro Señor, Su Señoría manda se notifique a las madres abadesas, priorizas y vicarias de dichos conventos tengan especial cuidado en evitar

semejantes devociones y castiguen a las que contravinieren y quebrantaren el tener de este auto. (Qtd. in Rubial, *Los libros* 417)[31]

Here the archbishop also addresses the danger of particular friendships between nuns and their female servants. Sor María Josefa was involved in a *mala amistad* with a servant girl of the convent, a *moza* named María Gertrudis Rodríguez. Mexican convents were in fact small cities themselves, within the confines of the larger city, in which secular women and female religious lived side by side on a daily basis. Although there were many rules in effect barring the presence of secular women and girls, or at least restricting their numbers, these rules were often flouted or were difficult to enforce. Servants were a convent fixture in both the lenient orders, such as the *concepcionistas*, as well as in the more rigorous ones such as the *carmelitas descalzas* (discalced Carmelites). The Church hierarchy often regarded servants with suspicion and made many attempts to control their lives, as they were thought to contaminate the pristine ambiance of the convent through commerce with the outside world. According to Salazar, in theory servants must receive papal dispensation, or at least episcopal permission, in order to enter the cloister, although in practice many exceptions were made ("Niñas" 170–71). The general feeling among the ecclesiastic authorities was that the presence of private servants in the cloister made the nuns' lives too easy.[32]

Returning to the archbishop's edict, one can see that the punishment he threatened to mete out to those who contravened his *auto*—"excomunicación mayor"—was severe. To make sure all inhabitants of the convent were aware of his edict, he ordered them to be gathered together in the *coro bajo*, whereupon an official would read the edict to them so that they could not claim "ignorancia" of his instructions. Moreover, a copy was to be placed on the door of the *coro bajo*, "de donde ninguna de dichas religiosas, niñas o mozas sea osada de quitarlo ni romperlo, so las dichas penas de excomunicación mayor" (qtd. in Rubial, *Los libros* 418).[33] Obviously the archbishop was taking the problem of *mala amistad* very seriously indeed.

Fray Andrés de Borda, writing in 1708, also singles out servants as being the primary cause of these illicit relationships in the convent.[34] His text *Práctica de confesores* is ostensibly a manual for confessors, although it is apparent that the nuns themselves are his intended audience. In a style that echoes Núñez's in his *Cartilla de la doctrina religiosa*, it is written in the form of a didactic dialogue between a paternal and patriarchal priest and an eager and ignorant nun, in which the latter poses a series of questions regarding correct behavior in the convent.[35] Borda devotes one section to the topic of particular friendships with servants. To the opening question, "¿Padre, y en estas amistades con las sirvientas que en algunos conventos hay, y llaman *madres de amor*?" (Father, and what of these friendships with the servants that they have in some convents and who are known as *mothers of love*?), the priest replies, "no lo son de él, de Dios, porque no lo dicen sus costumbres conque lo son del amor del mundo" (these are not of God's doing, because they do not follow his traditions and as such constitute earthly love) (45–46). He offers the following clarification:

> Este puede ser honesto, como cuidar la moza a la religiosa, sazonándole un bocado, y es otras cosas necesarias si para sólo es esto no es prohibido, pero si pasa permitirle a la criada algunas acciones indecentes y pocas honestas, si la hace archivo de sus secretos y medianera de sus inquietudes, siento que es pecado mortal, perdición de las religiosas, relajación de los monasterios. (45–46)[36]

As with all the texts, the allusions to illicit acts are vague, but the warnings are explicit.[37] In another moment in his text, Borda describes these relations as constituting two "pecados mortales": one "de sacrilegio contra la virtud de la religión" (a sacrilege against religious virtue) and the other "contra la virtud de la castidad" (against the virtue of chastity).

In the texts above, most of the admonishments against *mala amistad* focus on the idea of "ruina espiritual" and "gravísimo inconveniente" (a very grave problem), implying that these relationships provoke a dereliction of duty—of the dedication to the worship of God as befitting a bride of Christ—and pose a danger to the harmony of the community. All three authors invoke the devil as a guiding force in these unhealthy encounters, tempting the righteous away from the path of perfection into evil.

Yet beyond these warnings concerning community and spiritual life is a subtext that has sexuality at its core. Janice Raymond's analysis of the prohibitions against particular friendships distinguishes two categories. The first category involves the sanctity of the virtue of charity. The Church believed that the possible creation of factions through these special relationships "would be injurious to the love of all the community" (92). The second claim against these special friendships, according to Raymond, was that the Church considered them "a violation of the vow of chastity" (92). Although the vow of chastity was usually interpreted as "illicit relations with the opposite sex," there was an implicit belief that within the cloister "chastity was often interpreted as refraining from illicit intimacy with the same sex" (Raymond 93). The threat of sensuality embedded in the prohibition against particular friendships has a complicated history and exists even in present-day female religious communities. In her book *The Nuns*, Marcelle Bernstein shows how modern nuns also face prohibitions against particular friendships, which they interpret in several ways. The nuns understand that such prohibitions are superficially intended to safeguard the reputation of the community (114). However, as Bernstein says, "Others see it as far more direct," and she quotes a nun who claims: "When we were novices, we knew it meant sensual friendships, we didn't just think it meant having friends sensibly" (114). It is this idea of particular friendship as "sensual friendship" that underlies all the warnings in the texts I have examined so far and that stimulated the mistrust and fear with which their authors viewed these relationships.

In Sor María Josefa's case, the authorities never openly articulate the sexual misconduct associated with the charge of *mala amistad*, yet in my opinion this drives the investigation forward, coloring the perception of the nun in the eyes of the Inquisitors, and rendering her a subversive and aberrant body. There is no way to know the exact details of her relationship with María Gertrudis Rodríguez, especially as all her testimony was produced under duress. There can be no doubt that strong feeling existed on Sor María Joseta's part, as she speaks of her desire to leave the convent to be with her friend, "por no separarse de ella" (f. 6). It is also evident that in the minds of the ecclesiastical hierarchy, this was an aberrant relationship, a *mala amistad*. In the following section of this study, I analyze how this taint of aberrance is compounded by the authorities' belief that Sor María Joseta's illness played a role in her *mala amistad*. Eventually, the two issues, illness and the illicit relationship, will become inextricably linked in the minds of the authorities.[38]

Retraction and Humiliation: "Por mi mucha fragilidad y miseria"

As I mentioned in the introduction to this study, this case is characterized by an impressive array of twists and turns and stops and starts. Following the *Fiscal*'s report (dated March 10, 1794), the next document in the file is a letter from the nun herself to her confessor, dated 1794 with no month specified. The letter, written in Sor María Josefa's tiny handwriting, details a retraction and an apology to the Holy Tribunal. Given her poor mental state, she was led into falsely writing the denunciation against Tomás: "Por mi mucha fragilidad y miseria y estando preocupada de la pasión del desconsuelo, vine por fin a caer en la falsedad de escribir a este Santo Tribunal" (f. 17).[39] She states she had deceived the Inquisition: "engañé siendo falso este conocimiento" (I lied as this information is not true), despite the fact that "me hizo jurar las dos veces" (he made me swear twice). In her incoherent and rambling letter, she claims that she knew Tomás, his sorcery, and the magic book were her inventions, "aunque a la dicha persona que nombré aunque no me acuerdo si nombré también el apellido por no acordarme en el día del apellido y es cierto conocí a la tal persona más no es cierto de que esta persona era mágico ni yo he tenido tal conocimiento de ningún mágico ni es cierto tal papel"(f. 17).⁴⁰ She wants the Inquisition to drop its case against Tomás, as "no hay nada y sólo lo hice perturbada con la pasión como he dicho" (there is no case and I only did it because I was overcome by emotions, as I have said) (f. 17).

Attached to her letter is one from her confessor, Padre Pablo Patiño. He informs the Inquisition that he instructed Sor María Josefa to write her letter. It is he who sends along the retraction with "otra denuncia de una niña que confesó pocos días ha en Santa Inés" (another denunciation of a girl I confessed a few days ago in Santa Inés) (f. 18). He writes that "Días ha que se lo hice escribir como era justo informado de la falsedad de la denuncia que había practicado contra el inocente de quien depuso diciendo que era mágico" (f. 18).⁴¹ He decided to wait, however, before sending it, to make sure this was indeed the truth, owing to the fragile mental state of the nun: "para reconocer si estaba constante en la retracción por ser mujer joven y sumamente apasionada y melancólica" (in order to confirm if her retraction was consistent as she is a young woman who is highly emotional and melancholic) (f. 18). He waits a long time indeed to make this determination. Her letter is dated 1794, Padre Patiño's, April 20, 1797.

Despite her earlier denials, Sor María Josefa now blames her false denunciation of Tomás on the effects of her illness. The Inquisitors had already made a connection between her illness and her illicit relationship ("el engaño de una fantasía lastimada por la enfermedad o por la misma vehemencia de los deseos que hubo de salir de la clausura para estar en la mala compañía de una moza con que hubo ilícita correspondencia" (f. 19).⁴² Of interest to me here is the interplay between the charge of *mala amistad* and the imputation of mental infirmity to Sor María Josefa. In the following section, I examine the mechanisms at play in this connection and review eighteenth-century opinions on hysteria to consider how they figure in the Inquisition's specific handling of Sor Maria Josefa's case.⁴³

The long-held theory that attributed hysteria to the infamous wandering womb, *mal de madre*, had been overthrown by the eighteenth century. It was replaced by the premise of a weakness in the nervous system as responsible for the disease, however "poorly defined and ill-understood" the concept of the nervous system may have been (G. S. Rousseau 147).[44] However, what Rousseau has dubbed "Enlightenment hysteria" was certainly not free of prejudices, ignorance, or, specifically, negative imaging of the female body. Moreover, medicine had not drawn a clear line between madness and hysteria: "The line between melancholy and madness was delicate and thus greatly feared" (153). Rousseau chronicles a list of terms—"melancholy, madness, hysteria, hypochondria, dementia, spleen and vapors, nerves"—all of which were, by the eighteenth century, "jumbled and confused with one another as they had never been before" (153). The documents describing Sor María Josefa's case perfectly illustrate this confusion. Her illness is described variously as "hipocondría," "una especie de mal que le priva de los sentidos" (a type of illness that deprives one of one's senses), "Histérico o de lo que vulgarmente se llama Latido" (hysteria or what is commonly called *latido*), and "una imaginación perturbada" (a disturbed mind). She is also depicted as being "sumamente apasionada y melancólica" (highly unstable and melancholic) (f. 20).

The confusion of hysteria and its offshoots with madness, of which Rousseau speaks, led to a stigma that seemed to attach itself particularly to the female patient, as had the uterine theory of centuries past. Although by the eighteenth century it was accepted that men too could be hysterics, the disease was still very much thought of as a female one. However, in an age that held the process of scientific inquiry so dear, it was necessary to clarify just why women were so much more susceptible than men. The answer the experts came up with showed that science still adhered to long-held stereotypical views of women, what Rousseau classifies as "so-called incontrovertibles: women's innate propensity to nervousness; their domestic situation in a private world conducive to hysterical excess; their insatiable sexual voracity granted from time immemorial" (174). It is possible to see all these factors at play in the minds of the Inquisitors as they question Sor María Josefa on the nature of her illness.

Michel Foucault reads this gendered diagnosis as encapsulating a moral and ethical judgment:

> The resistance of the organs to the disordered penetration of the spirits is perhaps one and the same thing as that strength of soul which keeps the thoughts and desires in order. This internal space which has become permeable and porous is perhaps only the laxity of the heart. (*Madness and Civilization* 149)

In the same vein, the Italian physician Georgio Baglivi (1668–1707) held that women's vulnerability to the disease arose from what he termed "passions of the mind." In his 1704 treatise on hysteria, Baglivi declared: "Women are more subject than Men to Diseases arising from Passions of the Mind, and more violently affected with them, by Reason of the Timorousness and Weakness of their Sex" (qtd. in Rousseau 148).

These "passions of the mind" implied a specific connection between passion and the imagination and, as a consequence, provoked somatic change (Rousseau 162).[45] Passions and imaginations—or, one could perhaps say, passionate imaginations—were often considered the result of lovesickness or erotomania, a view that became particularly popular in the eighteenth century. Rousseau describes the eighteenth-century belief that in such cases "the nervous system had flared out of control as the result of passion" (173). Melancholy, a disease that was often confused or conflated with hysteria and with which María Josefa had also been "diagnosed," was often believed to result from excessive desires.[46] Women, of course, were far more susceptible to this type of condition. Katharine Hodgkin writes: "for women in particular it [melancholy] was shadowed by the suggestion of excessive and unseemly sexual desires" (70). As with hysteria, the cause was thought to be located in the nerves or the nervous system, a theory that finally triumphed over the centuries-long diagnosis of the imbalance of the corporeal humors (Starobinski 50).

Another renowned physician of the eighteenth century, Pinel, believed the cure lay in the removal from the patient of the object that had caused the disturbance: "Melancholy cannot be completely cured unless the causes are destroyed. The first essential is therefore, to know at the outset what these causes are" (Starobinski 52). For Pinel, the melancholic was a "victim of an idea of his own making which lives inside him as a parasite" (Starobinski 52). In this case, the parasite is the *mala amistad*, the obsessive affection for the servant. It was believed that erotomania was brought about by excessive focus on the object of desire. Prominent eighteenth-century physician Jerome Graub wrote the following of the sufferers of erotomania:

> How the force and continuity of the functions slacken, how the condition of the body languishes and all the powers of the economy weaken and collapse when an ardent wish for some desired object is too long drawn out! [...] How often do beautiful maidens and handsome youths, caught in the toils of love, grow ghastly pale and waste away, consumed by melancholy, green-sickness, or erotomania, when delays occur or the hope of possession is lost?"[47]

If María Gertrudis, the servant girl, did in fact leave the convent as she had planned, the Inquisitors may have attributed María Josefa's illness to a case of erotomania caused by the devastation of an illicit lost love.

This view of Sor María Josefa Ildefonsa as a subject whose unruly passions or unseemly sexual desires brought on a nervous illness is one held by the male ecclesiastical hierarchy, including the Inquisitors and her confessor, who have definitely made a moral and ethical judgment. They consistently discredit her as a witness and treat her more as the accused, while bringing greater focus to bear on her illness and how it must have tainted her testimony. The Inquisitors had established a definite connection between *mala amistad* and the nun's illness, between her unseemly desires and her "imaginación perturbada" (f. 20). This reaction is typical of the eighteenth century—an age when "Women in their disorders are [. . .] emblems of the disorders of their ungovernable bodies and unruly passions" (Hodgkin 74).

The reports of María Josefa's ungovernable body and disordered mind appear at various points throughout these documents over the seven-year period during which the Inquisition officials examine her case. The Inquisitors cannot decide quite how to interpret her illness. Did her illness disorder her imagination ("el engaño de una fantasía lastimada por enfermedad")? Or was it the perversity of the illicit relationship that caused the illness ("la misma vehemencia de los deseos que hubo de salir de la clausura para estar en la mala compañia de una moza con que hubo ilícita correspondencia") (f. 19)?[48] The two interpretations are of course inextricably related. In the minds and words of the authorities, sexual aberrance and mental illness have run together in indistinguishable confusion. From here on in, the sick mind and body of the nun begin to take center stage in the documents, as the crimes of the mysterious Tomás Barreto fade increasingly into the background.

Illness and Discredit: The Second Investigation

To follow the chronology of this case is no easy task. Incredibly, seven years after the initial investigation began with Sor María Josefa's letter of denunciation in September 1792, and two years after the nun's confessor Padre Patiño submitted her retraction in 1797, the case was being investigated again. The Inquisitors had not brought to light any new evidence, so one can only speculate that a confluence of factors led to a reawakening of the Inquisition's interest: an unresolved case with many hours of investigation wasted, a missing defendant, and more importantly, a witness who was an easy target.

The first task the Inquisitors undertake is to interrogate the nun as to why she made the two conflicting statements: the one in which she denounced Tomás and the other in which she retracted her denunciation. The Inquisitors' statements reveal their preconceived notion, apparent from their statements, that all false testimony was a direct result of her deluded state of mind. In her first interview on August 31, 1799, with Padre Pico, she is asked why she made the first statement in 1792, in which she denounced Tomás. She replies that although she recognizes the letter as being written in her hand, she can offer no further clarification as to the veracity of its contents. The Inquisition report states:

> Se le manifestó y entregó la esquela que corre en estas diligencias para que la leyere y reconociese y habiéndola leído y visto a su satisfacción dijo que todo esto da en su letra y que supone por su contexto que la escribió para enviarla a los Santos Inquisidores pero no se acuerda si así fue, ni tiene presente con quién la remitió. (f. 20)[49]

They bombard her with questions, asking her whether the denunciation of Tomás or the retraction of the charge is the truthful version. She says she cannot be sure. She is instructed to spend the next day "thinking" about this matter, in consultation with her confessor, whereupon the Inquisitors will return for her answer. Not surprisingly, when they return two days later, the nun explains she has clarified things in her own mind "habiendo contestado con su confesor" (having consulted her confessor) (f. 20) and that after seeking advice from him she could confidently answer that the initial denunciation was indeed false. Echoing the Inquisitors' own words, she asserts that she made this denunciation under the influence of poor mental health: "teniendo preocupada la cabeza con sus enfermedades" (her mind being distracted by illness) (f. 20).

Padre Pico's report of the interview, dated September 14, 1799, makes reference to the Madre Abadesa's report to the Inquisition concerning Sor María Josefa. Apparently, the abbess had met with Padre Pico before the interrogation of the nun, "en la reja en presencia del Notario" (at the grill in the presence of the notary) (f. 21), to bring him up to date on the particulars of Sor María Josefa's illness. Her report is inflammatory. According to Pico, the abbess recounts the following:

> Que esta Religiosa padece un histérico excesivo, de modo que tiene la cabeza muy débil y llena de especies las más irregulares de que es difícil disuadirla: que una vez dio en que una moza entraba en su celda por una

ventana, estando cerradas las puertas de la misma ventana; y otra, que había visto en un tránsito a las cuatro de la mañana un hombre de capa encarnada; y a este modo afirma y asegura con la mayor certeza otras cosas semejantes: que estando ya tocada de esta enfermedad la acaba de rematar un cáustico que le pusieron en el cerebro, con motivo de un mal fuerte que le daba, que acaso la desflaqueció, o lastimó los nervios de una parte delicada: Que todo esto lo prevenía la Madre Abadesa para que no se diese fácilmente crédito a lo que dijera en orden a estas especies, ni a las que contenía la denuncia que había hecho. (f. 21)[50]

The report is unfavorable to Sor María and deals a further blow to her credibility, coming as it does from the head of her community. (One cannot help wondering if the "delusion" described in the report of the girl who entered her cell through the window was indeed a delusion or was actually the flesh-and-blood servant girl, María Gertrudis Rodríguez.) The treatment and the *cáustico*'s aftereffects described in the report sound both unpleasant and unhelpful and are completely in keeping with the ignorance and confusion that characterized the eighteenth-century response to this illness.[51] María del Carmen Simón Palmer has pointed out that in the eighteenth century in Spain, moral and religious imperatives often took precedence over scientific advances in the treatment of women's illness: "El choque entre los deberes morales y las necesidades físicas se saldó siempre a favor de la salvación del alma, por encima del bienestar del cuerpo" (71).[52] It seems that this was the case for María Josefa, that a desire to cure her of her delusions and/or her illicit relationship and restore her to a life of perfection in the convent precipitated this treatment.

At the end of his report, Padre Pico offers his opinion of the nun. He judges her comments to have been "propios de una imaginación perturbada, y en este concepto considero a esta Religiosa libre enteramente de malicia y de culpa y digna de compasión" (f. 22).[53] Incredibly, although he deems her free of guilt and worthy of compassion, the matter is not to end here. The Inquisition once again asks the nun's confessor, Padre Patiño, to intercede. He asks her for any further information she can dredge up from her fevered mind concerning Tomás Barreto, in further pursuance of the circumstances surrounding her false denunciation. She writes him a letter, apologizing for the delay, explaining that she has suffered from memory loss ever since "me echaron el cáustico en el cerebro" (they applied the *cáustico* to my brain) (f. 25). She repeats verbatim the same information she offered seven years ago about Tomás, explaining that she had indeed wanted to consult with a "mágico" because of her "desconsuelos" (unhappiness), that is, her desire to be with the *moza* who had resolved to leave the convent.

This time, however, she adds by way of explanation that, as best she can recall, her then-confessor pressured her into making the denunciation: "Batalló mucho para que diera el aviso al Santo Oficio pero por fin lo hice" (He strove to make me inform the Holy Office, which I finally did) (f. 25). Her confessor had misunderstood, she says. She had told him she wanted to consult a sorcerer, but he understood this to mean that she had already consulted one: "le dije deseaba tener comunicación con un mágico por mis desconsuelos pero él se entendió que la tenía" (I told him I wanted to make contact with a sorcerer because I was unhappy but he understood me to mean I already had) (f. 25). Either in an effort to please him or through fear, she finally admits to having consulted a *mágico*: "así ya después si dije que tenía y ésto fue porque como lo entendió" (afterwards I did say I had done so, because that is what he thought I had done) (f. 25). According to Sor María Josefa, she denounced Tomás because she had seen him a few times before she entered the convent: "y el coger el nombre del sujeto que he dicho no me acuerdo, si fue por pensar que si vivía estaría muy lejos o si por haberle visto algunos lugares cuando estaba yo en la calle" (f. 25).[54] She seems confused and frightened ("tengo mil dudas") (f. 25). Finally, she gives her mother's name and address—"porque me mandó le diera razón de mi madre" (I was told to give information about my mother) (f. 25)—and also offers the name of her aunt, a nun in the Balvanera convent who can also "dar razón de todo" (give a full account) (f. 25). This is the last we hear from Sor María Josefa Ildefonsa de San Juan Bautista.

The group of documents comes to an inconclusive end. It is not known what the fate of the young nun may have been. Did the Inquisition let the matter drop, following Padre Pico's recommendation to treat her with compassion? Or do they continue to hound her, perhaps even prosecute and imprison her? There is no record.

Confession and the Search for Truth

Which version of María Josefa's story represents the truth? As fanciful as María Josefa's original denunciation of Tomás may be with its story of the magic book, it is not impossible that she was the victim of an unscrupulous confidence trickster who preyed on a gullible teenage nun and her desire to leave the convent so as not to be separated from the servant girl, María Gertrudis Rodríguez. After all, there is motive for such a scheme. According to her initial statement, he had told her that if he were to liberate her from the convent, he would offer them accommodation ("tenía donde ponerla en compañía de la moza" [he had a place for her to stay with the servant girl]) on the condition that "estando en la calle, había de hacer lo que el Tomás le dijera" (once in the street, she had to do whatever Tomás told her) (f. 6). If we are to believe what the investigation turned up about Tomás (that he possessed "alguna afición desarreglada a las personas del otro sexo" [an improper interest in members of the opposite sex]) (f. 28), this scenario may not be entirely implausible. Yet, it is also not implausible that the nun denounced Tomás in a desperate and misguided attempt to draw attention away from her illicit relationship with the servant girl. That she was very naïve is obvious from the documents. What interests me here is how the Inquisitors arrive at what they accept as the truth (that she lied in her original denunciation owing to her illness) and what role Sor María Joseta's confessor plays in this search for the "truth."

It is important that we consider Sor María Josefa's case against the historical background of the Inquisition in Mexico. First officially established in 1571, the Mexican Inquisition finally ground to a halt in 1820, although it had been in decline since the 1760s: "the activities of the Holy Office were severely hampered because of the tendency of royal and ecclesiastical officialdom to embrace philosophical eclecticism" (Greenleaf 258). According to Richard Greenleaf, an inability to tackle large-scale problems led to "a sense of frustration," which in turn led officials to "concentrate on smaller ones" (Greenleaf 259). Greenleaf depicts an organization characterized by "hair-splitting and tedious controversies" as well as the "preoccupation with protecting the position and dignity of the Tribunal of the Inquisition" (259). This description perfectly sums up how the Inquisition treated the case of Sor María Josefa. Elías Trabulse has characterized the late eighteenth-century Inquisition as mirroring the changes that were occurring in Mexican society. Inquisition archives reveal that the kind of cases that it prosecuted—an increase in blasphemy and heresy, for example—were strong indications of transformations in "las costumbres, las ideas y las mentalidades" (habits, ideas, and thought patterns) (9). Obviously, the fact that the Inquisition's records provide us with this glimpse into changing attitudes is precisely because they were trying to counteract these changes. Yet, there is no doubt that the Mexican Inquisition was not at the peak of its oppressive powers in this period. Ruth Behar describes the Mexican Inquisitors of this period as "lenient and paternal" ("Sex and Sin" 42), their central goal being to inspire a sense of guilt and shame in penitents and through confession to bring them back to the correct way of life (Behar, "Sexual Witchcraft" 183–84).

Nonetheless, it still had a powerful grip on society and on the conduct of its members.

The Inquisition penetrated into all areas of eighteenth-century Mexican life, leading to what Behar has termed an "interiorization of inquisitorial ideas" ("Sex and Sin" 36). She bases this theory on the large number of self-denunciations found in the Inquisition's records (36). This "self-censoring process" (36) was particularly prevalent among women. It was a process that "began with a prohibited act" and "ended with a desire for integration into the Church" (36). The role of the confessor was fundamental in facilitating this process as the case of Sor María Josefa demonstrates. Mabel Moraña has described the figure of the confessor as "Figura paternal protectora y tiránica, imagen de autoridad que representa la fe y la represión, la salvación y la condena, la iniciación y el fin, la posición del confesor se ubica en la zona oscura e impenetrable de la intimidad, en la frontera tenue que separa pecado y santidad" (*Viaje al silencio* 143).[55] Moraña refers here to the relationship between Sor Juana and her erstwhile confessor Antonio Núñez de Miranda, but we can apply her analysis to the general relationship between the nun and her male confessor, as well as to the specific relationship between Sor María Josefa and her confessor, Padre Pedro Patiño.

The nun is unable to act without first consulting her confessor; he is the one who guides all her actions. The power structure of the convent served to promote the subordinate role the nun occupied in this dyad. María Águeda Méndez writes: "En tal ámbito, los guardianes de almas tenían injerencia y regían su modo de actuar, pero, más grave aún, su forma de pensar, expropiándoles la libertad tanto física como mental" ("La palabra persuasiva" 103).[56] It is important to note that not all relationships between nun and confessors can be characterized in this way. The relationship could be an extremely complicated one, not always characterized by a one-way power dynamic (Sampson Vera Tudela 46). Indeed, some confessors elevated their own stature by directing the spiritual lives, and often *vidas*, of spiritually advanced women (Sampson Vera Tudela 47). Moreover, women writers in the convent often secretly and strategically manipulated their narratives to subvert and resist the male ecclesiastical power structure, while at the same time superficially collaborating with their confessors (Myers, "The Mystic Triad" 482). However, María Josefa does not fall into the category of exceptional nuns, and her relationship with her confessors cannot be characterized as one of mutual intellectual stimulation and benefit.

According to Sor María Josefa, she never approaches the Inquisition without first consulting with her confessor. In the initial examination by the Inquisition following her denunciation of Tomás, she is asked "¿Cúal es el objeto de su denuncia?" (What is the purpose of her denunciation?) (f. 4). She claims ignorance: "Dijo: que no entiende de estas cosas" (She said that she doesn't understand these matters) and that she was simply carrying out the instructions of her confessor: "que la denuncia la hizo porque el Licenciado Don Fernando Martínez de Soria, con quien está haciendo confesión, le previno que la hiciera" (f. 4).[57] Her subsequent retraction is made on the orders of her confessor, now Padre Patiño. When the Inquisitors revisit the case in 1799 and Sor María Josefa is unable to recall whether the original denunciation or the later retraction is correct, she is told to consult with her confessor in order to clear her mind. The result, as the Inquisitors expect, is that she tells them what they want to hear: "habiendo contestado con su confesor ya está asegurada de que puede decir con verdad y sin temor alguno que efectivamente fue falsa su denuncia" (f. 20).[58]

The rhetoric of humility Sor María Josefa employs to address her confessor exemplifies the comments made by Mabel Moraña cited earlier. She is unable to act without first consulting her confessor; he is the one who guides all her actions. Moreover, the fear in her words demonstrates her desire to keep within the boundaries laid out by him and by the Church. On one occasion, for example, she writes to him: "Mi muy venerado Padre, me alegraré no tenga novedad en su apreciable salud. Estimado Padre, pensará V.M. que él no haberle escrito antes así ha sido de desidia o cosa semejante. Más no ha sido así sino que quería darle razón a todo pero esto no es posible por falta de memoria" (f. 25).[59] Moreover, she states that one reason for her inability to remember past information, such as Tomás's last name, is that she had no confessor at that time: "Sólo por obedecer a VM escribo esto y lo hago con bastante mortificación por no poder acordar pero no me parece que entonces tenía confesor con quien quedarme" (f. 25).[60] Here she makes a connection between the truth and the guidance of a confessor. Seemingly one is not possible without the other.

Peter Brooks has written of the "bond" between confessor and confessant: "It contains, and activates, elements of dependency, subjugation, fear, the desire for propitiation, the wish to appease and to please. It leads to the articulation of secrets, perhaps to the creation of hitherto 'unrealized' truth—or perhaps the simulacrum of truth" (35). All these elements exist in Sor María Josefa's relationship with Padre Patiño and have resulted in the production of several "truths," one or more of which must be a simulacrum. These elements of which Brooks speaks, especially subjugation and fear, are heightened by the presence of another, equally powerful, bond: that which exists between the nun's confessor and the Inquisition. The links between the role of the confessor and the institution of the Inquisition go back to the Fourth Lateran Council of 1215, which promulgated yearly confession for all Christians. At the same time, it established the institution of the Inquisition to eradicate heresy (Brooks 45). Confession and the Inquisition are thus inextricably linked. Brooks writes: "The urge to confess is thus put to work both toward the absolution of the sinner's individual conscience and toward the policing of religious orthodoxy. Confession is the way to contrition and absolution, which permits a reintegration into the community of the faithful" (46). From the evidence provided by the documents, it seems that Patiño's actions serve the ends of the Inquisition more than they help the nun. In the minds of the Inquisitors, María Josefa's status as a complaining witness was discredited early on in the case, and they avail themselves of Patiño's role as father figure, relying on her desire to please him, to obtain what they have deemed to be the truth.

It was obviously important for them that she corroborate their version of the truth. To cite Brooks again: "Commonsensically, we might assume that the evidence against the accused produced from his own mouth is always the most reliable evidence we can have. When someone confesses, his judges may proceed to condemn him with good conscience" (21). However, Brooks's entire analysis of the act of confessing undermines what is commonly held to be "confessional truth." He lays bare "confessional truth," revealing it as a product of many different factors, least of which is the "truth":

> Confessions rarely are products of free and rational will. They arise in situations of constraint, whether physical or psychological. They are motivated by inextricable layers of shame, guilt, disgrace, contempt, self-loathing, propiation and expiation. Their truth is often not straightforward but deviated from its apparent referent: a truth of performance and dialogue, a truth created by the bond of confessant and confessor. (63)

All these elements have entered into the production of María Josefa's "confession": her retraction of her original denunciation of Tomás. The Inquisitors' interrogations systematically undermined her credibility and self-confidence. They tried to compel her to admit that her denunciation was the product of mental illness and that her mental illness was the product of an illicit and shameful relationship. They use the relationship with her confessor to extract the relevant information they are seeking. A confession under circumstances such as these is, according to Brooks, an "alienated production" (78) and a result of what he deems "the overborne will" of the person making the confession. By this he means that "voluntariness" has been lost from the confessional act in a situation where, by whatever means, "free choice has been constrained or impaired" (69).

As we read the last letter Sor María Josefa wrote, there is no doubt that her will has been "overborne." She has been overwhelmed and frightened by an investigation that has lasted seven years and in which she has had ranged against her not only the Inquisitors but her own confessor and the abbess of her convent. Never mentioned, but surely discussed with her confessor, is the importance of salvation to this process. The sins of María Josefa were to be expiated if she were to confess. According to the Church, her sins were many: her desire to break her vows, her lies, her illicit same-sex relationship. The Inquisition relied, according to Brooks, on "a nexus of consolation and discipline," and in this case, they readily employed these tools in the service of the[ir] "truth."

Conclusion

This case from the Inquisition archives of Mexico is characterized by a dizzying series of stops and starts and twists and turns that, at times, seem inexplicable. The inconsistencies in the nun's story form a contrast with the constant effort on the part of the Inquisition to undermine her and to cast her in the role of the accused. From the very beginning, the Inquisitors seem unwilling to believe her, based on the stigma she carries because of the charge of *mala amistad*. Sor María Josefa is never able to shake off the mistrust accorded to her because of this illicit and aberrant relationship. It is the taint of aberrance that fuels the Inquisition's interest over a period of seven years—even when there is nothing new to discover, and years have gone by with nothing new added to the case.

The category of *mala amistad* is part of the obscure and contradictory evidence that exists with regard to same-sex relationships between women. A phallocentric view of human behavior led to a reluctance to accept the existence of women's same-sex activity. Such was the fear attached to the female body and sexual instincts, however, that any type of aberrant behavior was deemed possible, and prohibitions had to be constructed to guard against it. The topic of perceived female aberrant behavior was approached with reluctance, euphemism, and even squeamishness. However, it both informed and provoked negative views of women, in particular with reference to female coexistence in the convent.

To trace the details of same-sex relationships between women in history is a difficult task. Women were not often able to express their feelings openly, so written evidence of these feelings told in their own words is rarely available. The critic or historian is often faced with the difficult task of piecing together a story from the words of others—most often, as is the case with María Josefa's story, from the words of those who would censure these types of homoerotic relationships. The Inquisition provides a perfect example of this. As Mary E. Giles has written of the stories of women in the Inquisition in Spain and the New World: "In words recorded by notaries who were present at their audiences with the inquisitors and in chambers of torture, women step forward, like ghosts in a dream, to claim existence and identity in the reader's imagination" (1). Such a ghostly figure is Sor María Josefa Ildefonsa de San Juan Bautista. Despite the access we have to letters written in her own hand, she is never really able to tell her story. An even more ghostly and dreamlike figure is that of the servant girl, María Gertrudis Rodríguez, whose name is never mentioned without the accompanying phrase of *mala amistad*. The details of their relationship will never be known. What is clear is the extreme displeasure and condemnation their relationship provoked in the authorities, predicated on its threat to the coerced community, which is our only window onto their story.

4

Mobilizing Community

The Fight against *vida común*

Between the years of 1625 and 1637, an English Dominican friar by the name of Thomas Gage traveled through Mexico and Guatemala, all the while recording his impressions for posterity. In 1648 his book bearing the title *The English-American or A New Survey of the West Indies* was published in England. By the time the book began to circulate, Gage had become an ardent Protestant, and in the text he singles out the Catholic Church for severe criticism, casting aspersions on all he describes. Gage's main target was the convents, which he depicted as being a heavy financial drain on the communities they supposedly served, as well as neglecting their spiritual mission. In one passage he accuses a particular community of nuns of overemphasizing the importance of the secular accomplishments of music and drama and of putting on entertainments with their pupils as protagonists. He fulminates: "They [the nuns] teach these children to act like players; and to entice people to their churches, they make these children act short dialogues in their choirs. [. . .] No delights are wanting in that city abroad in the world, nor in the churches, which should be the house of God, and the soul, not the sense's delight" (72). He also criticizes the fraternization of monks and nuns, portraying the convent as a salon where men come to be entertained by amenable ladies:

> It is ordinary for the friars to visit the devoted nuns, and to spend whole days with them, hearing their music, feeding on their sweetmeats, and for this purpose they have many chambers which they call *locutorios*, to talk in, with wooden bars between the nuns and them, and in these chambers are tables for the friars to dine at, and while they dine the nuns recreate them with their voices. (72)

Gage's most vehemently critical remarks are reserved for nuns alone, especially the cloister of La Concepción in Antigua, Guatemala, and one of its inhabitants, the beautiful Doña Juana de Maldonado y Paz, who so captivated the bishop with her personal attractions that he risked scandal to make her abbess of the convent. The prelate lavished gifts upon her, as did her rich father, and she built herself "a new quarter within the cloister with rooms and galleries, and a private garden-walk, and kept at work and to wait on her half a dozen Blackamoor maids" (190). Her private chapel, according to Gage, was decked with jewels and lined with gold, which "was enough for a nun that had vowed poverty, chastity and obedience" (191). Her money, claims the Englishman, bought her power and influence, and she was able to "win the hearts of the common sort of nuns" (191). He ends this anecdote on a typically hyperbolic moralizing note: "Thus is ambition and desire of command and power crept into the walls of the nunneries, like the abomination of the wall of Ezekiel, and hath possessed the hearts of nuns, which should be humble, poor and mortified virgins" (191).

There can be no doubt that Gage's book, written at a time of fanatical Protestantism in Oliver Cromwell's England, was "deeply influenced by political and religious considerations" (Gage xv, Thompson introduction). Although the circumstances under which he recorded his comments are singular—he was a recent convert to Protestantism eager to prove his commitment to his new faith—his observations, especially those on the dissolute life of communities of female religious, are not unique to writers of anti-Popish rhetoric. Such observations have dogged the New World convents throughout the centuries and are seemingly not specific to any one religious preference or historical moment. Writers from Carlos de Sigüenza y Góngora to Octavio Paz have leveled accusations of overly luxurious living at the convents. In the eighteenth century, the Church claimed this was the chief motivation behind its reform of the New World convents. The so-called common life, or *vida común*,[1] they declared, would introduce a simpler and more orthodox way of life by curtailing the luxuries nuns enjoyed in the convent and severely limiting their contact with the outside world.

What was really at stake in these enforcements, I argue, was the issue of control of the female orders. The rule of *vida común* implied a life that was communal in all its aspects. Houses that adhered to it—such as those of the more austere *descalzado* (discalced) orders—had communal facilities for sleeping, eating, doing laundry, and handling money. The less rigorous *calzado* convents obeyed cloister and other vows, yet were able to maintain their own establishments within the convent walls.[2] These women observed what was known as *vida particular*. They had servants and slaves, and their cells were sometimes like small houses. They also administered their own finances with allowances based on donations given to the convent by their families. Moreover, every convent was run according to the specificity of its own *constituciones* (Sierra Nava-Lasa 196–97), which helped bestow each convent with a source of pride in its own particular community.[3]

The polemic concerning the imposition of *vida común* continued for several decades, generating hundreds and hundreds of documents from both sides of the debate and from both sides of the Atlantic. This chapter does not purport to be a history of the controversy, but rather will study some of the documents generated by each side to elucidate the belief each held as to how convent communities should be constructed and lived in, as well as what means each side employed to achieve its ends. I examine documents that detail both sides of the debate: the ecclesiastic authorities on one hand and the nuns on the other. The two sides were seemingly unevenly matched in terms of access to power; nevertheless, the nuns mobilized power and authority via acts of alliance and community to counteract the patriarchal advantage. I also study in detail the tale of two communities that emerges from the debate, which reveals the enormous chasm between the image of community the male ecclesiastic authorities desired and the community women in the convent actually formed, the latter being something the nuns fought very hard to preserve.

Gender and Religious Reform

Margaret Chowning's work on the *vida común* places these particular eighteenth-century reforms within the long tradition of Catholic reform of monasticism. She describes this as "a timeless tug of war between rigor and relaxation" (*Rebellious Nuns* 123). Throughout the history of monasticism, both male and female orders have been the subject of criticism. Yet, the concept of reform—ever present in the institutions of the Church—was unmistakably shaped by gender bias as I discussed in chapter 1. From the very first centuries of the Early Church, there was an inexorable move toward the eradication of female autonomy of any kind, facilitated by continuous programs of reform. These reforms—their unifying factor being disregard for the opinions of the women who were to be subject to them—populated the ecclesiastical landscape for centuries.

In the early modern period it is, of course, the Council of Trent (1545–1563) that stands as the watershed moment in early modern religious reform. As with other issues pertaining to nuns, such as enclosure, the desirability of *vida común* in the Counter-Reformation period was debated at the Council of Trent.[4] The discussions held at Trent set the tone for several centuries of stringent amendments of female religious spaces, including the *vida común* reforms. Of the significance of the reforms promulgated at Trent, Antonio Domínguez Ortiz writes: "Todo arranca de Trento, donde ellas [the nuns] no tuvieron la oportunidad de hacer valer su punto de vista" (Everything stems from Trent, where they [the nuns] did not have the chance to air their point of view) (121). The Tridentine reforms were the showpiece of the Counter-Reformation, a campaign that "clothed as it was in the imagery of war and military organization [. . .] was thoroughly masculinized" (McNamara, *Sisters* 489). Convents of female religious, invested as they were with symbolic values pertinent to the health of society as a whole yet mistrusted as being populated with weak creatures prone to sin, were thus perfect subjects for reform. Reformers usually used excessive and hyperbolic language. While there seems to be a propensity for words such as *relajación* (laxity) and *decadencia* (decadence) in the reformist tracts of early modern Spain, specific examples of such tendencies among the nuns themselves are scarce (Lehfeldt 72). Authors of the reformist texts from the *vida común* scandal in Mexico examined in this chapter exemplify this tendency to hysteria and hyperbole, as they depict seemingly inconsequential acts as presaging the downfall of religious values.

A pervasive and unquenchable desire to control the female convent community characterized male reform of female religious houses. The male ecclesiastical hierarchy couched their reforms in an overblown language that betrayed the anxiety the female convent community inspired in them. Reform was also used as a staging ground for male power plays that, taking advantage of the supposed powerless state of the convent community, launched reform projects that had much to do with personal ambition and little or nothing to do with the desires or even well-being of the women whose lives they wanted to change. McNamara has characterized male reforms of female convents in the following terms:

> [The] genuine idealism [of reform] was shaped and often warped by the ambitions of the popes and his legates, bishops, monastic orders, and secular magistrates. They often used the rhetoric of morality, ranting about loss of chastity and filthy depravities. But when they thrust themselves indecorously and sometimes violently into women's communities, what they imposed was control. The property, the political authority, and the independence of female monastics were the chief target and the chief victims of these reforms. (*Sisters* 419)

While McNamara specifically treats reformist projects in fifteenth-century Europe, her comments perfectly encapsulate the program of reform that took place in eighteenth-century Mexico. The struggle over the configuration of convent community here has all the elements McNamara outlines: violence, rhetoric of morality, accusations of indecorous behavior, and the desire to curtail any political power female monastics had previously enjoyed in the New World.

Vida común reforms also came at a time of general restructuring in New Spain, as the metropolis tightened its control on the colonies in a variety of ways. We must thus consider the *vida común* polemic within the larger context of the so-called Bourbon reforms of the eighteenth century and take into account how this specific situation affected the lives of women living in convents.

The Convents and the Bourbon Reforms

The Austrian House of Hapsburg's rule in Spain and its dominions came to an end in 1700 with the death of Charles II. Charles had bequeathed his kingdom to Philippe, Duke of Anjou, of the French House of Bourbon, and thus in 1701, as Felipe V, he ascended to the throne of Spain. The new king survived onslaughts from other interests in the War of Spanish Succession (1701–1713) to establish the Bourbon dynasty in Spain. By the time of Carlos III (1759–1788), the Spanish empire emerged from the inertia of the Hapsburg era (Lynch 337) and began to consolidate its authority, passing laws that strengthened the power of the state while weakening criollo participation in government (337). The Bourbons initiated a period of reform in which, in the particular case of New Spain, administration was streamlined so as to consolidate Spanish control of its overseas territory. For David Brading in *The First America*, the Bourbon reforms, with their goal of colonial economic revitalization and exploitation of American resources, had as their aim the revival of the Spanish monarchy as a European power to be reckoned with (4). The Church in particular was singled out, as the Crown asserted its power over an institution it regarded with jealousy and suspicion. The reforms aimed to bring the Church's immense wealth and power firmly and definitively under metropolitan control.[5] And the convents, as we will see, were not to be spared.

Margaret Chowning traces this particular reforming impulse to the influence of Enlightenment ideas on the traditional gender biases in ecclesiastical reform: "To the time-honored condemnation of cloistered convents as allowing a style of life that was too worldly and too comfortable (even decadent) were added the complaints that they perpetuated a style of worship that was too 'baroque,' too full of pomp and excessive celebration, and that they were parasitical, socially-useless" (*Rebellious Nuns* 153). Interestingly, the other group often targeted for their love of baroque excesses was the Indians (Brading, *The First America* 494). The irrationalities of women and indigenous peoples did not enter into the rational, masculinist project of the eighteenth-century reformers. However, to what point Enlightenment ideals truly informed the Church reformers is open to debate. It is difficult to view reforms that strengthened the hand of an absolute monarchy as being truly "enlightened." The reformers seemingly did not consider that it was the ecclesiastical authorities themselves who had, through their insistence on enclosure and being "dead to the world," condemned the convents and their inhabitants to a life of social ineffectiveness.[6] Ironically, these so-called enlightened reformers embraced some of the reforms enshrined at Trent—specifically, the "reformed" female convent.[7] The juxtaposition of these so-called enlightened reforms with the ideals of the post-Tridentine Church, which they claimed to repudiate, was a curious one indeed.[8]

The Crown's policies demonstrated a clearly secularizing bent that resolved to limit the power of the Church in both Spain and its colonies, and thus the reforms seemed to set the two institutions against each other.[9] However, a movement in the Spanish Church of powerful reforming clerics helped to bridge this gap and bring the two sides—or at least elements therein—together. Common ground seemed to be found in the desire to move the peninsular Church away from the stranglehold of Rome and accept the protection of—and thus dependency on—the Spanish Crown (Loreto López 87; Brading, *The First America* 503–4; Chowning, "Convent Reform" 14). The position of the New World Church in these reforms is more ambivalent. For Chowning, the Church in New Spain was not just the passive recipient of Peninsular reforms, but rather actively engaged in its own "improvements." Most scholarship, she argues, has focused on reform as external—that is, "sponsored by the Crown" ("Convent Reform" 4). She offers an alternative view, contending that the earliest and most "clear and comprehensive" expression of reform took place in Mexico itself with the setting up of the Fourth Provincial Council in 1771.[10] However, it must be said that the cleric responsible for convening the Council—Archbishop Lorenzana of Mexico (1766–1772)—was, of course, from Spain.[11] He and his fellow Spaniard and friend Bishop Fabián y Fuero of Puebla (1765–1773) were to be the most fervent adherents of convent reform.

Criticism of moral laxity was leveled at the male orders in the eighteenth century in both Spain and her American dominions (Lavrin, "Ecclesiastical Reform" 182). Yet curiously, the only wide-scale reform project undertaken at this time was the overhaul of the living conditions of the female orders. They were never criticized for moral laxity, which one would imagine to be the far more serious charge, but rather for what Lavrin calls "a lack of proper observance of their Rules and Constitutions" (182). Given the ambiguous relationship between the Crown and the New World Church, it seems that there may well have been some gender bias in selecting the subject of reform. At a time when abuses in the New World Church were coming under scrutiny from the metropolis, it appears that perhaps a "kill two birds with one stone" philosophy prevailed among reform-minded prelates. The ecclesiastical authorities could offer up the convents as an oblation to satiate the need to curb the power of the Church within the New World. At the same time, these too-autonomous cities of women could be controlled and monitored more effectively. According to Esteban Sánchez de Tagle, the climate of incipient secularization and economic reform had a particular impact on the convent. He claims it became "el sitio más susceptible, el más expuesto" (the most vulnerable, the most exposed place) (149). Moreover, he sees the nuns as scapegoats for what he considers a "régimen condenado, [...] un régimen cuyo fin se acercaba inexorablemente" (a condemned regime, [...] a regime whose end was inexorably approaching) (149).[12]

The first specific instructions regarding the implementation of *vida común* in the New World came in 1560 with a *real cédula* (royal decree) Felipe II issued in Toledo.[13] Pope Benedict XIV (1740–1758) also sent out an edict that made its way to the New World.[14] Although he directed his tract at both male and female religious, it is nuns who come most under fire for their abuse of the vow of poverty. Speaking of the private monies of these women he writes:

> No todas las monjas que reciben estos anuales adelantamientos de dinero, lo gastan siempre en sus necesidades sino que también algunas veces esta con no provido concejo sin mirarlo para adelante se desperdician y gastan mal gastado, para colmar de regalos y dádivas a los amigos y conocidos que viven en el siglo, la cual ciertamente le infiere y causa a la vida claustral y religiosa el postrer desastre y ultima destrucción. (f. 72)[15]

With its infantilization of women (shown here as impulsive and destructive in handling money) and hinting of greater dangers ahead if such freedoms continue, this text echoes the words of Antonio Núñez de Miranda. The hyperbolic connection the pontiff makes between women, money, and the destruction of the cloister is one that belongs to a bigger prejudice that has traditionally connected women and luxurious living to licentious behavior and immorality. The *vida común* reforms of the eighteenth century were the most vigorous attempt so far to implement an austere life in the convent, which would stamp out the kind of luxuries Thomas Gage detailed in his book.

Gendering Luxury: "Criollas regalonas y chocolateras"

Since ancient times, society has linked the pursuit and enjoyment of luxurious living to immorality. Plato attributed the decline of civilization to the licentious desires that arose from a decadently luxurious lifestyle. Women have often been singled out as the embodiment of this connection, and the eighteenth century produced writers who espoused this viewpoint. A particularly lurid example of the gendering of the association between luxury and licentiousness is found in the work of a French doctor, M.D.T. Bienville, whose treatise, published in English in 1775 as *Nymphomania, or a Dissertation Concerning the Furor Uterinus*,[16] spelled out the connection between luxury and rampant female desire. Bienville claimed to have discovered a connection between nymphomania—*furor uterinus*—and a taste for luxury. He wrote:

> [*Furor uterinus*] generally happens when the woman is accustomed to pleasure, and high living, but particularly to rich sauces and spiced meats; for we may take it for granted, that a thousand little indulgences she allows herself, added to a table luxuriously set out, and at which a delicate appetite may be gratified in every taste, must excite the most voluptuous desires. (Qtd. in Peace 251)

Bienville also listed the drinking of chocolate as one of the major causes of the disease (244). Interestingly, Bienville's English translator, Edward Sloane Wilmot, saw fit to clarify the degrees of danger of different types of chocolate, calling "Spanish chocolate" the most dangerous as its "compound" nature made it "doubly inflammatory." Meanwhile English chocolate "is the most plain and innocent" of them all (qtd. in Peace 256). The New World ecclesiastical authorities were also critical of the consumption of chocolate in the convents, using it as an indication of excessively luxurious living.[17] A Mexican nun, María Ana de la Encarnación (1571–1657), writes of a cleric who had accused the nuns in certain convents as being "criollas regalonas y chocolateras" (gift-giving and chocolate-drinking criollas) (qtd. in Ibsen, "The Hiding Places" 257).

The Church's disapproval of luxurious living is echoed in texts such as Núñez de Miranda's, which rail against the possession of *alhajas* and the giving of gifts. A modern historian, Luis Sierra Nava-Lasa, describes the habits of the nuns in the *calzado* convents as being overly opulent, with huge "escapularios" (scapulars) and good-quality fabrics. He also criticizes them for the excess they displayed in choosing their religious names—"largos y recargados" (long and overly elaborate)—which he attributes to "la tendencia al barroquismo y la exhuberancia, que consideramos rasgos típicos de la idiosincracia femenina mexicana" (the tendency to baroqueness and exuberance, which we consider to be typical traits of the idiosyncratic Mexican female nature) (199). Despite such comments, the convents were not isolated islands of luxurious living in a sea of austerity, and Mexican women were not alone in displaying a tendency for "barroquismo y exhuberancia." The combination of aesthetic excess and religion was not by any means exclusive to houses of nuns, but was, as is well known, a defining characteristic in the artistic and architectural representations of the so-called *Barroco de Indias* (baroque of the Indies), a style that persisted well into the eighteenth century. Kristine Ibsen has written of the period:

> The eyes of the imagination were inspired and enriched by artwork that penetrated every corner of churches, convents and private homes. Constructed at the height of the baroque sensibility, the colonial church played out sensuality in concrete form with golden altars, velvet-robed saints and the scent of incense. ("The Hiding Places" 257)

The nuns who inhabited the convents were members of society's elite who, choosing life in a *calzado* convent, were expecting to replicate, to a certain degree, the standard of living to which they were accustomed. In a society that presented women—in this case elite women—with very few alternatives, religious life offered "one of the few available outlets for autonomy and dignity" (Ibsen, *Women's Spiritual Autobiography* 6), as well as, perhaps, "an authority inadmissible in marriage" (6).

It was the scale upon which this lifestyle took place that seemed to most horrify the authorities. Nuria Salazar has written of the New World convents: "Eran verdaderas ciudades que se desarrollaban al interior de la urbe" (They were veritable cities that sprang up inside the metropolis) ("Niñas, viudas, mozas..." 162). While the Church perceived luxurious lifestyles and the immorality they supposedly entailed as threatening, a larger problem was also at stake. This problem was the size and power of the New World convents and the implicit threat a city of women represented.

The Specter of the City of Ladies

In the opening passage of her 1405 text *The Book of the City of Ladies,* Christine de Pisan places herself in her study "surrounded by books on many different subjects" (3). There, she begins to muse on the fact that "so many different men—and learned men among them—have been and are so inclined to express both in speaking and in their treatises and writings so many devilish and wicked thoughts about women and their behavior" (3–4). Vexed by these accusations, she consults other women: "princesses, great ladies, women of the middle and lower classes in great numbers" (4). While this community of interlocutors evinces the decent behavior and good character of women, Christine is nonetheless unable to resolve the great dichotomy between her empirically gathered evidence and the great weight of the textual information legions of male scholars have offered.

Caught in this quandary, Christine begins to consider herself unfortunate because "God had made me inhabit a female body in this world" (5). Lost in her misery, she is suddenly startled by the appearance of "three crowned ladies" who stand before her: "the splendor of their bright faces shone on me and throughout the entire room" (6). The ladies gently admonish her for thinking pessimistically of her own sex. They tell her that male authorities who were her sources often contradicted both themselves and one another. They also resorted, claim the ladies, to the use of fiction, which rendered their arguments unconvincing. The ladies then announce the true purpose of their visit, which has "another greater and even more special reason" (10). This, they explain, is to help Christine construct a city of ladies, a place that will function as

> a refuge and defense against the various assailants, [for] those ladies who have been abandoned for so long, exposed like a field without a surrounding hedge, without finding a champion to afford them an adequate defense, notwithstanding those noble men who are required by law to protect them, who by negligence and apathy have allowed them to be mistreated. (10)

The aim of the city of ladies is clear: it is to be a self-sufficient space that will protect women. The city is to be beautiful and strong: "We will bring you sufficient building stone, stronger and more durable than any marble with cement could be. Thus your City will be extremely beautiful, without equal, and of perpetual duration in the world" (11). It will function as a fortress, repelling all those who would try to penetrate its walls: "This City, which you will found with our help, will never be destroyed, nor will it ever fall, but will remain prosperous forever, regardless of all its jealous enemies. It will be stormed by many numerous assaults, but it will never be taken or conquered" (11).

Christine seizes on the metaphor of a fortified city that protects and provides for its all-female citizens. She uses it to exemplify what Natalie Zemon Davis calls a "walled city of defense: of arguments and examples that women use to think well of themselves and to answer their detractors" (xix). However, the New World male critics did not favor the image that served Christine de Pisan so well and had allowed her to mount her defense of women. Instead, the authorities used this term to describe the houses of female religious in their ecclesiastical jurisdiction in disapproving terms. The frequent comparisons of the convent to a city—a city of ladies—provoked fear in the Church authorities. What was so terrifying about the specter of a city of women that led the authorities to want literally to tear these so-called cities down? The answer lies in the symbolism attached to the image of the city. Elizabeth Grosz defines it as

> a complex and interactive network that links together, often in an unintegrated and ad hoc way, a number of disparate social activities, processes, relations, with a number of architectural, geographical, civic, and power relations. The city brings together economic flows, and power networks, forms of management and political organizations, interpersonal, familial, and extrafamilial social relations, and the aesthetic/economic organization of space and place to create a semi-permanent but everchanging built environment or milieu. (105)

A city of women implied the autonomous existence of all these activities, which in turn would leave room for both the type of improvisation and ad hoc behavior the Church tried so hard to guard against with its discursive controls. Additionally, its very self-sufficiency would be perceived as emasculating the male Church. Grosz describes the city as "the most immediate locus for the production and circulation of power" (109). The specter of the city of ladies threatened the very source against which masculine power configured itself: the male-controlled, subservient female convent.

A popular view of the city promulgated in the Enlightenment was that of a "parallelism between the body and the city, or the body and the state" (105).[18] This formulation, explains Elizabeth Grosz, was codified in the following terms: "The King usually represents the Head of State; the populace is usually represented as the body. The law has been compared to the body's nerves; the military to its arms, commerce to its legs or stomach and so on" (106). Grosz claims that, as it is rarely attributed a sex, this coding of the body politic is "implicitly masculine" (106). She writes: "While claiming it models itself on the human body, [it] uses the male to represent the human, in other words, its deep and unrecognized investment in phallocentrism" (106). It is this masculine formulation that operates in the colonial city, consequently rendering the concept of a city of women both anomalous and perverse. If the male body represents the city, then a city of women symbolizes a grotesque and aberrant body that society must cure or even destroy. This is precisely what some of the most powerful clerics in the New World Church set out to do as they seized on the metaphor of the city of ladies, attempting to reform the convents and oblige them to accept the rule of *vida común*.

Inhabiting the New World City of Ladies

In 1772 the Consejo de Indias (Council of the Indies) spoke with evident displeasure of the convent of Santa Clara in Puebla: "con muchas niñas y mozas que había, más parecía pueblo que claustro de religiosas consagradas al retiro" (With so many girls and servant-girls there, it seemed more like a town than a cloister of nuns devoted to retirement) (qtd. in Salazar, *La vida común* 51). The convents did indeed resemble small cities, housing a heterogeneous population that grew constantly on an ad hoc basis. As a result, the need to expand and modify convent architecture often arose.

Alongside the nuns lived a large number of secular women of various types. Nuns who followed the rule of *vida particular* were exempt from having to eat and sleep in communal spaces. The nuns had private cells, which became the target of some of the more vitriolic criticism directed at them. These cells and their furnishings allowed the women—in some cases—to approximate the lifestyles they had enjoyed before entering the convent. Moreover, these were the only spaces where some kind of private life might be enjoyed in the convent (Loreto López 159). These private living arrangements, with their attendant food purchases and preparations, also required the presence of private servants in the convent. Sierra Nava-Lasa, not without an element of disapproval, describes a typical nun in the *calzado* convent as being "una señora con servicio de mandaderas y recadistas" (a lady with messengers and errand-girls at her bidding) (199). He describes how, in some cases, "la convivencia se torna abuso de hecho" (cohabitation is, in fact, abused) and details how in some convents certain nuns were allowed up to three servants each (199). Reciprocally, for servant girls, or *mozas*, life in the convent could be a better alternative to the harsh world outside that existed for women of lower rank (McNamara, *Sisters* 533).

Women of a different class sought not employment but rather a place to live in the convent, among them widows or the so-called *niñas*—a rather vague category that described secular girls and sometimes women.[19] For some of these girls the convent functioned as a boarding-school, where their families sent them for lack of any other educational establishments available for female pupils.[20] Other less fortunate girls—orphans, girls of upper-class families fallen on hard times—also lived in the convents, their room and board paid for by wealthy individuals or *cofradías*.[21] These girls constituted an important part of the community for the nuns. As I show later in this chapter, many of the complaints made by the nuns during the *vida común* polemic concerned the mistreatment of the *niñas*, for whom the nuns acted in loco parentis, by the ecclesiastic authorities. Sigüenza y Góngora describes the relationship between a teaching nun, Sor María Antonia de Santo Domingo from the convent of Jesús María and her charges: "enseñaba a sus discípulas [...] con tan gran cuidado, caridad y amor como si fueran nacidas de sus entrañas" (she taught her pupils with such great care, charity and love as if they had sprung from her own body) (315). On completing their education, they had the opportunity to either profess or leave to get married.[22] Many, however, simply stayed on—without ever professing—to an age when they could not reasonably be called *niñas*.[23] Having started out living in dormitories, the *niñas* often slept in the cells of individual nuns with whom they formed close relationships. Sierra Nava-Lasa writes disapprovingly of this arrangement: "La compasión original degenera así en faccioncillas y celotipias" (What may start out as compassion degenerates into little factions and intense jealousy) (199). Octavio Paz's reaction to this arrangement is more extreme and somewhat salacious in its implication. He describes the living arrangements thus: "Cada una de sus grandes celdas albergaba a una religiosa, a la niña o niñas confiadas a su cuidado, las criadas de su servicio y las favorecidas."[24] He then adds: "Esta última categoría *me laisse rêver*" (This last category boggles the mind) (162).

Each woman who professed entered the convent with a dowry. In most cases, this was given by the nun's family. In other cases—such as that of Sor Juana Inés de la Cruz—a wealthy benefactor would bestow what the family could not. As people often remembered them in their wills, whole convents were also recipients of generosity and largesse from the *siglo* and could often amass considerable wealth over the years. The nuns were given money in the form of a daily allowance or *peculio*, which the families, guardians, or benefactors set up at the time of profession.[25] Despite the continual charges of luxurious and opulent living leveled at the inhabitants of the convents, Sierra Nava-Lasa himself points out that although the convents may have been rich, this did not mean that "el modo de vida de sus moradoras sea suntuario" (their inhabitants led a sumptuous life) (200). He quotes information from a Mexican lawyer, Baltasar Ladrón de Guevara, who represented the nuns of Jesús María in Mexico City in their fight against the imposition of *vida común*. Ladrón de Guevara states that each nun was given the modest sum of twelve *reales* daily in the form of *peculio*, of which four were spent on food for her and any servants she may have had. The rest of the money went to the upkeep of her clothing, laundry expenses, and sugar (201).

Another New World traveler and monk, the Italian Capuchin friar Ilarione da Bergamo, who visited Mexico from 1763 to 1768, also dedicates some of his book to the lifestyles of Mexican nuns. His comments describe the convent as a space of commerce and economic activity:

> Nearly every nun has her own servant, and some even two, all of them young and in secular garb. Each nun has her servant prepare meals for her. For that reason at the gate of these convents it looks like a perpetual fair is going on from morning until night because there are hawkers of every kind. One person is carrying vegetables, another fruits, another meat, another mats, another blackbirds, another ribbons and fabrics, so that the two gates of the convent stay open practically all day long and are packed with nuns and servants. The same thing even goes on at the grilled windows. One person calls out for an item, and some other person for something else, and those whose faces cannot be seen because of the crowd raise their arms. In sum, there is a clamor unlike any you have heard before. (151)

The Church authorities greatly disapproved of this economic activity in the convent space and tried constantly to control the events that took place at the *portería*. This type of social interaction challenged the Church's wish for nuns to be "muerta al mundo," buried alive within the four walls of the convent. Moreover, the presence of secular women, in the form of servants and *niñas*, provided a conduit to the outside world. The Church believed these secular women to be even more imperfect than the nuns themselves, therefore increasing the possibilities for cross-contamination within a community of women. All these factors contributed to the need for constant vigilance on the part of the Church officials.

Tearing Down the New World City of Ladies

The *vida común* reforms were designed to go one step beyond the virtual panopticon of masculine power relations, making it less virtual and more real. This transformation implied the literal destruction and dismantling of the cities of women. The plans were to remove all private spaces and make every activity—eating, sleeping, and working—communal. Furthermore, there was no longer to be any contact with the outside world. The convent was to be hermetically sealed, as a result turning it into the tomb Núñez de Miranda desired. Windows were to be bricked up, and access to the *locutorio* and the *portería* was to be severely curtailed—for all women, including the servants. This would help to stamp out the nuns' participation in commerce and was to be carried out as part of the plan to raze the city of ladies to the ground. This was all to be performed in the name of community and the benefits of the so-called common life.

There is something apparently unpalatable to many in the idea of female religious living relatively autonomously in comfort and, perhaps, luxury. Critics of an all-too-comfortable life enjoyed in the convent deem this lifestyle incompatible with the pursuit of a spiritual life. Many contemporary historians have upheld this as the motivating factor behind the *vida común* reforms. David Brading writes of the Church's "justifiable concern that life had become too comfortable and lax in these wealthy establishments" (*Church and State* 101). Bernard E. Bobb comments, disapprovingly, on an "easy mode of existence" that "offered both peace of mind and physical comfort" and "was not as austere as might generally and logically be presumed" (64). The unmistakable tone of disapproval at work here leads the reader to question if peace of mind is deemed too much of a luxury for nuns.

Hierarchies, Genealogies, and the Exercise of Masculine Power

The first indication that the ecclesiastical authorities were to single out the convents of female religious as targets for reform came from the Bishop of Puebla, Francisco de Fabián y Fuero. In 1765 he issued his first set of instructions regarding what he saw as excessive expenditure in the *poblano* convents (Salazar, *La vida común* 15). Three years later, on August 10, 1768, he followed up on these dictates, writing a detailed letter addressed to all the mother superiors of the *calzado* convents affirming the authority of "los Sumos Pontífices y Concilios Generales [y] el Santo Concilio de Trento" (the Sovereign Pontiffs and General Councils and the Holy Council of Trent) (100).[26] These supreme entities, he argued, would never have ordered the common life if it were "tan difícil y llena de esperanzas" (so difficult and full of expectations) (100). He then cites St. Augustine, "el glorioso padre," who said "no tengáis cosa propia, todo sea común entre vosotras" (you must not possess anything, all should be shared among you), as well as the "seráfico" (saintly) Padre San Francisco," who along the same lines claimed "que nadie reciba dineros de ningún modo" (on no account must anyone receive monies) (101). Further on in the letter, he quotes "el glorioso San Antonio de

Florencia," who, according to the bishop, claimed that those who live according to the rules of *vida particular* are "en mal estado por que viven secularmente y quieren perseverar así" (in a predicament because they live according to secular rules and wish to continue in this way) (104). Invoking these "Santos Patriarcas," he marshals what appears to be an impenetrable wall of authority against any objections the mother superiors may raise against the common life. He intimates that any battle between patriarchal and matriarchal power is one that they, the patriarchs, are destined to win.

To further bolster the strength of his argument, he sets up a series of rhetorical and moral extremes that leave no doubt as to which "life" he deems correct. (This placement of the two lifestyles at opposite ends of rhetorical and moral spectrums is common to all the documents the authorities issue throughout the many years of the polemic.) He claims that *vida común* "no es un monstruo espantoso y terrible" (is not a menacing and terrible monster), but instead possesses "hermosura, apacibilidad, y buen trato" (beauty, tranquility and benevolence) (106). Moreover, this way of life will "apartar todo vicio y aún sombra de propiedad" (keep away all sins and even the shadow possessions cast) and will allow the nuns to live in "la perfección de la pobreza" (poverty's perfection) (107). Although he does not say so outright, he implies that the direct opposite of the saintly *vida común* is the monstrous and vice-riddled *vida particular*. He makes clear that the nuns should desire only what the authorities tell them to desire: "Cada religiosa debe tener preparado su ánimo a no repugnar, ni poner obstáculos a la *vida común* cuando los superiores manifiestan en ésto su voluntad" (107).[27] Yet he cloaks this message of privation in a language that purports to benefit the community of nuns. The rule of *vida común* "no es para destruir sino para perfeccionar la vida religiosa según la santa regla con indecibles alivios de la comunidad" (107).[28]

What are the *alivios* of which he speaks? His enumeration appears to offer little benefit to the community though much to the authorities. There can be no clearer indication of this than that the Church considered the convent community to be a reified entity, a community imposed from outside. This community of women was to be the projection of the patriarchal authorities' wishes. The image of community that Fabián y Fuero proposes is one that the nuns can only attain through the improvement of their "vida religiosa" (101). He spells out exactly how they should accomplish this, framing his instructions with the phrase "nuestro amoroso intento es que . . ." (our loving intention is to . . .) (101). Chief among his concerns is a reduction in the population of the city of women, "dejando número de criadas correspondientes a él de las religiosas, se guise en comunidad a las sanas como que lo están y a las enfermas como lo pidiere su necesidad" (102).²⁹ There is to be a common *ropería* (clothes room), so that the washing and repairing of garments can be carried out on a communal level—again removing the necessity for every nun to have her own servant (102). Fabián y Fuero also proposed wide-ranging and explicit architectural changes to the convents, which a reduction in the convent population was to make possible: "Se edificarán y destinarán piezas proporcionadas para las oficinas convenientes" (103).³⁰ To be gone were the individual cells and private cooking and dining areas. In their place were to be communal dormitories and refectories.

The bishop is quick to point out that the Church has no intention of abandoning these secular women once they no longer live in the convent: "[No] es nuestro ánimo desamparar o dejar en la calle alguna de las pobres seculares que habitan en nuestros conventos que a todas las tiene nuestra compasión muy presentes y daremos nuestra providencia para que no se pierdan ni se aflijan" (103).³¹ As we shall see, the fate of the secular women expelled from the convent became one of the more hotly debated issues between the two sides as the nuns tried to protect the women, whom they saw as an integral part of their communities, from the dangers of the *siglo*.

Money was at the heart of the flourishing of the city of women. Many of the New World convents had amassed great wealth through their business dealings, and many of the nuns were also independently wealthy. The Church needed to shut down this circulation of money if they were to eliminate the city of women, and the bishop addresses this in his letter. "La comunidad de corazones" (the community of hearts), claims Fabián y Fuero, is not attainable without the "comunidad de las bienes" (community of possessions) (105). Citing San Antonio de Florencia, he outlaws the use of *peculio* with which the nuns ran their individual households. From then on, the authorities would centralize everything, and no female religious would have the funds even to purchase her own food. This, he says, should be of no consequence to the nuns: "ésto [no] pudiera faltar a unas almas entregadas por medio de los votos solemnes a un Dios infinitamente rico" (this will not matter to individuals, who through solemn vows, have given themselves over to a God with infinite riches) (103). What use would they have for earthly riches when heavenly ones await them? Obviously, it was far simpler for the ecclesiastical authorities to oversee and control this common fund. Under the new regime, the bishop tells them, they will not want for anything—they will have "comida y vestido suficiente" (sufficient food and clothing) (103). But it will be, he asserts, within the bounds of a decent religiosity ("una decencia religiosa") (103), again not so subtly implying that what they enjoyed before most certainly went beyond these bounds. We will see, however, that the nuns insisted that what was given to them under the new regulations left them ill-nourished and in poor health.

Fabián y Fuero finishes his letter by telling the mother superiors exactly what they should say to introduce the practice of *vida común* into the convents, insinuating that to do otherwise would endanger their spiritual health. He writes: "El superior y las preladas tenemos obligación de procurar que se introduzca la observancia de la *vida común*, y así no lo hacemos no estamos seguros en conciencia" (105).³² The use of the first person plural is obviously nothing more than a rhetorical device, as the hierarchical division of power between the *preladas* and himself in his capacity as "el superior" was very clear-cut. He warns them to follow his instructions exactly so as to avoid possible discord as they implement these wide-ranging reforms:

> En vista de lo [. . .] que queda expuesto, cómo podremos menos de esperar que tengan buen efecto nuestras insinuaciones cuando admita la *vida común* se evitan tantas distracciones del entendimiento, tantas solicitudes del ánimo y tantas ansiedades de corazón, así es y en esta confianza, y en los alivios que ahora podemos conceder y acaso no tendremos después de nuestra mano, está nuestro consuelo, como en su resignada ejecución está vuestra felicidad y la de todas las hijas. (105)³³

The unsubtle intimation here is that he will brook no argument with regard to these "reforms." He closes the letter by exhorting the women to promote community on the Church's terms, cloaking it in the language of Christian love and charity: "Con la unión de bienes se facilita en gran manera la unión y comunidad de corazones en que consiste la caridad, que es el vínculo y lazo de la perfección y el fin de cuanto Dios nos manda" (106).³⁴

Fabián y Fuero was convinced that his carefully structured letter would get the process smoothly under way. On September 8 work on the architectural changes he proposed began, and on December 3 he sent special food for a celebratory dinner to be held in each convent to mark the official beginning of the new rule of *vida común* (Salazar, *La vida común* 18–31). The King, Carlos III, was evidently highly impressed by the zeal and efficiency with which the bishop had imposed these sweeping changes and wrote him a congratulatory letter in which he applauded his subordinate's actions (Salazar, *La vida común* 31). It was to be, as we shall see, a premature celebration.

Other lesser luminaries in the male ecclesiastical hierarchy also jumped onto the bandwagon of reform. The lowly parish priest of Córdoba, Mexico, also pestered the nuns of Puebla to put "en práctica el instituto apostólico de la vida común" (into practice the apostolic institution of the common life), doing so in verse perhaps in an attempt to get himself noticed.[35] His poem shares some points in common with his superior's letter. Moreover, in its unsubtle and overblown verse, the poem sheds further light on the male clergy's view of the female convents.

To shore up his argument in favor of *vida común* and in a gesture identical to the bishop's, the priest starts off with an appeal to a genealogy of learned men. He begins, or so he claims, at the very beginning: "Nuestra Madre la Iglesia fijó en todas las comunidades de uno y otro sexo una memoria venerable del modo de vida que tuvieron los apóstoles, obispos, presbíteros, diáconos y demás fieles de la primitiva Iglesia" (107).[36] Despite the mention of "comunidades de uno y otro sexo," the preferences or opinions of any women members of the "primitiva Iglesia" are noticeably absent, although perhaps there is a half-hearted gesture made toward including them under the rubric of "demás fieles."

The introduction sets the tone for the poem, in which women will be either chastised and lectured or reified and immobilized. He next appeals to that bastion of male power and control, the Council of Trent, invoking its mandate of *vida común*: "mandada del Sacrosanto Concilio Tridentino en la sesión 25, capítulos 1 y 2" (107). As if that were not enough, he finishes off by summoning up the power of the supreme patriarch himself, the Pope, or rather multiple popes: "renovados sus sagrados canones por siete Sumos Pontífices" (seven Sovereign Pontiffs renewed its [Trent's] sacred canons) (107–8).

His authority established as an albeit lowly member of this illustrious male lineage, he moves on to the nuns of Puebla. He opens his first verse speaking directly to the nuns, describing them in a way that contrasts with the powerful battery of male ecclesiastic power he marshaled in his introduction. He describes them as "Cándidos lirios del plantel florido, / Nítidas rosas del jardín sagrado" (Spotless lilies of the flowery seedbed / Gleaming roses of the holy garden) (108). Here the poet-priest seizes on the well-known correspondence between the female body and the enclosed garden, the *hortus conclusus* (Stallybrass 129). With his description of the nuns as flowers in a sacred garden, the poet conjures up the image of the contained, and thus monitored, female body. The comparison between the New World convent and the garden is not a new one. Sigüenza y Góngora also invoked it in his history of the convent of Jesús María in *Paraíso Occidental*, in which he posits a pristine American paradise populated by decorous New World virgins. The same elements of control and containment are operational in Sigüenza's text too, as he makes the convent into an artificial New World Garden of Eden. Kathleen Ross describes it in the following terms:

> The occidental paradise is founded on virginity, on the conscious suppression of desire. Much as the plants in this garden are controlled and rational, so are the bodies and natures of the women who inhabit it. Planting a better Paradise in a convent supposes an essential dichotomy in female sexuality, the vision of woman as either virgin or temptress. If Eve lost the original Paradise, Mary will regain it in the New World and in doing so will elevate it to a higher level, beyond the corruptions of the flesh. (*The Baroque Narrative* 66)

Our poet-priest also introduces the essential dichotomy of Eve and Mary into his poem. He describes the nuns as "Castas ramas del tronco esclarecido / De María Virgen, timbre de ese estado" (Chaste branches of the illustrious trunk / Miniature examples of the Virgin Mary's state) (108). The image of the nuns as chaste limbs of the tree of Mary stresses the importance of a female genealogy that starts with the Virgin. The tree also suggests the nuns' family tree—their *árbol genealógico*: "Matriarca cuyo ejemplo os ha franqueado / Tanto blazón heroíco y distinguido" (A matriarch whose example shows you the way / Such heroic and distinguished ancestry) (108). The Virgin Mary is the matriarch of this female family, and it is her coat of arms they must proudly wear. The invocation of chastity, along with the Virgin Mary as its supreme embodiment, functions to strengthen the male hierarchies of power through the immobilization of women. Furthermore, the tree also brings to mind the image of Mary's opposite—Eve. The two are never far apart in the imagery the Church employs.

After these two stanzas of circumscribing praise, the poet sets out to lecture the nuns on the importance of their status as brides of Christ: "Sepa el mordaz que sois con vuestro Esposo, / De imitación y amor raro portento, / Y que sabéis emplear vuestro talento / En copiar un dechado tan piadoso" (108).[37] The example they must follow is that of poverty: "¿Pobre no fue al nacer? Claro se advierte: / Y ¿que tuvo al morir? Suma pobreza" (Was he not poor at birth? / And what did he possess when he died? / The greatest poverty) (108). The implication here is that they must eschew all the trappings of luxurious convent living and embrace holy poverty. The priest then returns to the core of his argument, the male genealogy of power upon which he builds his defense of *vida común*. He praises the reforming bent of "Nuestro Príncipe Ilustre" (Our Illustrious Prince), whom he likens to Theseus: "Con el hilo sútil de un buen deseo / ... / Penetró (haciendo de su celo alarde) / Laberinto mayor, mejor Theseo" (With the subtle thread of good intent / ... / He entered (displaying his zeal) / A bigger labyrinth, he a greater Theseus) (109). Of course, if the "Príncipe Ilustre" is a "mejor Theseo" who, armed only with his thread of "buen deseo" and his zeal to reform, enters a greater labyrinth than the real Theseus did, what then is the Minotaur he comes to do battle with? I would argue that the poet here portrays *vida particular* as the monstrous Minotaur. Not coincidentally, the evocation of the Minotaur's labyrinth calls to mind images of those vast, maze-like cities of women against which the authorities railed and that symbolized all the evils of *vida particular*.

In his next stanza the poet mentions yet another hero in support of his argument—this one a little closer to home. The priest mentions the illustrious prince of the previous stanza: "Glorioso imitador del Borromino / Con la divina luz que en su pecho arde" (Borromeo's glorious imitator / Who has the divine light aflame in his breast) (109). By "Borromino," he means Carlo Borromeo (1538–1584), an Italian cleric canonized in 1610 renowned for his zeal in the Counter-Reformation. He was a fervent supporter of the Council of Trent who worked hard to enforce its decrees and reforms. Despite coming from an extremely wealthy family, he was highly critical of the luxurious lifestyle that both members of the Church and aristocracy enjoyed in Italy. Thus, for the parish priest of Córdoba, he was the perfect role model for the "Príncipe Ilustre" to imitate when "Resucitó sagaz (y no muy tarde) / La disciplina antigua (¡santo empleo!)" (Wisely he revived [and not before time] / the ancient discipline [o holy task!]) (109). The reforms were timely, he implies here, given that, as he claims in the next stanza, the rules had been long ignored ("¡y qué olvidadas!"). He again addresses the nuns directly in the following stanza, telling them that the "Prince" has desired the common life for them, and for that they must give him "mil alabanzas" (a thousand compliments). On this foundation, then, will be built "edificio tan santo y peregrino" (such a holy and astonishing building) (109), that it will stand in contrast to the sinful cities of women that the convents have become. He ends his poem, drawing a none-too-subtle connection between the common life and eternal life: "Ésta es la VIDA que COMÚN se llama: / ... / Y la que os asegura inmortal VIDA" (This is the LIFE that COMMON is called / ... / And which will ensure you all immortal LIFE) (110).

The poem posits an ideal female body, enclosed and immobilized by the chastity and the enclosure that a powerful masculine genealogical network of theologians, popes, and saints have under surveillance. As Peter Stallybrass points out: "the surveillance of the women concentrated upon three specific areas: the mouth, chastity, the threshold of the house" (126). Moreover, the three terms were often collapsed into one. Thus: "Silence, the closed mouth, is made a sign of chastity. And silence and chastity are, in turn, homologous to woman's enclosure within the house" (127). With this image in mind, the poet's exclusivist masculine genealogy is even less surprising. As far as the Church was concerned, the chaste and enclosed nuns could not speak out on this matter, even though it concerned their way of life and no one else's. Yet, as we will see, no matter how many poetic and rhetorical commands to silence there were, the nuns were not willing to keep their mouths closed.

Mobilizing Community: The Fight against *vida común*

The nuns did not accept the dictates the Church issued in the form of letters such as Fabián y Fuero's and the parish priest's poem. In response, they crafted their own carefully written texts to complain about specific events that took place during the dispute, or as one nun called it, the "guerra civil." Although each text uses different tactics and strategies to take on the enemy, there is a common strategy we can identify in all: the mobilization of the community to resist the sweeping changes to be imposed on it from outside. The ecclesiastical authorities intended the discourse of powerful figures such as Fabián y Fuero to ensure the status of the nuns as docile bodies. As detailed in their letters and other documents, the nuns' actions demonstrate their rejection of a role of passive victim to the Church's machinations. Instead, they overtly confront the prevailing power structure. The nuns, using community as their point of departure, challenge the gendering of authority as exclusively masculine and speak out for what they want.

In the early modern New World, relations of domination were constructed along gender lines. Men dominated women—either independently in marriages and families or via institutions under their control such as the Church. Power was exercised through a series of discursive controls that constructed, sanctioned, and propagated power. In this period, with the domain of discourse firmly in patriarchal hands, the dominant power was masculine, or so it seemed. Foucault theorizes power as something that is multiple and thus not centralized and which creates subjectivity via discursive practices. Subaltern groups, therefore, do have access to power, for it is not monolithic. However, feminists have long taken issue with elements of Foucault's premise. Nancy Hartsock, for example, criticizes Foucault for not taking into account the unequal levels of participation in these constellations, in which access to dominant discursive practices is not equally available to all. She writes: "the image of the network in which we all participate carries implications of equality and participation rather than the subsequent domination of the many by the few" ("Community" 40). Yet, she does agree with Foucault on the presence of "counter-space"—that wherever there is power there must be resistance ("Foucault on Power" 168). Resistance, according to this theoretical paradigm, can be undertaken by confronting the "congealment" of dominant power in the "loose network of power relations" that constitutes society (Allen 44).

Hartsock identifies a difference in the types of power mobilized by dominant groups and by oppressed groups. According to her, we can characterize the power that is wielded in a historical and patriarchal context as domination and violence. Basing her analysis in part on Hannah Arendt's theorization of power and violence,[38] she asserts that power can often be confused with and collapsed into violence. However, she claims that power can also be operational without domination and violence, instead enabling itself through the institution of community.[39] Power without violence, she claims, following the theories of Hannah Arendt, is only possible via communal action. Power through domination, such as that which tyrannical regimes exercise, can be attained by violence, but it will destroy the community as it does so. Hartsock, citing Arendt, describes this nullification of the community in the following terms: "Tyrannies are characterized by the powerlessness of subjects who have lost the human capacity to speak and act together" ("Community" 33). The community, she claims, is held together by a different kind of power. Whereas power through domination functions by "moulding the opinions and practices of others through various forms of psychological pressure" (Emmet, qtd. in Hartsock, "Community" 35), power mobilized through community works to stimulate activity in others and raise morale.

The type of power displayed by the Church, and the resistance with which the nuns counter it, offers a concrete example of this theory. The Church attempts to coerce the women to accept the way of life it wants for them, at times resorting to psychological pressure and even physical violence. Simultaneously, the nuns mobilize power through their communities to resist changes to their way of life. Sometimes the alliances unite whole convent communities; sometimes they extend between different convents, whereas others are smaller. The common factor is the security afforded the nuns by their action in concert, which they felt gave them a platform from which to voice their opposition to the reforms.

There can be no doubt that Hartsock's model resonates with the utopian impulse that lies behind some theorizing of female community.[40] The idea that hierarchies of power are not operational in female communities is a naïve one at best. There can be no doubt that women dominated other women and that there were vertical power structures in place in the New World cloister. This notwithstanding, female communities did provide the forum for the empowerment of women, allowing them to authorize both their voices and their actions. The community, by mobilizing to protect itself, demonstrated that the care of its individual members was of paramount importance. Furthermore, the women contrasted their care for members of their communities with the cruelty and disregard with which the ecclesiastical authorities treated them. They turned the tables on the Church, empowering themselves while they simultaneously worked to prove that the actions exercised by Church officials to assert authority in fact rendered that authority null and void.

The Nuns of La Santísima Trinidad: Re-gendering Authority and Re-configuring Power

The key to the women's opposition was their voices, which they used to resist the psychological, physical, and legislative violence certain ecclesiastic officials in the Church attempted to exercise against them. One of the manifestations of the power they mobilized through their communities was the authority they awarded themselves through their textual resistance. As Foucault has pointed out, power is brought to bear through the imposition of "dominant knowledge." The ecclesiastical authorities subjugated and disqualified the nuns' knowledge. In order to raise the status of their knowledge, the nuns lent authority to the means of its communication. The nuns of the convent of the Santísima Trinidad in Puebla undertook a series of clever rhetorical strategies that challenged the patriarchy's control of authority in a letter of bitter complaint they wrote to the viceroy, Antonio de Bucareli, in 1774.[41] Here, they complained about the way the officials of the diocese of Puebla had gone about implementing the new rules of *vida común*.

The letter details a series of violent abuses of power by ecclesiastical authorities whose victims were the nuns. In their salutation to the viceroy, the nuns appear to keep within the paradigms of patriarchal correctness. They know their place their letter says. In the opening paragraph, they cast themselves in the role of defenseless, and unworthy, supplicants to the all-powerful viceroy:

> Excelentísimo señor: Las religiosas de este convento, las que en ésta se firman, puestas a sus pies con el mejor rendimiento llenas de confianza por estar enteradas de la gran caridad y santos procederes de Vuestra Ex-

celencia, pues publica al mundo entero que ha sido y es el amparo de estos reinos, nos hacemos presentes las más afligidas y desamparadas en la tierra que puede haber ni ha habido. (119–20)[42]

This seemingly innocuous *captatio benevolentae*, however, contains the seeds of their challenge to patriarchal power. Using the strategy Josefina Ludmer has termed the "tretas del débil" (tricks of the weak), they undercut the power that they claim to obey so unquestioningly. They, the most "afligidas y desamparadas," are manipulating the authority of the viceroy to challenge another source of authority: the Bishop of Puebla.[43]

Kathleen B. Jones defines authority in "modern western discourse [. . .] as a set of rules governing public life issued by those who are entitled to speak" ("What Is Authority's Gender?" 77). In terms of New World society, as nuns, the women of the Santísima Trinidad had no authority; they were not entitled to speak. Yet with this letter, they authorize themselves to carry out a systematic verbal attack on the bishop's attempts to enact the reforms of *vida común*, undermining his authority in the process and replacing it with their own. Jones expands her definition of authority in the following terms:

> An authority is someone who is *official* (occupies a public, professional role recognized as having the capacity to issue rules), *knowledgeable* (has knowledge that meets a certain epistemic criteria [*sic*] in order to issue rules), *decisive* (possesses singularity of will and judges dispassionately so that the rules will be enforced, and *compelling* (constructs political obedience to the rules ordering public life through institutionalized hierarchy). In other words, those who are "in authority" are perceived to be "in authority" because they exhibit the signs of office, knowledge, judgment, and will associated objectively and formally with the practice of ruling. ("What Is Authority's Gender?" 79)

In their letter, the nuns seek to undermine the bishop on each one of these points, in the process authorizing themselves to decide their own fate. At the very beginning of their letter, the nuns indicate that the bishop is someone who has been, from the outset, highly negligent in exercising his *official* role as bishop. Again, they are careful not to be seen as straying beyond the limits of established power; they stress their obedience to all previous prelates, to those who have deserved their authority. Fabián y Fuero is different, however. He has not kept his end of the bargain:

Primeramente diremos que habiendo llegado a esta ciudad cuando esperábamos hallar un padre y pastor amoroso *como los antecesores*, llegó el día en que nos visitó en un locutorio, en donde bajamos todas a rendir la obediencia, habiéndole prevenido algunos obsequios correspondientes a el estado religioso con demostraciones de hijas, padecimos el sonrojo de que nada admitió, y habiendo estado tan corto tiempo en dicho locutorio, que no llegó más de medio cuarto de hora, sin mas demonstración que saludar políticamente a la Prelada, dejándonos a todas bien desconsoladas y no habiéndonos honrado con otra visita. (121, emphasis mine)[44]

The implication is clear. The nuns fulfilled their official capacity as submissive daughters anxious for approval from their "padre y pastor amoroso" (loving father and priest). But he neglected the demands of his office. In another instance, they claim they begged him to visit them and thereby tried to speak with him about their desire to not take on *vida común*, but "jamás lo conseguimos" (We never managed to do so) (122).

The nuns also question his authority in terms of his *knowledge* of how life in the community should be conducted. They indicate myriad examples of his forcing them, against their will, to break the sanctity of their vows and other Christian precepts. They thus question his ability to carry out his official duties, in this case as prelate to a convent of cloistered nuns, basing their judgment on his lack of necessary knowledge. He is shown violating established rules of enclosure on more than one occasion by arriving at the convent with dozens of workmen to destroy women's individual cells in order to make the changes necessary to the precepts of *vida común*. He fails to warn the nuns about the entry of these workmen: on one occasion they number eighty and on another one hundred. So violent and unexpected was their appearance, the nuns claim, that during the violation of the passive enclosure and the wrecking of the cells several nuns were injured and even killed: "Este destrozo y la violencia de la novedad quitó la vida primeramente a una religiosa sin más enfermedad que haberse contristado y espantado al ver tan lastimosos destrozos" (122).[45]

Fabián's overzealous actions in pursuit of his goal of *vida común* have also undermined the vow of chastity. The nuns write of how his actions have led to their receiving inappropriate letters: "Seguidamente nos envió a todos los conventos un cuaderno o carta impresa tan indecorosa, que algunas que la leían se afligieron demasiado" (He immediately sent out to all the convents a pamphlet that was so unseemly that some of those who read it were seriously distressed)

(122). The author of this offensive document was "un fulano Posadas, religioso del orden de Santo Domingo, quien dice la escribió a religiosas relajadas de esta ciudad" (some man called Posadas, a Dominican monk, who claims to have written it for the undisciplined nuns of this city) (122). It is, the nuns say, the bishop's reckless actions that have left them open to such scurrilous and unmerited attacks. Anyone, however undeserving they imply, now believes he has the right to criticize the nuns and to do so in such a way that violates their decency and modesty. Other actions taken by the bishop have also exposed the nuns to unseemly ridicule, imperiling the virtue of chastity they guard so dearly.

> No omito el decir a Vuestra Excelencia el que padecimos, el mayor sonrojo, antes de entrar a la *vida común*, y fue de un escrutinio que mandó su Ilustrísima nos hicieran, poniendo por lista de ropas que teníamos, interiores y exteriores, de modo que cada una mandó se le dijera que teníamos al uso. La cual mortificación fue tan grande al considerar se leía y publicaban nuestras desdichas en la Contaduría del Obispado, tan público, que fue ocasión de que con ultraje nos hicieran los zánganos algunos versos. (130)[46]

Finally, in the same vein, they claim that the most dreadful of these obscene letters ("el caso el más grave") (132) was addressed to them by two priests, José Ortega y Moro and Joseph Larios. Its offense, they claim, was terrible. They describe it as "desdorando nuestro honor y él de todos los confesores" (tarnishing our honor and that of all our confessors) (132). It was so offensive that they judge it "digna de que a voz de verdugo se quemara en las plazas" (fitting that the executioner burn it in the city squares) (132). Worst of all, the bishop is heavily implicated in its circulation, having paid for its printing out of his own pocket (132). Not only was it, as were the others, a threat to their chastity ("habiendo sido causa y aún lo es, de que padezcamos todas las religiosas deshonras públicas" [having been and still being the reason why all we nuns have suffered such public disgrace]) (132), but it has also left them without confessors willing to guide them. They claim to have suffered "desconsuelos grandes en el alma (great sadness of soul) since, because of the letter, "pues por esta no hay confesor que nos quiera confesar ni gobernar" (no confessor will confess or direct us) (132).

This lack of access to the confessor is one of the most important points raised by the nuns and one that they repeat over and over again in the letter. As we can see in the texts of Antonio Núñez de Miranda, the vow of obedience was almost entirely centered on the deference the nun owed to her spiritual father. Again, the letter writers call into question Fabián y Fuero's authority based on his knowledge, or lack thereof, that this relationship was crucial to convent life:

> Después empezó a quitarnos confesores, suspendiendo de licencias a los más o todos los que nos gobernaban, y habiendo ejecutado éste, mandó que en todas las sacristías de nuestros conventos se pusieran unas cartas con prevención de tintero para que los pocos que nos venían a confesar pusieran sus firmas y nombres de las que confesaban, *sin saber nadie por qué motivo se practicaba tan grande novedad.* (121–22, emphasis mine)[47]

They question his ability to understand the importance of the confessor/nun relationship, as well as the protocol associated with such an activity. They again fall back on their strategy of "tretas del débil" to show how they have suffered without the guidance of confessors. Writing of their receipt of another unpleasant letter, they claim not to know what to do, for they cannot rely on the knowledge of learned men as they are always counseled to do: "Hallándonos todas sin la luz que nos pudieran comunicar los confesores doctos que teníamos, llenas de tribulación clamamos a Dios que nos la comunicara" (Finding ourselves without the light the learned confessors brought us, deeply troubled we beg God to show us the way) (122).

Gravest of all and owing to the bishop's ungoverned actions, many nuns have been forced to die without first confessing and receiving the Last Rites and Extreme Unction. In his attempts to force them into accepting the rule of *vida común*, he issued a "mandato" in which he withheld the sacrament of confession for those who were dying:

> Para que a las religiosas que morían no se les permitiera que las auxiliara de noche su confesor, ni otro ninguno sacerdote, imponiéndoles a éstas pena para que ni un momento se recostaran a descansar, con éstos se veían precisados a dejar a la agonizante, la que moría llena de desconsuelos, pues vimos en una que clamó por confesor para reconciliarse y mientras fueron por dicho confesor expiró con grandes aflicciones y de este modo han acabado muchas (127–28).[48]

Careful to show how *they* possess knowledge of the correct way to conduct themselves within the patriarchal hierarchy of the Church, the nuns stress their reliance on the spiritual guidance of a confessor.

As the letter continues, the nuns also challenge the bishop's ability to be *decisive*, which, if we follow Kathleen Jones's definition, requires the ability to dispassionately enforce impartial rules and regulations that will replace order with disorder ("What Is Authority's Gender?" 78). The bishop, they claim, has been anything but impartial or dispassionate. He has sought to punish those who do not comply with his illegitimate commands, showing himself to be cruel and violent. The catalogue of suffering the nuns set out depicts scenes of chaos in which the bishop displays a devastating lack of Christian charity. Repeated references are made to the terrible hardships the women have endured. At one point in the text, they compare the bishop's catalogue of cruelties as exemplified in his series of *mandatos* to a "claro quebrantamiento del quinto mandamiento de Dios" (clear violation of God's Fifth Commandment) (128). The meaning is clear: They are accusing the bishop of murder.

At the beginning of the petition, the nuns beg the viceroy to hear them:

> Para que como nuestro verdadero padre y señor en la tierra, nos atienda, nos consuele y remedie; que no dudamos de sus santas entrañas el que si hubiera sabido antes cuantas desdichas, trabajos y desconsuelos nos hemos padecido éstas sus hijas amantes, sus fieles vasallas, creemos ciertamente, el que no nos halláramos en tan lamentablemente estado como sabrá su Excelencia. (120)[49]

The viceroy is their real earthly father, as opposed to that cruel usurper, the bishop. Once the viceroy bears witness to the lack of objectivity with which the bishop has enforced illegitimate rules, he will rescue them from their plight. The nuns are not asking for special treatment. They will, they say, follow the rules their order, the Council of Trent, and the patriarchal ecclesiastic establishment laid down, if the rules are applied fairly and dispassionately.

They indicate further abuses: how the bishop's henchman tried to force them, "con violenta precisión" (with violent precision), to sign a paper accepting the rule of *vida común*. When they refused, he conspired with his subordinates to produce a fake letter of the nuns' intent to accept the rule of *vida común*, in which their signatures were forged. They also tell of how they were lied to and told that the other four convents in Puebla had agreed to accept *vida común*, which was untrue (125). All these attempts to secure their consent having failed, the bishop then entered the convent and destroyed their private property, which caused much suffering in the community. The workmen were ordered to commence con barretas echar de abajo las piezas del noviciado todo y los dormitorios nuestros y muchas celdas de harto costo, con tanta violencia que no dieron tiempo ni aún para que se sacaran las cosas necesarias que allí había, de modo que con gran trabajo se puede sacar a una pobre religiosa que estaba enferma en una de las celdas. (131)[50]

Their own funds were withheld from them, and all personal items were removed. These included devotional objects, "imágenes de Niños Jesuses," and even such nonluxury items as "platitos de barro ordinario" (ordinary little earthenware plates). The bishop treated the "niñas doncellas" (young ladies) as servants, forcing them to dress in "ropas inferiores" and ordering them to "sirvieran a las religiosas igual como las criadas" (wait on the nuns as if they were servants) (129). Moreover, some of these "doncellas," if they were poor or orphans, were no longer given access to proper food and instead were forced to survive on "las sobras que salían del refectorio" (the leftovers from the refectory) (130). Not content with demeaning and starving these young secular residents of the convent, the bishop demonstrates an even more flagrant example of his cruelty as he expels them altogether.

The nuns take great care to indicate to the viceroy the importance to the community of these *niñas* and the pivotal role they play in convent life: "La compañía de las niñas nos servía de grande alivio y consuelo así para cuando estábamos enfermas que nos asistían y servían con esmeros, como para que pudiéramos estarnos en coro sin cuidar de cosa doméstica, y ésto con grande quietud se practicaba siempre" (143).[51] The nuns' regard for the *niñas* is not quite as self-serving as these remarks suggest. There seems to have been a genuine desire on the nuns' part to protect the *niñas* in the safe haven of the convent. When Fabián y Fuero issues an order giving the *niñas* only twenty-four hours to vacate the premises, the nuns bewail the fate awaiting the girls outside the safety of the convent walls. They report: "Empezaron a salir de éste y de todos los conventos la cosa más lastimosa que se debe llorar para siempre, porque muchas que se criaron en las claúsulas huérfanas de padres no tenían donde irse, ni por la violencia se les buscó, y paradas en las calles lloraban su desamparo" (130).[52]

The tragedy of the *niñas*' expulsion is compounded, the nuns are quick to inform the viceroy, by the terrible end some of the girls met once they left the safety of the convent, an end very different from the kind the bishop had promised them:

Le juramos a su Excelencia que de muchas y las más sabemos él que su necesidad las obligó a ofender a Dios gravemente, y algunas han muerto en partos mal habidos, otras por su necesidad se casaron sin inclinación al estado; unas han muerto y otras viven desamparadas, y aunque algunas se metieron en colegios y se decía que todas se mantenía en ellos su Ilustrísima, fueron pocas y éstas sólo les daba cuatro pesos cada mes. (130)[53]

It is clear from their letter that the nuns fulfilled a parental role for these girls, and once the bishop took this from them, the *niñas* suffered grave consequences that compromised their hitherto pristine rectitude. The nuns highlight the bishop's cruelty by emphasizing the Christian charity of others toward these poor unfortunates. Not only do the nuns help their former charges ("muchas religiosas movidas de santo celo las socarrían con el bocado que les quedaba" [driven by religious fervor, many nuns have helped them out with the little bit of food they themselves have left]) (130), but so too do others, who moreover may not have had the wherewithal to do so ("algunos de los criados y criadas mandaderas de las porterías las amparaban" [some of the servants in the porter's lodge who run errands have come to their aid]) (130). Yet not only is the bishop unwilling to help these poor unfortunates himself, he wants to stop anyone else helping them either. When the bishop finds out the nuns have been helping the *niñas* from their own scant resources, he harshly finds a way to put an end to their charity: "Lo supo su Ilustrísima y envió otro mandato con precepto de obediencia para que ninguna religiosa pudiera dar ni por vía de limosna, ni un mendrugo, el más pequeño de pan, ni nada" (130).[54]

The nuns themselves have also endured much, they claim. They accuse the bishop of withholding decent and adequate nourishment from them, which has put their health into great jeopardy:[55] "Empezó a extrañar los alimentos que antes teníamos, bien cocidos y sazonados, y éstos, siendo calderos para más de cien personas, no pueden tener el cocimiento y sazón que tiene para porción" (129).[56] As a final exposure of his cruelty and violence, the nuns report how at another convent in Puebla, Santa Inés, one of his henchmen ("el señor su Secretario y Vicario") entered the convent "con muchas de su familia y más de cien hombres de todas las calidades" (with many members of his family and more than a hundred men of all types) in order to force twelve dissident nuns—those who according to the letter could not be intimidated—into accepting *vida común*. They tell of the violence and cruelty the bishop's men inflict on the convent's inhabitants:

> Entrando por la puerta de las doce separadas, les empezaron a descerrajar las puertas interiores del convento y las de sus dormitorios, entrando hasta ellos la multitud de hombres que iban repartiéndose con hachas y faroles hasta sobre las azoteas del convento; y rompiéndoles las puertas de las pie-

zas en que estaban durmiendo las fueron prendiendo para lo que metieron cordeles, grillos, cerrojos y candados, con tanto ultraje que a una le dio el señor Vicario tales bofetadas, que fue necesario el que al segundo día le hicieran dos sangrías porque le lastimó gravemente la cara; a otra porque iba a favorecer a otra religiosa que estaba gravemente enferma, le dio el señor Redondo tal tirón de un brazo, que le dislocó el hombro [. . .] de modo que está inhábil; a otra religiosa le dio otro de los señores tal golpe en el pecho que estuvo privada muchas horas. (137)[57]

These violent acts were not the last torment the clerics inflicted on the nuns of Santa Inés, according to the nuns of La Santísima Trinidad. The "señores" then proceeded to imprison the disobedient nuns: "a éstas les encerraron con cerrojos y candados, dando orden de que las mortificaran con ayunos a pan y agua" (they held them under lock and key, giving orders they be fed only bread and water) (137). Lest the reader forget who is responsible for these outrages, the nuns take us to the bishop's palace, where they describe a very different scene: "Después de ésto al segundo día hizo nuestro Ilustrísimo un banquete en su Palacio, en que se comieron once platillos y tres géneros de vinos" (On the second day after all this happened our Illustrious Bishop held a banquet in his palace where guests ate eleven courses and enjoyed three different types of wine) (137). This scene of gluttony and excess stands in sharp contrast to the one depicted at the convent, where imprisoned nuns are fed only bread and water. To make this banquet scene even more egregious, some of the guests had also participated in the night of bloody violence at Santa Inés (137). The juxtaposition of cruelty and excess makes the bishop seem more like a corrupt Roman emperor than a sober and holy clergyman. Painting the bishop as a Caligula serves to undermine his authority as a zealous and pious reformer. The bishop does not enforce rules and regulations dispassionately, but rather demonstrates a complete lack of self-control in his excesses of greed, cruelty, and violence.

The cruelty and violence, the very opposite of dispassion, with which the nuns claim Fabián y Fuero enforces the rules is also connected to the final point on which they attempt to undermine his authority. Jones classifies this as authority based on the ability to *compel*—that is, to construct political obedience to the rules ordering public life through institutionalized hierarchy ("What Is Authority's Gender?" 79). This authority they clearly deny, again using multiple examples to show up the bishop. To start with, the very existence of their letter, which goes above the bishop's head to the viceroy with the implicit request that he inform the King, shows that while the bishop is not mindful of the institutionalized hierarchy of imperial society, the nuns are: "Diremos a Vuestra Excelencia cuanto sea posible para no cansar su atención [. . .] a que mirando primero la mayor honra y gloria de Dios Nuestro Señor y el que no se pierdan tantas almas, le haga presente a nuestro Rey y señor natural, a quien Dios nos guarde" (120).[58] They are exceptionally careful to stress at all times that they know their place in this hierarchy. They refer to themselves as "hijas amantes" (loving daughters) and "fieles vasallas" (loyal vassals), always assuming the lowliest position in this hierarchy that the bishop himself refuses to respect. Although their position may be humble, they show themselves to be cognizant of this hierarchy of power and its well-established laws. In this regard, they devote a considerable part of their letter to a detailing of the abuses suffered by the confessors who have tried to continue guiding their spiritual daughters—as the Church indeed mandates them to do. The nuns tell of confessors who have been jailed for confessing them: "Pues llevó dicho que, así por los temores de castigos que en cárceles han muerto muchos y otros innumerables curas" (It has been said that many [confessors] and countless other priests have died in prison because of fear of punishment) (133). The bishop, on the other hand, is shown to belong to another hierarchy—a hierarchy of outlaws—that cannot thus compel the obedience of others as it remains outside the law. The bishop is seen to be ignoring the rules of the *cura monalium*, mandated centuries previously, in which the male clergy were charged with supervision of female religious, including administering the sacraments to them and acting as their spiritual advisers. They accuse the bishop of perverting these well-established laws by punishing those clergy who try to fulfill their official roles.

The bishop has, however, won over to his side some confessors who are also willing to break the rules and act outside the law. The nuns accuse this group of manipulating Church doctrine to suit their nefarious purpose. They charge the bishop's group with corrupting the sanctity of the confessional by using it as a forum to force women to accept the rule of *vida común* by declaring them in danger of mortal sin if they do not: "Les han hecho creer a muchas que deben abrazar la vida común y sus preceptos y constituciones por ser hijas de obediencia, y la que no lo hace peca mortalmente, y no sólo nos afligen en el secreto de la confesión, pero en los púlpitos y pláticas interiores" (140).[59] This unlawful manipulation, they claim, has led some of them to a conclusion they never would have reached in other circumstances:

> Hay religiosas tan arrepentidas de haberlo sido que se les oye a cada paso maldecir la hora e instante en que se entraron a la religión: y le juramos a

> Vuestra Excelencia, como arriba, él que las más hemos perdido el gusto y consuelo de nuestra vocación; que quizás fuéramos mejores mal casadas que no religiosas desesperadas según el monstruo que esto se ha formado. (140)[60]

It is this monster of *vida común* that has forced them to question their very vocations. This they blame squarely on the bishop and his (mis)rule of (out)law.

The nuns further undermine the bishop's place in patriarchal society by showing a contradiction between his actions and those of their fathers in the *siglo*. This matter is raised with relation to the destruction of the individual cells, bought for each nun by her father. He is thus guilty of causing an affront to another branch of patriarchal law. They make several references to the destruction of their property, which, as they are careful to point out, represents the destruction of their fathers' property. They speak of the "destrozo de las celdas que tanto costaron a los padres de las religiosas" (destruction of the cells for which the nuns' fathers had paid so much). Moreover, the power of the bishop's outlaw hierarchy has reached beyond the walls of the convent to the *siglo*, where its members have threatened and mistreated the nuns' families "hasta de nuestros deudos estábamos desamparadas, porque aún estos huyen de nosotras del gran temor que tienen, por lo que han visto han padecido algunos" (134).[61]

The bishop is also shown to have perverted other kinds of systems of law. First, he has interfered in the election process in the convent, something that goes against the laws of the "Santo Concilio." The nuns accuse one of the bishop's henchmen, his secretary Victoriano López, who has been promoted to *vicario*. This man, the nuns claim, is no better than his superior and does not treat the nuns with the respect their status as *Sponsa Dei* merits: "Este señor nos ha tratado no como religiosas, sino como a negras de obraje" (This man has not treated us like nuns, but instead as if we were black labourers) (133). They make this allegation based on the way he interferes with the convent elections, which took place in all five *poblano* (Pueblan) convents. At first he stops the elections. He then allows them to take place, but makes sure to influence their outcome:

> Después de que en ningún convento dejó que eligiéramos preladas a nuestro gusto, como lo manda el Santo Concilio, sino que con rigor mandó se eligieran aquéllas que su Ilustrísimo quiso, nos hizo el día de las elecciones una plática de tantos ultrajes, amenazándonos con los mayores castigos, a las que no quisimos ni queremos la vida común. (134)[62]

Finally, the nuns accuse the bishop of withholding from them "recurso jurídico a nuestro Soberano" (judicial recourse to our sovereign) (135), thus dealing a final blow to his reputation as an official able to carry out his duties according to careful observance of rules and hierarchy. By exposing the bishop as one who is not simply ignorant of but dares to flout official hierarchy, the nuns drive the final nail into the figurative coffin of his professional life. The nuns imply that he has put himself in the place of the sovereign by making decisions that only the latter is authorized to make. Citing the right of appeal the state gave the nuns of Mexico City at the fourth Concilio Mexicano after the King issued the first royal *cédula* in 1770,[63] the nuns of La Santísima Trinidad claim that, unlike the nuns of Mexico City, they did not avail themselves of this right because of the terrible price the nuns of Santa Inés had paid when they attempted to do so: "no lo hicimos nosotras porque supimos que lo habían hecho las madres ineses, las que han sido las que más han padecido y padecen" (we didn't do it because we had found out that the nuns from Santa Inés had done so, and suffered and still suffer for it the most) (135). According to the nuns of La Santísima Trinidad, the ecclesiastical authorities had punished the nuns of their sister convents for following the King's ruling and appealing: "el nuestro Ilustrísimo empezó a dar órdenes a su Secretario para que apretara el rigor con ellas, y fue tanto que llegaron a la mayor desesperación" (our Illustrious Bishop began to give orders to his Secretary to treat them more harshly, and he did so to such an extent that they became most desperate) (135).

They dedicate the last few pages of their letter to a summary of all that has gone before, emphasizing their wish that the viceroy—"Señor y Padre"—communicate their letter to the King. In order to do so, they again use their double strategy of abnegation and authority. On the one hand, they are his "fieles esclavas todas nuestras vidas" (loyal slaves for our entire lives) (146), who beg indulgence for "nuestro sexo mujeril, de nuestra delicadeza y complexión" (our female sex, our fragility and disposition) (142). Yet, at the same time, they put forward a litany of demands that would return them to the life they had previously enjoyed. They want control of their own money—*vida común* has placed them all in poverty (142). They want the *niñas* returned to the convent, their cells rebuilt, and access to their confessors as well as to the possessions their fathers had bequeathed them. This, they claim, is all legitimately theirs, as this is the life under which they professed: "esperamos nos ponga en el estado de vida que se practicaba desde nuestra profesión" (we hope you will restore to us the way of life we were practicing since our profession) (143). Moreover, for those few that willingly embraced *vida común* owing to a lack of personal fortune, they request that they be given the monies the bishop promised them—fifty pesos—for their annual clothing expenses, which were never forthcoming. This act of solidarity with those nuns who chose to observe *vida común* shows that their conception of community is not based on the same criterion of lack of individuality fostered by the ecclesiastical authorities.

Only eleven nuns sign the letter. Although the majority desire to have their way of life restored to what it was prior to the bishop's interference, many choose not to sign for fear of repercussions. The core eleven therefore make the request not only for themselves but also for their unnamed sisters in La Santísima Trinidad, as well as for "todas las de los cuatro quienes como nosotras padecen" (all those in the four [convents] who suffer as we do) (146). They end the letter with the demand that their old way of life be restored. If it is not, they claim, the very image of the nun in colonial society is in jeopardy:

> Que nos dejen en quietud seguir la distribución religiosa que hallamos, en la cual florecía mucha virtud y era público al mundo entero la unión, paz y caridad que en todos los conventos calzados reinaba; y ahora es tan contraria la fama, que ni aun hay quien pretenda el ser religiosa por lo espantosos que se han puesto todos los conventos. (146)[64]

Thus, having artfully but ruthlessly stripped the bishop of his authority, they stake a claim of their own. But theirs is an authority very different from that which the bishop attempts to wield. In contrast to the hierarchical top-down power structure marshaled by the Church, the nuns' power is grounded in the community and marshaled in the acts that bind the community together.

For Kathleen Jones, the authority women establish and assert through community is not simply a function of the number of people in the group, but comes from the connections between group members—connections maintained by the compassion one member feels for another ("On Authority" 121). Women's compassion has, she claims, been used as a weapon against their claims for authority: "In the dominant discourse, much of compassion is taken as nonauthoritative, marginal pleadings for mercy—gestures of the subordinate" (121). To rebut this discourse, Jones looks at differences in women's responses to issues that come from differences in socialization: "[if] women approach ethical dilemmas and make decisions with a fundamentally different language and logic, then the female voice of would-be authority may speak in compassionate tones" (121).[65] She rejects the notion that compassion is synonymous with sentimentality, instead positing that it informs a democratic and communitarian approach to the quest for authority (131). Compassionate authority as Jones defines it has neither need for compulsion nor to assert control over bodies, creating instead a space for human agency via communal connectedness. Moreover, such authority calls into question the assumption that "masculine bodies best represent the body politic" ("What Is Authority's Gender?" 79). This is the authority the nuns establish for themselves in their letter, while in a simultaneous gesture they deauthorize the ecclesiastical body politic.

With the strength of their community behind them, the nuns had fired a successful salvo in the battle with Fabián y Fuero over *vida común*. Yet, as we will see, the war was far from over.

The *Real Cédula* of 1774

Letters such as that from the sisters of La Santísima Trinidad prompted the King to call for an inquiry into the handling of the matter in all the convents in Puebla. The recently appointed Archbishop of Mexico, Alonso Núñez de Haro, carried out an investigation, reporting to the King that, in his opinion, both Fabián y Fuero and his successor, Victoriano López, had treated the nuns shamefully. Accordingly, the King issued a *real cédula* of May 22, 1774[66] in which he clarifies his position: "Deseo y quiero que en todos los conventos de mis dominios de América se observe y guarde la vida común que ordena y manda el mismo Santo Concilio y Sagrado Canones" (f. 263).[67] However, he is clear that the nuns already living in the convent should be able to make this choice freely and independently, and if so desiring, to continue living privately. He cautions the ecclesiastical authorities to leave the nuns "en absoluto y plena libertad" (with absolute and complete freedom) to decide "el admitirla o, sin admitirla, a continuar en la costumbre de vida que había en cada uno de ellos cuando tomaron el santo hábito y profesaron" (to accept it, or if not to accept it to continue the way of life there was in each convent when they took the holy habit and professed) (f. 263). The King declares that the nuns should make this decision—which should be "madura y bien considerada" (sensible and well thought out)—after fifteen days of deliberation.

The King's actions seem benevolent compared to the tyranny that Fabián y Fuero and his successor inflicted on the nuns. Nonetheless, he insists that the patriarchal ecclesiastical authorities should guide the nuns' decision. A paternal dictator, the King does not allow the women, whom he benignly infantilizes, to decide their own fate: "Se permitirá a todas, y a cada una de las religiosas, tratar para el efecto de informarse en el asunto con sus confesores, directores y con otra cualesquiera persona de virtud, ciencia, y consejo" (f. 264).[68] Moreover, he severely limits the participation in community life of those nuns who choose to stay living under the rule of *vida particular*, decreeing that only those who observe the *vida común* may hold elected office in the convent. The King uses a vocabulary of sickness and health to show which group he favors. Those who accept *vida común* belong to the "parte más sana" (most wholesome group) (f. 264) and are, moreover, "más dignas y beneméritas" (worthiest and most meritorious). From this moment on, all novices must profess according to the rule of *vida común*, and thus the King hopes to simply phase out those nuns who profess *vida particular*. More subtle than the *poblano* bishops, he strives nevertheless to censure and thus dissuade those who will not conform to the controlled community: "siempre las que guarden la vida común que se propone como la parte más sana, deben ser preferidas a las que no la observen" (those who live according to the common life, which is the most wholesome group, should be favored over those who do not) (f. 264).

Ironically, after dividing the convent into two groups—the "parte más sana" and that which must be, by default, "menos sana" (least wholesome)—the King charges the prelates with maintaining harmony in the convent community: "Deberán asimismo los Prelados respectivos cuidar mucho de que en los conventos de sus jurisdicciones se observe gran paz y caridad fraternal entre las religiosas, cuidando del alivio temporal y consuelo espiritual de todas con total indiferencia" (f. 265).[69] He warns that there should be equitable distribution of "bienes temporales" (disposable goods) and that the nuns living in *vida particular* should receive their *peculio* as always. On one matter, however, he is unequivocal. All *niñas* should be expelled and servants kept to a minimum, "habiendo manifestado la experiencia que cuan dañosa es y perjudical a la misma religión el trato y comunicación de personas seculares con religiosas esposas de Jesús Cristo" (f. 265).[70] Only the male prelates may authorize exceptions, but they should always bear in mind "que en el mismo convento no habiten muchas personas seculares" (that few secular persons should inhabit the convent) (f. 265). The King is not, it seems, in favor of the city of ladies.

The monarch indulges in a great deal of double-talk in his letter as he strives to appease the different factions involved in the quarrel. After all, many powerful aristocrats and landowners housed their daughters in the New World convents. While seeming benign, the King leaves little doubt as to which mode of convent life he favors. His methods for enforcing *vida común*, however, are less overtly coercive than those of the *poblano* bishops. He makes clear to the ecclesiastic authorities that they must persuade by psychological means rather than by physical violence. Although one can only imagine the pressure brought to bear during the grace period, many nuns chose not to opt for *vida común*.

A document devoid of windy rhetoric and ornate argument but stunningly powerful in its affirmation of community and the power wielded by many individuals united in a cause is that which details the response of the nuns of the convent of Santa Clara in Puebla to the Church's desire to impose the new rule.[71] At the end of the fifteen-day "consultation" period the *real cédula* designated, a representative of the viceroy called the nuns together to vote "en plena comunidad y a son de campanas" (in full community, with bells ringing) (f. 25). There, the decree was again read to them. The text details the responses of the nuns, listing "las diligencias hechas" (the steps taken) (f. 25) in response to the decree. Although, as the document clearly states, they are illegally threatened with the "nulidad en su profesión" (annulment of their profession), they all decline to accept *vida común*. With the exception of the signing nun's name, each entry is identical: "Fue llamada la señora Sor María Josefa de la Concepción y preguntada sobre lo mismo respondió: no admite la vida común" (Sister María Josefa de la Concepción was called upon and asked the same question to which she responded that she does not accept the common life) (f. 27).

The document's vivid illustration of the political force female community can exercise is extremely suggestive. Of all the ninety-five nuns listed, each one is asked whether or not she will accept the rule. The same question and the same answer is repeated and written out ninety-five times, with the name of each nun given next to her signature. The few that do not sign directly express their dissent via proxy, as they were unable to write because of injury or blindness. The document ends with the statement and signature of the Madre Abadesa Sor Micaela de San Jerónimo, who reiterates the desires of the entire community:

> Preguntada sobre lo mismo respondió que no admite la vida común y que en todo lo demás a su nombre y él de toda su santa comunidad está pronta a obedecer todos los preceptos de nuestro soberano (que Dios guarde) y así lo expresó y lo firmó. (f. 35)[72]

Where the nuns of the convent of Santa Clara are concerned, the authorities were unable to promote schisms in the community by favoring one group over another. In the cases of other convents, where some nuns did opt for *vida común*, the authorities tried to convince more nuns to do so by overtly favoring "la parte más sana," all the while doing so in the name of community. This was the case in the convent of Santa Inés in Puebla.

Santa Inés: A Tale of Two Communities

In 1774 a group of nuns from the convent of Santa Inés sent a letter to the viceroy complaining of the mistreatment the ecclesiastical authorities in Puebla had inflicted on them for not accepting the rule of *vida común*.[73] The letter claims their investment in the integrity of their community, a community they occupied on their own terms. It also ironically demonstrates that the authorities had attempted to destroy the community by their desire to implement something called *vida común*. They begin their letter stressing its communal nature: "Las religiosas del convento de Nuestra Madre Santa Inés de la ciudad de Puebla que firmamos este escrito *en consorcio de las demás que eligieron permanecer en el método de vida que se observaba cuando profesaron*" (f. 362, my emphasis).[74] The issue of maintaining the life under which they had originally professed is one of the most important ones for all the Mexican nuns in spelling out their opposition to the *vida común* reforms. The nuns believed that the changes were illegal given that they had taken their vows under the rule of *vida particular*. Their reliance on precedent demonstrates the importance the nuns placed in their individual understandings of religious community and elucidates their refusal to accept the imposition of the Church's point of view. Their shared experience of both convent life and ecclesiastical oppression offers them a staging ground for resistance. They argue for a community that goes beyond a simple communitarian construction of shared identity, instead promoting one that is based on the shared experiences of individuals.

Marilyn Friedman distinguishes between "communities of place," which are essentially involuntary and founded on an a priori identity, and "communities of choice." It is in these latter communities that individual subjects can come together and "reconstitute" their identities (Friedman 289). The nuns used the convent communities they formed as a counterpoint to "communities of place," establishing relationships and enjoying life experiences there. I do not suggest that the convents constituted a proto-feminist utopia, but rather a voluntary community in which both good and bad experiences were lived out through unimposed relationships. According to Jean-Luc Nancy, the community is "the ground of all possibility" (60). Yet it is "an unstable and shifting ground" (60). On this unstable and shifting ground, both positive and negative experiences will be lived, but there does exist a space for negotiation as to what can be shared and how it will be shared (Phelan 248). Attempts to fix and reify the community's characteristics will, however, result in "flights from community toward identity" (Nancy 61). This is not an identity created on voluntary terms, but one that is essentialized and imposed from outside. Nancy has termed this the "flight from being-in-common to being common" (qtd. in Phelan 241). The nuns obviously wished to "be-in-common," and thus rejected the Church's attempts to make them instead "be common."

The nuns were happy for each member of the community to choose their own lifestyle. This, not unexpectedly, did not conform to the ecclesiastical authorities' wishes, as it challenged their plans for the increased efficacy of the panopticon that *vida común* would bring them. It also challenged their authority. The nuns paraphrase the words of the royal *cédula*, stressing first how the King had advocated tolerance on the part of the officials. Twice they repeat the word "benígnamente," setting up their reader for the contrast of the less-than-benign actions they describe further on:

> En la Real Cédula del 21 de mayo del año próximo pasado de 1774 en que se mandó que eligieran las religiosas, se previno también que los prelados admitiesen benignamente tanto a las que quisieran la vida común como a las que escogieran permanecer en la antigua, y que cuidasen mucho de que se observase gran paz y caridad entre unas y otras del alivio temporal y consuelo espiritual de todas con total indiferencia atendiendo igualmente a las de la vida común y a las de la vida antigua. (f. 369)[75]

What follows in stark juxtaposition to this careful paraphrase of the *cédula* is the nuns' report on the actual actions taken by the ecclesiastic authorities. They show how these officials have blatantly flouted the King's orders:

> No se ha cumplido en este convento ni los demás calzados de esta ciudad dándonos trato con el mayor desafecto las Preladas y las demás de la vida común que disfrutan el favor de nuestro Prelado mortificándonos lo que toleramos con resignación por no aumentar las discordias ocasionadas de la división. Y aunque lo que ha expuesto nunca lo reclamaríamos por que siempre ha sido nuestro ánimo suplir estas adversidades en cuanto alcanzan nuestras fuerzas pero también se extienden las que padecemos a otra mate-

ria que toca en daño espiritual y en él de nuestra salvación y nuestras almas que no podemos abandonar. (f. 371)[76]

The letter writers call attention to the cruelties of the male clergy who are stopping them from living peaceably as a holy community. They themselves, following the King's mandate, wished to continue living harmoniously, albeit separately, but the authorities continuously undertook to jeopardize this by fostering divisions. Their overt favoring of one faction over another has created a schism that never existed before. While carrying out their reforms in the name of community, the authorities are willfully destroying it to achieve their own ends. The Church authorities inflict on them most grievous harm, they claim, by withholding from those who will not accept *vida común* the sacrament of confession and the guidance of a spiritual father:

> Muchos [confessors] comienzan a intimarnos que estamos en pecado mortal y no en estado de absolución aterrorizándonos y afligiéndonos en tanto grado que aunque no dejamos de conocer lo contrario y él que así lo tiene calificado SM en su Real Cédula porque respecto a que siendo pecado no nos hubiera dejado libertad ni concedido permanecer en la vida antigua. (f. 375)[77]

The nuns also use the example of the terrible treatment meted out to the sick and dying to again show how their view of community differs from that of the Church officials. They tell the story of two nuns, Sor Eulalia del Sacramento and Sor Marcela de San Felipe Neri, who endure needless additional suffering on their deathbeds owing to the Church's determination to configure community according to its wishes. There is apparently no limit to their egregious behavior as they resort to persecuting the dying. The nuns describe the coercion of Sor Eulalia during her last hours: "Habiendo padecido insulto en su repetición que temió le acometieran la entró a confesar el Capellán D. Antonio Romero quien nos hacemos juicio la apuraría en esta material pues luego ese día admitió la vida común" (f. 376).[78]

They offer even more disturbing details in the case of Marcela de San Felipe who, even as she lay dying, refused to submit to the pressure and machinations of the Church:

> [La] sacramentaron y olearon por estar enferma de mucho peligro asistiéndole su confesor lo que era el Padre D. Ildefonso Fuentes que la consoló de lo que provino que observando que el dicho confesor no había ejecutado

lo que otros, le metieron a el Padre D. Joachim Castro sin que ella lo pidiera, con disimulado artificio, para dos ocasiones para que la persuadiera. No conseguido el intento pidió la enferma le volvieran a meter a su Padre por que ese otro la había apurado. (f. 377)[79]

The awful story continues. Other confessors are sent to persuade her that she should die in the common life ("muriera en la vida común"), yet she resists:

> Siempre dio muestras de que Dios no la llamaba para esta mudanza de vida como lo comprueba que estaba tan serena su conciencia antes de morir, que volviéndole a instar el dicho padre en que muriese en la vida común respondió que no, lo que causa admiración por que no había ese día hablado nada en muchas horas, y se verificó que se murió en la vida antigua que profesó el día 23 de este mes de marzo. (f. 377)[80]

The nuns offer the dead body of Sor Marcela as a martyr to their cause. Although two separate male clergy members (Padre Castro and the sacristan of the convent, D. Ignacio Ibáñez) intimidate her as she lies dying, she is able to resist and find the strength, miraculously, to speak. Finally she dies, still observing the life under whose rules she had professed. The nuns bring their letter to a close with Sor Marcela's heroic death, providing a dramatic backdrop to their story of the courage of their community and the cruelty of the authorities. They are, they write, approaching Holy Week, when they will need the offices of the confessors to be able to fulfill their spiritual duties. As this has been refused them in the past, they have no choice but to turn for help to the King:

> Ahora nos hallamos en el conflicto de estar próxima la Semana Santa y sea preciso cumplir con la Iglesia y no haber otros confesores a excepción de los que no quieren absolver por que los demás se excusan como llevamos referido, por lo cual no nos queda más remedio que ocurrir a la justificación y Patrocinio de VE. (f. 389)[81]

Although they seemingly throw themselves defenseless on his mercy ("suplicamos rendidamente a su benígnidad"), they are also clear in stating that they feel they are entitled to help, given what they have sacrificed to be cloistered nuns: "de ella depende la salvación de unas religiosas que por buscarla dejaron sus casas y se sacrificaron a una perpétua clausura (on it [your kindness] depends the salvation of nuns who, in search of this same thing, left their homes and surrendered themselves to permanent cloister) (f. 391).

In this letter, the nuns' strategy is twofold. They wish to communicate their understanding of community, as well as emphasize the power the solidarity of this community has given them. The other community, the one the authorities have co-opted, is not the real community. It is a simulacrum of the Church's abusive power. Just as they start their letter with a reminder of their solidarity—"en consorcio de las demás" (in partnership with each other)—they end it with an affirmation of the same. Moreover, they offer a wall of female solidarity in the shape of a chain of united convent communities as a challenge to the intimidation of the authorities. As did the nuns of La Santísima Trinidad, who referred to the strife at Santa Inés, they too link the sufferings of their community to that of another convent, Santa Caterina de Sena, showing how this community was punished for daring to speak out: "de esto se siguió que las religiosas que habían firmado la representación padecieron la mayor aflicción" (it thus ensued that the nuns who had signed the petition were those who suffered the most) (f. 391). In order to avoid these repercussions, many of their number wish to withhold their names. Yet the implication is that they are many in number and resolute of purpose in their desire to preserve the integrity of their community: "Con el temor de que vistos sus nombres se les castigase y se vieron en conflicto más grave y así suplicamos rendidamente a la benignidad y paternales entrañas de VE se digne mandar por este memorial se reserve nuestros nombres y convento que hace el reclamo" (f. 392).[82] The letter is signed by two nuns: Ana María de los Dolores, "primer velo y Madre de consejo" (of the first veil and Nun Councillor), and Joachina María de la Santísima Trinidad, "tercer velo y Madre de consejo" (of the third veil and Nun Councillor). They represent "las 28 que somos las que no estamos en la vida común" (the 28 of us who do not observe the common life) (f. 392).

Conclusion

In 1775 two nuns of the convent of Santa Caterina de Sena in Puebla, Sor Guadalupe del Espíritu Santo and Sor Catalina del Rosario, wrote to the Bishop of Puebla claiming they were suffering hardships owing to the imposition of *vida común* in their convent. The letter has to do with the issuance of *peculio*, which the Church had halted with the imposition of *vida común*. The nuns write to the bishop complaining that the new way of life he has imposed on them is detrimental to their health: "cada día se halla más quebrantada" (every day it is worse) (f. 13). Moreover, they feel their treatment has been unfair: "No habíamos de estar como esclavas debajo de la ley sino libres al amparo de la gracia al de

VP" (We should not have been like slaves but rather free under Your Reverend's fatherly protection) (f. 13). The prelate's reply seems to suggest that the nuns' very act of writing is inappropriate to their status. In a curt warning, he elaborates their duties as brides of Christ, linking their desire to maintain their way of life to diabolical temptations:

> Vuelvan sobre sí y háganse cargo de esto es conocida tentación del demonio para apartarle de lo más perfecto y privarlas de las imponderables utilidades que les ofrece su primera intención. Pongan ustedes la consideración de los bienes eternos con esta suerte cargarán gustosas su cruz siguiendo las huellas de su esposo Jesús, esto es de un esposo mortificado coronado de espinas no de flores gustando hieles puesto en su cruz. (f. 16)[83]

Dismissing their claim, the priest points out that he is not required to dignify their letter with a response, but does so out of spiritual generosity: "Y aunque como Prelado no debo dar satisfacción de mi conducta ni responder de mis determinaciones sin embargo procediendo como amoroso Padre" (And although as your superior I do not have to explain my conduct nor be accountable to you for my decisions, I do so, however, as your loving Father) (f. 18). This remark sums up the attitude of Church authorities to the many letters nuns dispatched to challenge compulsory changes to their lifestyles. The Church believed that the community was there to be manipulated and that the nuns should be "docile bodies," dead to the world and dead even to life in the cloister. Obviously the nuns had other ideas. What emerges from their texts is an incredibly firm commitment to a community lived on their own terms. Not only are they determined to safeguard their vision of community, but the community itself becomes a powerful tool in this undertaking, providing the point of departure from which they mobilize their power and authorize their voices. Far from being "sepultadas vivas" (buried alive), these women showed themselves to be dynamic political actors.

It is difficult to assess the success the nuns had in standing up to the imposition of *vida común*. The 1774 *cédula*, issued in response to their many protests, gave them the opportunity to stay in the life that they had chosen when they professed. Moreover, enthusiasm for the rigid implementation of the reforms appears to have weakened once the two main proponents—Fabián y Fuero and Lorenzana—returned to Spain in 1773 and 1772. Still, the Church would accept only those incoming novices who agreed to observe the new rule. This meant, though, that the Church had to settle for the gradual implementation of *vida común*, waiting patiently for the nonconformists to die off in order to replace them with more perfect models of female religious. Asunción Lavrin has provided evidence that nuns continued to keep private servants and that the reformation regarding the expulsion of *niñas* was only really "half-fulfilled and only for a limited amount of time" (201). She asserts that from the time of the polemic until the convents were declared unconstitutional in 1863, "there is no evidence to suggest that the common life was ever completely accepted by the nunneries" (202).[84] What is certain is that female religious communities provided the base for a political mobilization that resisted the imposition of identities from the outside and fought to maintain, as far as possible, the integrity of a group of individuals being in common.

5

Sor Juana, Serafina de Cristo, and the Nuns of the Casa del Placer

Intellectual Alliance and Learned Community

> *Pero yo, queridas mías, más quisiera veros muy*
> *observantes religiosas, que grandes cortesanas y teólogas.*
> *(My dears, as far as I am concerned, I would rather you were*
> *observant nuns than great court ladies and theologians.)*
>
> Antonio Núñez de Miranda, *Cartilla de la doctrina religiosa*

In the *Respuesta a Sor Filotea de la Cruz* (Reply to Sister Filotea), Sor Juana seems to bemoan the fact that although she has a room of her own, she is still plagued by interruptions and unable to dedicate sufficient time to her intellectual pursuits:

> Estar yo estudiando y pelear dos criadas y venirme a constituir juez de su pendencia; estar yo escribiendo y venir una amiga a visitarme, haciéndome muy mala obra con muy buena voluntad. [...] Y esto es continuamente, porque como los ratos que destino a mi estudio son los que sobran de lo regular de la comunidad, esos mismos les sobran a las otras para venirme a estorbar. (ll. 400–408)[1]

Critics such as Octavio Paz and Dario Puccini have taken this one assertion as the principal point of departure for their criticism of the life and work of Sor Juana,[2] depicting her as a necessary victim of solitude—a woman so unlike her female counterparts that her only choice was to withdraw from the community of gossipy, idle women and dedicate herself to the masculine pastime of study and writing.[3] I argue, however, that this vein of criticism needs to be rethought, that these lines in particular must be read in the context of a highly structured rhetorical response to the attacks perpetrated on Sor Juana by a misogynistic ecclesiastic establishment—what critics have called "el magisterio exclusivista de la elite clerical masculina" (the exclusive education of the masculine clerical elite) (Sabat Rivers and Rivers 681). The statement must be considered in the context of the self-defense that it was.

Frederick Luciani has called attention to the formulaic quality of the anecdotes in the letter, arguing that they be reconsidered as "topoi within a set of generic conventions" (75), and warns of the dangers of "overextrapolating from potential textual sources for the anecdotes, a meaning or intent where there is only a coincidence or an echo" (77).[4] He shows how many of the anecdotes contained in the *Respuesta*, instead of being straightforwardly autobiographical, correspond to common tropes of the day, such as religious self-mortification as exemplified in the hair-cutting incident (75). Similarly Rosa Perelmuter in an exploration of the rhetorical structures of the *Respuesta* has shown that the document corresponds to a carefully structured formal argument prescribed in the rhetoric manuals of the day and following the strict discursive structure of "salutación, *captatio benevolentiae*, narración, petición y conclusión" (salutation, *captatio benevolentiae*, narration, petition, and conclusion) (152). Likewise, it employs contemporary rhetorical techniques such as *fastidium, ethos,* and *pathos* (155–56). She urges a reconsideration of the *Respuesta* with these techniques in mind, seeing it not as a spontaneous and natural outpouring of personal information, but rather as a meticulously planned and carefully conceived piece of forensic rhetoric (158).

It is on this basis that I would like to challenge the critical and historical use of the *Respuesta* to isolate Sor Juana within the convent walls. There can be no doubt that she *was* a remarkable figure in the strength of her talent and the spread of her fame. She is recognized as the most talented poet and intellectual, male or female, to emerge from the Mexican colonial context. However, it would be wrongheaded to use her exceptional talent and fame to overshadow other women's writings or the importance of intellectual community and acts of solidarity to those who did write or read other women's work. As Electa Arenal and Stacey Schlau have pointed out, the convent itself could and did function in many cases as a stimulus to female intellectual activity. They cite the focus on women's writing in this period that developments in gender studies of the last twenty years have brought to light: "Las investigaciones de los últimos años han hecho patente la existencia de miles de mujeres que a través de los siglos, y a veces en comunidad, alentaron la creación y el pensamiento culturales, al tiempo que colaboraron en su desarrollo" ("Escribiendo yo" 281).[5] Instead of using the example of Sor Juana's fame to obfuscate other women's contributions to scholarship and literature, they suggest we use her as a point of departure for exploring the cultural contributions of other women writers of the period, especially those writing from within convent walls. Arenal and Schlau caution that treating Sor Juana as an isolated phenomenon "pasa por alto una larga tradición—seglar y religiosa—de siglos y de la que Sor Juana misma nos dio la pauta" (ignores a long tradition—both secular and religious—which Sor Juana herself helped uncover for us) ("Escribiendo yo" 281).

I argue for taking Arenal and Schlau's idea one step further to highlight the importance of intellectual solidarity—in whatever form it may have taken—to those women who dedicated themselves to the pursuit of knowledge and culture. Critics have often discarded these less renowned texts as being of little or no intellectual importance. Antonio Alatorre, for example, has described what he calls "la poesía monjil con sus suspiros y sus noñerías" (nuns' poetry with its laments and fussiness) (*Sor Juana Inés de la Cruz* 14), and Enrique López Martínez refers to the nun poets of the Casa del Placer, whom I discuss later in this chapter, as "las monjitas" (little nuns) (55) and to their poetry as "bastante limitada" (quite limited) (57). However, mindful of what Virginia Woolf made very plain in *A Room of One's Own*, any judgments about intellectual and literary quality must be made in the context of women's access to education. Minor poets or writers of their autobiographies at the behest of others they may have been, but this does not negate the existence of intellectual activity and intellectual community in the convent.[6]

Nina Auerbach has written that the conventional ideal of a solitary woman "living for and through men, attaining citizenship in the community of adulthood through masculine approval alone" (13) has often been more culturally palatable than the image of a community of women that, she says, stands as a rebuke to patriarchal society (5). This has most definitely been the case with Sor Juana. Depicted by her male contemporaries as a "rara avis" and a "mujer varonil" (manly woman), she has been studied throughout history and up to the present day as both solitary woman and honorary man. The purpose of this chapter is thus twofold. On one hand, I offer an alternative reading of Sor Juana's solitary life in the convent, showing instead how her bonds with other women enabled her to challenge the coerced community imposed by the authorities in which her writing was deemed illegitimate. Secondly, I intend to show how intellectual activity in the convent was conducted as a communal activity among women, whereby they defined a space in which to work, to defend this work and their right to engage in it, and in some cases to judge their efforts superior to those of men. Writing in this case served as a "springboard for subversive thought, the precursory movement of a transformation of social and cultural structures" (D'Monté and Pohl 18).

In this chapter, I examine two recently unearthed texts in the field of Sor Juana studies: *Carta de Serafina de Cristo*, a text intimately linked to *Respuesta a Sor Filotea*, and *Enigmas ofrecidos a la Casa del Placer*.[7] The *Carta de Serafina de Cristo*, although of unknown authorship, marshals a female writing subject who enters the fray of the polemic surrounding the publication of the *Carta atenagórica*, defending Sor Juana's prerogative, as a woman, to write. I argue that it establishes a female intellectual alliance with Sor Juana, while simultaneously making a case for the legitimacy of women's writing in the seventeenth-century historical context from which both Sor Juana and Serafina wrote. In my reading of the second text, the *Enigmas*, I propose an analysis of the literary work of the nuns of the Casa del Placer in light of the solidarity implied by the mobilization of a virtual and utopian all-female writing community that challenged the Church's disapproval of female intellectual activity via the establishment of a learned community of scholarly women—in which Sor Juana and her friend and mentor the Condesa de Paredes were participants,[8] together with Portuguese nuns from several different convents.

The *Carta de Serafina de Cristo*: A Female Intellectual Alliance

In 1690 a theological treatise written by Sor Juana was printed in Puebla— against her wishes, one must add—at the instigation of the bishop of that city, Manuel Fernández de Santa Cruz, thus passing into general circulation among the lettered class. In this text Sor Juana tackled a theological problem, namely, which was the greatest of the "finezas" (gifts) of Christ? That is, which was the greatest proof of Christ's love for mankind? Her dense and baroque text stood as a refutation of another, written fifty years earlier by the renowned Portuguese Jesuit theologian Antonio Vieira.[9] Sor Juana's tract, published under the title *Carta atenagórica* or *Letter Worthy of Athena*,[10] was responsible for a scandal that ruffled many ecclesiastical feathers. It also forced Sor Juana to defend herself and her actions as a female intellectual with what has become her best-known piece of writing, the *Respuesta a Sor Filotea*, so named as it was a response to a text critical of her, the *Carta de Sor Filotea*, whose author was really the Bishop of Puebla, Manuel Fernández de Santa Cruz, masquerading as a nun.

According to Octavio Paz, Sor Juana had become caught in the crossfire of a battle of powerful male egos. Paz has traced the outlines of a long-standing enmity between Mexico's two most powerful prelates—Fernández de Santa

Cruz and the Archbishop of Mexico, Francisco de Aguiar y Seijas—which had intensified after the former was passed over for the archbishopric in favor of the latter, then Bishop of Michoacán. In an attempt to irritate his rival, who had strong ties to the Jesuits and who was a great admirer of Vieira (Paz 479), Fernández de Santa Cruz had Sor Juana write her text refuting Vieira's analysis of the "finezas de Cristo" (485). What Paz finds less easy to explain is the bishop's own letter, the *Carta de Sor Filotea*, which he published as a prologue to Sor Juana's text. Paz describes the letter—which mixes praise of Sor Juana for her critique of Vieira with criticism of her pursuit of secular literature—as both strange and ambivalent (489). As Sor Juana's response to this text shows, she herself obviously interpreted Sor Filotea's letter as a criticism and the publication of her critique of Vieira as a betrayal. Another writer also interprets the Bishop of Puebla's pseudonymous letter in this vein, coming to Sor Juana's defense in the lesser-known *Carta de Serafina de Cristo*, signed by a certain Serafina de Cristo, ostensibly a nun cloistered, like Sor Juana, in the Convent of San Jerónimo. The letter reads as a defense of the actions of Sor Juana as well as an attack on those who censured her. More generally, it boldly declares itself a manifesto for female intellectual activity and solidarity. Serafina, identifying herself as a fellow female writer, mobilizes rhetorical and emblematic forces against the male intellectual and ecclesiastic establishment that had seen fit to judge Sor Juana for actions they deemed ill-suited to her status as a woman and a nun.

It is my intention to read this letter in terms of such a female intellectual alliance, showing how it is carefully crafted to this end, as well as to elucidate the political capital such an alliance could create. Such a reading, however, is not possible without a discussion of the story behind the discovery and subsequent analysis of the letter, as well as an explanation of why I believe my reading is not only viable, but also crucial to a historically revisionist reading of female intellectual community and alliance in early modern New Spain.

The discovery of the *Carta de Serafina de Cristo* created little intellectual interest when a Jesuit priest first found it in 1960 in an antiquarian bookshop in Madrid.[11] However, in recent years it has become the center of a scholarly polemic, one that ironically mirrors the very textual wars of the seventeenth century with which it is concerned, with leading Sor Juana scholars offering very different views as to its genesis and intent. First to bring the letter into the scholarly spotlight was Elías Trabulse, who claims in his article and paleographic transcription of the letter that it was written by Sor Juana herself and addressed to the Bishop of Puebla, Manuel Fernández de Santa Cruz, also known as Sor Filotea.[12] He believes its intention was to reveal to her addressee that the real target of the *Carta atenagórica* was not Vieira, but rather her erstwhile confessor, the Jesuit priest Antonio Núñez de Miranda, a man never in favor of her intellectual activities and who, moreover, according to Trabulse, had been the anonymous "soldier," author of a text heavily critical of Sor Juana and her *Carta atenagórica*.[13] The soldier's text has never been found, but mention is made of it in Serafina's letter, as well as in Sor Juana's *Respuesta a Sor Filotea de la Cruz*.[14] According to Trabulse, Serafina's letter is the satirical counterpart to the *Respuesta*, in which a month later Sor Juana took her chance to boldly, and caustically, express all she felt she could not say in the first text ("La guerra" 204).

In a book published in 1998, *Serafina y Sor Juana*, Mexican scholars Antonio Alatorre and Lilia Tenorio, using critical, philological, historical, biographical, and even graphological tools, spend a great deal of time refuting Trabulse's theory that the letter had been written by Sor Juana herself. They also vehemently and scathingly disagree with Trabulse's theory of the purpose and recipient of the letter. They claim that his supposition "nos deja estupefactos" (leaves us stupefied) (82), arguing that the *Carta atenagórica* was indeed written to impugn Vieira directly. They also believe that the *Carta de Serafina de Cristo* was addressed to Sor Juana herself.[15] As far as the author of the letter, they settle on a minor poet and Sor Juana supporter of the time, Juan Ignacio de Castorena y Ursúa. They base their supposition on a comparison of his poetry and the letter, which similarly use a florid and convoluted baroque style. Comparing Serafina's text with some of Castorena's writings, they come to their conclusion, claiming: "están usando una prosa recargada y florida para decir cosas muy simples" (they are both employing an elaborate and flowery prose to say very simple things) (142).[16] While there is no doubt that Castorena was an admirer of Sor Juana—he edited her *Famas y obras póstumas* published in 1709—Alatorre and Tenorio's evidence is slight and unconvincing, given the uniformity of style that characterized much baroque writing.

Also part of the debate is Mexican historian Augusto Vallejo who bases his opinion on the difference in signature and rhetorical style between Serafina's letter and examples pertaining to Sor Juana.[17] He challenges Trabulse's research concerning the existence of a real Serafina de Cristo, who according to Vallejo was indeed a member of the convent community of San Jerónimo along with Sor Juana. Trabulse, unable to find any record of such a nun in the convent's *Libro de profesiones*,[18] had dismissed this possibility early on in his research. However, Vallejo adheres to the theory that she must have been a novice who never professed and for whom, therefore, there would be no record in the *Libro*.

Styles of the Flesh: Performing Gender

There can be no doubt that the detective work associated with pinning down elusive identities is a tantalizing pastime. Even so, Serafina's "true" identity may not be so crucial. Other more compelling information perhaps may be learned from the study of her letter. My reading of the *Carta de Serafina de Cristo* bypasses the polemic concerning the author's identity, focusing instead on the text as a declaration of a female intellectual alliance. First, though, I must address how a text by an unconfirmed author of unknowable gender can be read as an example of such alliance. Valerie Wayne, a critic of early modern English literature, has studied the antimisogynist play, *Swetnam the Woman-hater*, published anonymously in early seventeenth-century England. She questions whether a text expressing solidarity among women can be read as such if the identity, specifically the gender of the author, remains unknown:

> What does it mean, for instance, that some of the most articulate defenses of women against misogynist discourse in early modern England were written by authors whose gender is unknowable? To whom can we attribute agency in those texts? Can they offer instances of women's alliances if they also represent gender as indefinite and unstable? (221)

Wayne claims that a different reading strategy is required in the interpretation of an anonymous or pseudonymous text, one that resists "reliance on an originary, gendered author who stands outside the work" (222). She identifies the presence of a female intellectual alliance in *Swetnam the Woman-hater* by means of the theatrical performativity of gender, which she believes renders moot the biological sex of the authoring subject.[19] Judith Butler's theorizing of the performativity of gender helps illuminate the irrelevance of the biological, sexed origin of the writing subject. Questioning the essential properties of the gendered subject, Butler writes: "There is neither an 'essence' that gender expresses or externalizes nor an objective ideal to which gender aspires; because gender is not a fact, the various acts of gender create the idea of gender, and without these acts, there would be no gender at all" (522). Thus, construing gender as a series of performative acts rather than as a reified concept, one can look beyond the biological sex of authoring subjects to see what gender they are choosing to perform and why.

Elizabeth Harvey has studied the concept of gender performativity in early modern English writing from the specific viewpoint of male appropriations of feminine voice, raising some interesting points with regard to gender instability and performativity in early modern writing.[20] She poses a series of questions concerning the "origin" of the literary voice:

> Is there necessarily a difference between a feminine voice constructed by a female as opposed to a male author? If so—where—or in what—does the difference reside? Is there an essential distinguishing mark (a recognizably distinct female language), or is this difference signaled in its reception by the reader? What difference does it make who is speaking and who fashions a literary "voice"? (16)

Following Butler's theory of gender performativity, we can contest the essentialist notion of a feminine voice as a reified and preconstituted entity. It is thus possible to discard the notion of the biological sex of the author as "gendering" the language of the text; texts such as Serafina's mark a female cultural presence beyond that of the grammatical gender marker, even as they obscure identity. Of particular interest to me here is Harvey's questioning of a difference that is signaled by reception. This is relevant in the context of the political strategy of the performance of the female gender, especially in the baroque period in which Serafina was writing. My analysis of the letter foregrounds how Serafina manipulates the performance of female gender as a tactic to build female solidarity and intellectual community. She cleverly takes advantage of the reception accorded to her as a marginal female authoring subject, seizing on aspects of baroque discourse that allow her to subversively appropriate the tools of the patriarchy, to combat textual misogyny, and to stand in solidarity with another female author.

Battling Misogyny: The Female Authoring Subject and the Rhetoric of Marginality

Writing of the baroque in New Spain, Mabel Moraña has analyzed the constraints placed on those who wrote from the periphery of the hegemonic discourse. Among those constraints she has identified those internalized by the writing subject, what she terms an "aguda conciencia de la marginalidad" (acute awareness of marginality) (*Viaje al silencio* 45), which led the authors to be hyperaware of their text's reception or what she calls the "alteridad represiva del interlocutor" (the repressive otherness of the interlocutor) (44). She employs this analysis in her discussion of the writing strategies of Sor Juana, a subject marginalized variously by gender, status, and "nationality" (as a criolla). These limitations led to what Moraña has called "la retórica de la marginalidad" (46), present in Sor Juana's work, which she exercised from within the confines of the hegemonic discourse ("dominante, masculino, exclusivista, inquisitorial," 46). Moraña's rhetoric of marginality implies a subversion of this hegemonic discourse as the writing subject turns the very limits and constraints of this marginal locus of enunciation to her advantage. This we will see exemplified in the letter of Serafina de Cristo as she employs strategies that manipulate and flout the very limits patriarchal society imposed on her.

Surprisingly, some of the strategies employed by writers such as Serafina were also used by their misogynist counterparts. Stephanie Merrim traces this Janus-like phenomenon to a single origin in the *Querelle des femmes,* begun in 1403 with Christine de Pisan's *Book of the City of Ladies*. According to Merrim, the ideological issues taken up at this point and wielded by those on either side of the debate remained constant, as she demonstrates in texts from the early modern period (xiv). The only discourse available to antimisogynist writers was the discourse of the enemy—the discourse of patriarchy. Women writers skillfully availed themselves of this discourse in a maneuver Merrim calls "pitting the words of the patriarchs themselves against patriarchal misogyny" (xv). This maneuver involved the citation of texts in which authoritative *male* writers (biblical, classical, or contemporary, both secular and religious) defended and promoted women. Misogynist writers had long understood the value of the rhetoric of citation. Writing of early modern English misogynist texts, Diane Purkiss states: "Citation seems at once to act as an authenticating discourse which validates the misogynistic enterprise by aligning it with what is always already apparent" (69). The use of citation, especially in a period when originality in literature was not its most highly praised feature, bound texts together in a sort of textual network of misogyny. Moreover, as Purkiss points out, the rhetoric of citation acted as an "authenticating discourse" for misogynist texts, lending legitimacy to those newer texts that borrowed from more established ones. In this process of legitimation, the individual author is displaced by a group of established scholars who provide a textual safety in numbers that lends weight to the writer's argument.

The lure of the rhetoric of citation for the pro-female writer is obvious; the need for validation is much stronger in pro-female texts because they stand outside the cozy embrace of patriarchal tradition. The art of citation, however authoritative it may have been, was not enough to protect the author against a misogynist audience. Acutely conscious of the reception awaiting their works, pro-female writers were obliged to be much more inventive and subversive in their use of this technique than the misogynist writers, resorting to deflecting, and dodging, and circumventing strategies. As Merrim explains, "pro-female writers hard-pressed by the weight of patriarchal tradition against their position often resorted to manipulation of that tradition, taking proof texts out of context and/or glossing them willfully to suit their purposes" (xvi). Although women writers were forced to internalize patriarchal, and even misogynist, praxis in order to get their point across, they still found ways to subtly subvert them as is evidenced by the author of the *Carta de Serafina de Cristo*.

Sor Juana is the perfect example of a writer who, owing to her vast erudition, skillfully exploits the "dominant models" of language in order to subvert them. According to Moraña, the first step in the subversion of the dominant discourse from within begins with an awareness of the terms that constitute that discourse—a rigorous grounding, if you will, in the elements that constitute baroque writing:

> Para la oligarquía criolla del siglo XVII y su sector letrado, el Barroco es, como dijimos, un modelo expresivo, la imagen y el lenguaje del poder, al que se puede venerar o subvertir, según el grado de conciencia alcanzado. A través suyo se escucha la voz del escolatismo, la poética aristotélica y las formas de composición gongorinas. La apropiación de este modelo es, en gran medida, simbólica. Y reivindicativa. Toma connotaciones políticas cuando esos modelos dominantes adquieren, digamos, opacidad, llamando la atención sobre sí mismos; cuando lo que importa no es ya, solamente, los formas o grados de la apropiación del canon, sino los valores que ese canon institucionaliza, juzgados desde la perspectiva de un sector con conciencia de sí. (*Viaje al silencio* 48)[21]

We find this same kind of intellectual savvy in the *Carta de Serafina de Cristo*'s appropriations of extant discursive models. In the analysis that follows, I show how Serafina, working within the confines of a baroque discourse and employing its accepted techniques—among them, antithesis, *conceptismo*, and the rhetoric of citation—manipulates rhetorical tradition and practice to strike a blow against misogyny in defense of female intellectual alliance. It is my opinion, following Moraña, that Serafina exploits these "dominant models" to subvert the established gender binarisms and stereotypes that denigrated female authors and barred them from entering into theological debate.

Serafina, Sor Juana, and Camilla: Strength in Numbers

Using the "different reading strategy" I outlined earlier, I propose a reading of the *Carta de Serafina* as an example of intellectual solidarity among women and as a manifesto of female intellectual capability premised on the figure of Sor Juana. I argue that the content and intent of Serafina's letter mobilizes a female intellectual alliance to stand against the all-powerful community of men that had raised itself against Sor Juana following the publication, without her permission, of the *Carta atenagórica*. In the textual analysis to follow, I show how Serafina, in the name of female intellectual alliance and styling herself as a female authoring subject, subverts gender binarisms in favor of the female intellect.

The letter consists of a long introductory section in prose, followed by a liberal gloss on a section of Virgil's *Aeneid*, and then by a series of *quintillas*, or five-line stanzas, that sum up the argument and bring the letter to a close. The first strike by Serafina in the cause of female intellectual superiority comes with her early dismissal of the importance of Antonio Vieira, author of the text with which the theological polemic began, and the implication that it is Sor Juana herself, through her refutation of his analysis of the "finezas de Cristo," who has preserved his fame for posterity. This idea is elaborated, not coincidentally, around the concept of a funeral sermon that Vieira gave for a Portuguese aristocrat, Doña María de Ataide. Addressing herself directly to Sor Juana as she does throughout the letter, Serafina writes: "Vistas las athenagóricas cuentas que Vmd. le ajustó al orador más cabal entre los de maior cuenta del mundo, registre la suma de aquella numerosa Carta en el *Epítome platónico de doña María de Ataide*" (I, 37).[22] It is Sor Juana's text, her "Athenagorian accounts," that will thus enable Vieira's to live on. Serafina gleefully seizes on her funereal conceit, describing Vieira's waning intellectual fame with images traditionally associated with death: "Parece que se inclina allí a la tierra, mustia flor, la maravillosa fama de su gloria" (It appears that the marvelous fame of his glory now droops to the ground, a withered flower) (I, 37). In an antithetical move that carries with it the taint of faint praise (coming as it does immediately after the picture of his withered celebrity), she writes "Lo cierto es que, en la siempre floridíssima vega de los ingenios, nunca pudo ser ciprés difunto, sino siempre viva, y aun immortal, la gloria de su fama" (I, 37).[23] Although his fame appears to be "mustia flor," he is not a "ciprés difunto." But this doubling of death metaphors severely weakens her swift reassurance of the longevity of his fame, and Serafina leaves her reader in little doubt that Vieira's renown is moribund and only briefly receiving new life thanks to Sor Juana. Alatorre and Tenorio claim that Serafina's strategy here is to emphasize that Sor Juana always treated Vieira with respect. I think that they have missed the point, as Serafina swiftly dispatches Vieira and his importance to the matter so as to focus on the real target of her attack, "el soldado castellano" (the Castilian soldier).

The conceit of the fruits of a woman's intellect breathing new life into that of a man throws into disarray the strict binary opposites ascribed to male and female intellects in the seventeenth century. This idea, established by Serafina at the outset of the letter with regard to Vieira, is then developed to great effect in the next section, in which Serafina depicts the struggle between Sor Juana and a more dangerous adversary, "el soldado castellano." From the very beginning, she undertakes to undermine the attributes of masculinity in order to discredit him, disavowing in the process all rigid gender characterizations. She describes him as "el pobre," and in a short verse preceding the main poem that describes their confrontation, she writes of his attempt to challenge Sor Juana's intellect: "Su razón sólo es sentir; / su juicio, no parecer" (His intellect is pure emotion; / his judgment does not appear) (IV, 38). Here, she takes a traditional misogynistic view of women as ruled not by judgment but by passion and applies it to him. This idea is then taken further in the main poem, which glosses the section of Book XI of Virgil's *Aeneid*, in which the poet describes the confrontation between Ornithus, one of Aeneas's warriors (here Orphito), and the Amazon Camilla, who eventually slays him.

Before looking at how Serafina appropriates Virgil to her own ends, I would like to briefly digress to examine the figure of Camilla in the *Aeneid* and to see which elements of the original text made her so attractive to Serafina. Camilla first appears in Book VII of the *Aeneid*, where she is described as, among other things, "dura virgo." Unlike other women, she is accustomed to battle but unaccustomed to womanly tasks, such as the "distaff" and the "basket of wool." She is physically strong and fleet of foot, and other women marvel at her as she comes running by. Despite Camilla's masculine attributes, however, the poet repeatedly emphasizes her maidenhood, as Trudy Harrington Becker points out:

> Over and over again, Vergil reminds the reader carefully that Camilla is a woman, not a man at all. She is called *virgo* (virgin or maiden) or adjectival versions of that some 14 times in Book XI, a word declaring a stereotypical female virtue. She lives undefiled and preserves a love for her chastity (XI.584–85), which is of significance chiefly for women. (5)

It is clear why Serafina compares Sor Juana with Virgil's depiction of Camilla: she possesses the masculine strengths required to vanquish her foe while preserving the highest attributes of her own sex. She is, in essence, a double threat. In "The Dearth of the Author," Valerie Wayne discusses how the trope of the Amazon is deployed in antimisogynist discourse of the early modern period:

> Given the entrenched associations between women and weakness and all the other cultural constraints imposed upon women, the Amazon, who

combined masculine strength with feminine sympathies, was one of the most available candidates to perform the disorderly woman and mount an effective defense of women against men's physical and verbal attacks. (224)[24]

Employing the misogynistic technique of citation rhetoric to her advantage, Serafina invokes the comparison between Sor Juana and Camilla in a forceful performance of the Amazon trope as Wayne represents it.[25]

At the beginning of the gloss, Serafina strips her opponent of any virility his standing as a soldier would give him. He is described as "huyendo el lance" (fleeing the lance) (VII, 38). Worse, although he is young, his lack of courage makes him elderly: "El Joven, soldado viejo quiso parecer" (This young man wanted to look like an old soldier) (VII, 38). The figure of Camilla/Sor Juana appears in the next stanza as Serafina introduces the traditional images of the wolf and the lamb. However, as with other emblematic images, she subverts these to serve the theme of her text. The soldier *appears* at first to be the wolf, yet he cannot successfully maintain this appearance: "Y aunque los dientes afila, / queda *in albis* su fireza*"* (And although he sharpens his teeth, / his ferocity remains *in albis*) (VIII, 39).[26] The same holds true for the image of Sor Juana as the defenseless lamb. Although she appears to be this vulnerable creature, Serafina warns that she is not so docile and that the *soldado* misreads his opponent: "imagina ser cordera / su adalid como si fuera / aquella Camila YNES" (he believes his champion is a lamb / as if Camilla could be so) (VIII, 39). With "YNES," Serafina makes a play on the name "Inés" from "Sor Juana Inés," which derives from the Latin for "lamb": "as if Camilla were such a lamb."

In the next stanza Serafina directly addresses the issue of dueling texts, again losing no opportunity to discredit the courage and valor traditionally ascribed to the uber-masculine figure of the soldier: "Valiente / sólo en su papel salió" (He only appeared brave on paper) (IX, 39). He was never possessed of enough courage to face Sor Juana/Camilla directly. Nor was his text any match for hers: "El su papel hizo, y / se hubo Camila con él / como quien coge un papel / y lo tira por ay" (He carried out his role / and Camilla made off with it / like someone who grabs a piece of paper / and throws it away) (IX, 39). This line typifies Serafina's love of baroque wordplay. She amuses herself with the double meaning in Spanish of the word *papel*, here referring to the *role* the soldier plays, though badly, as a masculine man of action, as well as to his text, his *paper*, which Camilla throws away as if it were nothing.

In the last stanza of the gloss, Serafina crystallizes her ideas, proclaiming Sor

Juana/Camilla's victory as one that benefits a community of women. She continues with her tactic of investing gender stereotypes with new meanings, proclaiming Camilla's victory "mugeril" (womanly). Given all that Serafina has said heretofore in her letter, there can be no doubt that she intends the traditionally negative term "mugeril" to replace the positive "varonil," or "manly." Persisting in this subversion of stereotypes, Camilla proclaims: "la gloria / de los Padres es la mía" (the glory of the Fathers is mine) (X, 40). Here, in a daring jab at those who believe that women have no place in the masculine preserve of theological debate, Serafina has Camilla/Sor Juana assume the mantle of the Church Fathers. This is her most direct assault on those who chose to vilify Sor Juana for having the audacity to offer a reading of patristic theology, as she did in the *Carta atenagórica*. With this line, she sweeps away all competition in theological debate—Vieira, "el soldado," and all those clerics who were horrified to find a woman engaged in such a manly activity. Further underscoring her point and stressing the importance of intellectual alliance among women, Serafina extends the glory gained by Sor Juana's actions to the community of women to which she belongs: "Para gloria de las Madres / sepa en el mundo todo hombre / que hoy, en Camila, más nombre / han conseguido los Padres" (For the glory of the Mothers / let every man in the world know / that today, thanks to Camilla / the Fathers have gained more reknown) (X, 40). Driving her point home one final, defiant time, Serafina displays the figure of the woman illuminating members of her sex in reflected glory, proclaiming to all *men* that it is *she*, with her female pen, who has burnished the reputation of the Church Fathers. Subtle Serafina is not. Resolute and defiant, she is.[27]

Serafina returns to her prose format, reiterating what she has said in the last stanza of the poem: that Sor Juana's letter served to augment the glory of the Church Fathers. Referring to the writing as well as to the printing of the letter, she writes: "Que lo fue legítimo parto de la fecundidad del ingenio en lo escrito, no pudo ser desdoro, sino muy honrroso crédito de los Padres, impreso" (XI, 40).[28] Here she weaves a protective web around Sor Juana, claiming that the act of printing only served to honor the "Padres." Here she emphasizes the fact that Sor Juana refuted Vieira, who had contradicted the teachings of the Church Fathers with his sermon. Perhaps she also suggests—more indirectly by linking the "Padres" to the printing of the letter—that it was in fact the Bishop of Puebla who had ordered it so.

She brings the letter to a close with a series of *quintillas*, five-line stanzas— "Quinta esencia de la substancia de lo dicho" (the Quintessence of the substance of what was said) (XIV, 41). As I have already noted, subtlety is not Serafina's strong suit, and up to this point the reader must find him- or herself highly aware of the aim of Serafina's text. But the writer cannot resist one last attack on the now badly injured soldier. She ventures that perhaps the addition of these final poems will help to guide the poor unfortunate: "Puede ser que sirvan siquiera de pista a la flaqueza que en el dicho soldado se ha descubierto" (It could possibly serve as a guide for the soldier's weaknesses) (XIV, 41). In the second stanza, Serafina refers to "clarín de San Gerónimo" (San Gerónimo's trumpet), the name of the convent where Sor Juana resided, as the "señal de juicio" (sign of judgment), which "llena / por todo el mundo" (sounds / around the world) (XIV, ll. 8–10). Making sure her readers have no doubt as to who blows this trumpet, she tells us it is the "Ángel de la Cruz." The soldier hears the call to judgment, another play on words by Serafina, in which she refers to how he will be judged, as well as to his *juicio* (referring to intellect or judgment): "En juicio como debiera / con todo su juicio ha entrado" (With judgment, as he should / with all of his judgment gone) (XIV, ll. 24–25). As Serafina tells us, with his judgment gone and his number up, he finally succumbs to his fate: "vivo se entierra" (he buries himself alive) (XIV, l. 26). She makes clear, however, that Sor Juana is the agent of his destruction—"se atenagoricó" (he athenarized himself) (XIV, l. 27)—making a none-too-subtle reference to Sor Juana's *Carta atenagórica* with which the polemic began.²⁹

In the final three stanzas that conclude the letter, Serafina emphasizes her solidarity with Sor Juana, her affection for her. Employing the rhetoric of false modesty, perhaps, she recognizes the clumsiness of her verses. She casts herself in the role of willing acolyte to the great intellect and writer that is Sor Juana; her own verse can only be rendered worthy with the touch of a surer hand: "Si confuso caracol / es lo dicho, Madre Cruz, / apliquele su arrebol" (If what I have said is a confusing spiral, / then please, Mother Cruz, enlighten it) (XIV, ll. 51–53). For Serafina's text is not meant for the printing press ("la luz"), but rather for the eyes of her around whom she and others orbit ("el sol"). In the final stanza she places her own name and then as postscript writes: "En este convento que es de NPS Géronimo de México, en 1 de febrero de 1691 años. B.L.M. de Vmd. quien le ama en el Señor y todo bien le desea y espera" (XIV, 43).³⁰

For all its ludic content and satirical jibes, Serafina's letter is a text with a mission: to defend Sor Juana against her (inferior) detractors and to assert her talent and her right to the masculine pursuit of writing. Margo Glantz writes of the warring texts engaged in this battle for and against Sor Juana. She has likened Sor Juana's panegyrics—collected in the *Segundo volumen* and published in 1692, three years before her death—to a kind of textual fortress built for the express purpose of defending Sor Juana against the attacks and the envy of her detractors (*La comparación* 196). Serafina's text, too, has this defensive element, but it is also very much a text on the offensive, as we see in her merciless destruction of the figure of the *soldado castellano* and, less virulently, of Vieira. One of the elements with which she mounts both her defense and her attack is the weapon afforded to her by a female intellectual alliance. She stands with Sor Juana as a sister writer, a sister intellect, even as she disavows any talent of her own. Moreover, she shows a Sor Juana who writes for the benefit of her community, the community of nuns with whom she lives, thus positing strength in numbers.

Depictions of Sor Juana's isolated and lonely life in the convent, an intellectual island in a sea of bickering, simple-minded women, belong to a larger critical, historical, and popular school of thought that portrays discord and conflict among female convent dwellers as the norm. This image of conflict in the convent community belongs to a more general gender bias that casts alliances among women as something impossible given their conflictive natures and their desire to win the approval of masculine society at the expense of other women. Compared to a vast corpus of scholarship on male friendship and alliance, almost nothing exists on these types of relationships among women, and if such information exists, it is cast in the light of aberration or exception to the rule. In their collection of essays on alliances among women in early modern England, Susan Frye and Karen Robertson analyze the origins of this disparity:

> Men's alliances, formalized in such institutions as the guild, government, law, church and university, left behind records, architecture, and literature that have invited generations of scholars to codify them. As a result, entire libraries are filled with books analyzing men's connections. The relations among women [. . .] have proved not only less visible but also more difficult to reconstruct, often because women did not formally record their activities or seek memorialization in material structures. (3)

Different reading strategies are needed to reach both the lived reality of women and their thought processes. The strategy I employ in my analysis of the *Carta de Serafina de Cristo* disrupts the fixity of the assiduously created cultural constructions that were accorded women at the time and thus rethinks notions of power. Once we challenge the idea of power as a monolithic, all-encompassing force, we become aware of the existence of female agency. An examination of communal subversions of patriarchal control encourages us to see beyond the historically and socially constructed vulnerabilities of women in order to more fully elucidate their role in society. If Serafina de Cristo, whoever she may have been, stands in solidarity with Sor Juana to defend her right to transgress the male territory of the written word, the nuns of the Casa del Placer use a slightly different tactic, though with a similar end in mind. There is also commonality with Sor Juana in the clandestine way the nuns of the Casa del Placer set about the organization of their society. They establish a virtual writing community, known only to a select few, a safe haven in which Sor Juana can write, far from the censure of the ecclesiastic authorities. Their community was a far different place than the coerced convent community the Church desired. Perhaps for this reason, it was necessary to keep its activities secret.

Sor Juana and the Casa del Placer: The Pleasure of the Text

The Casa del Placer was a female literary academy formed by a group of aristocratic Portuguese nuns from various convents in Lisbon. It was a virtual academy in the sense that the nuns obviously communicated by letter because of the mandate of cloister. Little is known of the academy other than the texts that concern me here, a venture in which Sor Juana was involved. Owing to the connection between the Portuguese Duchess of Aveiro and the Condesa de Paredes, Sor Juana was invited to contribute her work to the group. The texts of eight Portuguese nuns and the Condesa de Paredes appear alongside Sor Juana's in what was meant as an homage to the Mexican poet, who by this time was a literary celebrity in all parts of the Spanish-speaking world (Sabat Rivers and Rivers 678). The result was the "Enigmas ofrecidos a la discreta inteligencia / de la soberana asamblea de la Casa del Placer / por su más rendida y aficionada / Soror Juana Inés de la Cruz, Décima Musa."[31] The Casa del Placer was also a secret society whose text was not to be disseminated. Its contents were meant only for the eyes of its members.[32]

Sor Juana's fame had spread to the Iberian Peninsula with the 1689 publication in Spain (owing to the efforts of the Condesa de Paredes) of a collection of Sor Juana's work, *Inundación castálida*. It was the Condesa who provided the link between the Soberana Asamblea de la Casa del Placer and the Décima Musa, facilitated no doubt by her powerful cousin the Duchess of Aveiro, a Portuguese aristocrat, married to a Spanish nobleman, who had also been in correspondence with Sor Juana.[33] Owing to the fact that the majority of Portuguese nuns were from aristocratic families, it is not difficult to see how this female network was constructed: from the connection between the aristocratic Portuguese nuns and the Duchess of Aveiro, and from there to Spanish court and the Duchess's cousin, the Condesa de Paredes. Finally, the latter provided the link from the court to the Convent of San Jerónimo, where Sor Juana lived. Georgina Sabat Rivers has called this endeavor "el testimonio más importante del reconocimiento de la fama de Sor Juana y de la solidaridad que existía entre mujeres nobles y monjas letradas" (Sabat Rivers 219).[34]

Through its inherent power, this female network was able to circumvent the usual channels of (transatlantic) communication controlled by men. As a female literary community, it facilitated the collection and production of a literary work composed entirely by women, the majority of whom were cloistered nuns. This endeavor speaks to the pursuit of a utopian quest and is underscored by the name of the Portuguese nuns' virtual literary academy, the Casa del Placer. Zygmunt Bauman has written of the division between the imagined community and lived reality:

> Paradise lost or a paradise still hoped to be found; one way or another, this is definitely not a paradise that we inhabit and not the paradise that we know from our own experience. Perhaps it is a paradise precisely for these reasons. Imagination, unlike the harsh realities of life, is an expanse of unbridled freedom. Imagination we can "let loose," and we do, with impunity—since we have not much chance of putting what we have imagined to the test of life. (3)

Although the Portuguese nuns, like Sor Juana, lived in the all-female communities of their convents, these spaces were not female utopias. The control Church hierarchies attempted to exert there speaks more to Bauman's "harsh realities of life" than his idea of a space of "unbridled freedom." I argue therefore that with the formation of the Casa del Placer and its creation of an autonomous female textual space, the nuns were reproducing community in an ideal form, different from the reality they actually lived.

The "house" imagined by these writing nuns—the Casa del Placer—affords them protection and shelter against the hostility of the outside world. Gaston Bachelard has written of the image of the house as one that "shelters daydreaming, the house protects the dreamer, the house allows one to dream in peace" (4). The house in this case offers its inhabitants the luxury of dreaming up an all-female universe where women write for other women, free from the disapproval that normally would accompany such activities. The house functions as a refuge and a redoubt from where they can challenge, as we shall see, male censure of women's writing. It is a house that demonstrates "human resistance at the height of the storm" (44).

This virtual female literary academy also opened up a multiplicity of speaking positions for women, promoting female agency under the auspices of a literary community. These "separatist spaces" can be used to empower women (d'Monté 93). Speaking of the kind of female separatist spaces created by Margaret Cavendish, a British noblewoman writing in the seventeenth century to whom I return shortly, d'Monté writes: "Inside these inner sanctums, the controlling male gaze has no strength and is transformed instead into a mutually supportive gaze between women" (93). In turn, this mutual support can be channeled into a legitimate space for creativity and learning, an activity often deemed unlawful or unseemly in other male-dominated spaces. It is from this point of view that I propose to study the purpose and intent of the Casa del Placer, analyzing how this separatist space was created as well as reading the texts that were conceived therein.

The creative production of the Casa del Placer consists of a dedicatory poem and a prologue in the form of a sonnet written by Sor Juana and four poems in praise of her by Sor Mariana de Santo Antonio, the Condesa de Paredes, Sor Francisca Xavier, and Sor Simoa de Castilla. The former texts were written in Spanish. There are also texts in Portuguese: two *censuras* (approbatory texts) in prose by Sor Feliciana de Milão and Sor Maria das Saudades and three *licenças* (permissions) in the form of *décimas* (stanzas of ten octosyllabic lines) by Sor Maria Magdalena, Sor Maria do Céu, and Sor Maria de Guedes.[35] Finally, there are Sor Juana's enigmas— twenty *redondillas* (quatrains) that offer riddles on the nature of love.[36] In describing the production of the Casa del Placer, I observe the exact order of texts in the manuscript, which is reproduced in book form.

The enigmas are the centerpiece of Casa del Placer's literary production. The preliminary texts provide the staging ground for the enigmas, establishing a separatist space that they infuse with the power afforded them by the mobilization of community. The gesture these texts enact is similar to that made by the nuns who mobilize community to protest the imposition of *vida común* in their convents. There, as here, the nuns empower themselves through action in concert, which enables them to challenge the supposed hegemony of the institutionalized power of the Church. The writing nuns of the Casa del Placer invent a virtual community from which to resist patriarchal injunctions to silence. It is, moreover, a utopian site that affords pleasure as well as power. The enigmas act as the defiant and parodic finale to the texts that precede them, setting the seal on the nuns' claim to writing by showcasing one of the best of their generation: Sor Juana. This they do as they create an exact replica of a book, mimicking every detail of what constituted a seventeenth-century published work: an illustrated cover, dedicatory poems, and the *censuras* and *licenças* that deem the book worthy of publication. In their separate, utopian space, they are free to enjoy at will the pleasure of their text, safe from the judgment of outsiders. In order to do so, they must make themselves completely self-sufficient, carrying out every element of their endeavor without outside help.

This painstaking gesture of imitation and reproduction of the printed book has a double purpose: it strengthens the hermetic all-female universe of the Casa del Placer, while simultaneously writing the women into the patriarchal discourse that prefers to exclude them. From the point of view of conferring legitimacy on their endeavor, nothing could be of greater import to the nuns of the Casa del Placer than to represent their work within the framework of the book. In seventeenth-century Western culture, the book possessed the status of a sacred object. Walter Mignolo has traced a trajectory in Western thought that posits the alphabet as the culminating moment in the history of literacy, a conceptualization that became particularly important to the Spanish mission to colonize the New World in the sixteenth century (57). The book, ever-laden with the symbolism of the original Holy Book, was regarded not only as sacred object but also as the "warranty of knowledge and truth" (57).

The Casa del Placer is legitimized as the voices of its participants are recorded for posterity within the leaves of a book. In an early modern culture where the written word was held to be so powerful that books were believed to hold sway over both the forces of good and evil (Mignolo 57; Chartier 50), no other act could endow the voice with such authority. Authority was, however, constructed most often as a masculinist discourse. And for women, there was no alternative to writing within the patriarchy, no feminist discourse into which women could inscribe themselves. Yet, as Stephanie Merrim has said, women did manage to open up discursive spaces for themselves in this period, within this dominant discourse, availing themselves of different tactics (xx). In their imitative gesture of a published book, the nuns of the Casa del Placer play with the paradox of their position as women who must write with the patriarchy's tools. It can be viewed in terms of a ludic maneuver that seeks to highlight the absurdity of the exclusion of women writers from the arena of writing and publishing (Sabat Rivers and Rivers call the dedicatory and approbatory texts "medio burlescos" [somewhat sarcastic]) (679). However, one must be careful to contextualize this seeming subversion within the historical and religious framework pertinent to these writers. If this was a satirical gesture, it was one to be enjoyed by only a very select group of like-minded readers: the nuns of the Portuguese convents and the aristocratic women who were their supporters and benefactors. The Casa del Placer was a secret society, for reasons of both expediency and desire.

The nuns of the Casa del Placer also imitated another exclusively male preserve: the literary academy. The existence of literary academies in the Iberian Peninsula was nothing remarkable in the seventeenth century.[37] José Sánchez describes the impetus behind their proliferation:

> Por razones psicológicas y sociales el hombre se asocia con sus semejantes para compartir con él sus goces y sentimientos; si la congregación de literatos, las expresiones del alma y del corazón asumen la forma de goces estéticos derivados de composiciones escritas con amor y con inspiración. Es natural buscar refugio en la compañía del amigo para contar o para oír algo que nos apena o que gozamos. (*Academias literarias*, 67)[38]

It is not surprising that Sánchez, writing in 1961, should use the generic "hombre" to describe the participants in Spain's literary academies. However, one cannot escape the fact that these literary academies *were* in fact the exclusive preserve of the male poet.[39] It is possible that some academy, at some time or other, included the participation of female poets, and there is evidence of Sor Juana's virtual participation in *certámenes* (literary competitions) in Mexico; yet an academy such as the Casa del Placer that provided a space—albeit virtual—for women writers was anomalous to the time. There is no doubt that the founders of the Casa del Placer set out to imitate the male literary academy in the formation of their own, although they reworked it to fit the needs of their particular female community. It is, as is the book, a satirical gesture. As Jean Franco has observed: "To write was to write within an institution. The only possible response was parody and mimicry" (43).

Observing a commonplace of the elitist literary academies of the seventeenth century, they relied on the patronage of the courtly order, although their patrons were exclusively *female* aristocrats. As we have seen, it is the sponsorship of two powerful female aristocrats that facilitated the compilation of the *Enigmas*,[40] with their initiation of contact between the famous Mexican poet and the literary academy of the Portuguese nuns. Literary academies of the time would often focus on a renowned poet who would bring prestige to their particular literary group (Sánchez, *Academias literarias* 12). The Portuguese nuns also adopted this practice with their celebration of Sor Juana, a poet well known by the lettered class of the Iberian Peninsula, owing to the publication of her works there (Sor Juana's first volume, *Inundación castálida*, was published to great acclaim in Madrid in 1689, and the *Segundo volumen* in Seville in 1692.)

One last example of this slippage between the imitative and the satirical can be found in the virtual academy's name. José Sánchez has identified the existence of a fictional literary academy, the "Academia de la Casa del Placer Honesto" (Academy of the House of Honest Pleasure), in the novel *La casa del placer honesto* (1620) by the Spanish writer Alonso Jerónimo de Salas de Barbadillo, who, according to Sánchez, was an aficionado of actual literary academies in Madrid (*Academias literarias* 30). The novel describes four young friends who abandon their family homes and university studies in Salamanca for Madrid, where they rent a comfortable and pleasant house. There they form the Casa del Placer Honesto and set down its laws, the most important of which requires an abandonment of all romantic pleasures in order to dedicate themselves to a study of the *bellas artes*. It is not impossible that the aristocratic nuns of the Lisbon convents had read or heard of Barbadillo's novel, and finding similarities in the life of artistic retirement chosen by the four young friends with their own lives in the cloister, chose this particular name for their literary academy.[41] This naming gesture also raises certain interesting questions if we are to indeed suppose a prior knowledge of Barbadillo's text. Is the Casa del Placer to be deemed not "honesto" in comparison with the Casa del Placer Honesto? Perhaps here the women were drawing attention to the idea of the clandestine nature of their academy, or maybe they were implicitly acknowledging and even celebrating the transgressive character of their endeavor. As intriguing as they are, we cannot answer these questions. Reviewing this naming gesture in light of Barbadillo's novel, however, one can also intuit a certain mischievous reworking of the perception of the convent space that unconsciously has more in common with the early modern English author Margaret Cavendish's utopian female separatist space, as depicted in her play *The Convent of Pleasure*, than with the realities of the cloister.

"Retiredness bars the life from nothing else but men": The Convent of Pleasure and the Casa del Placer

Margaret Cavendish, Duchess of Newcastle, was a seventeenth-century British royalist poet, as well as philosopher, scientist, and dramatist. Her prolific, sometimes audacious, writings and extravagant personality caused somewhat of a scandal in her day, although she often espoused conservative political and social beliefs. An underlying theme of Margaret Cavendish's fiction was the withdrawal of groups of women from society to a utopian space wherein these women could be self-sufficient. Texts such as *Blazing World* and the *Convent of Pleasure* depict a safe haven for women that encouraged female agency under the auspices of a mutually supportive female gaze, something that can be read into the formation of the similarly titled Casa del Placer. Although there are obviously striking differences on many levels between the fictional Convent of Pleasure and the virtual literary academy of the Casa del Placer, there are also similarities in intent in the creation of both of these utopian all-female spaces that warrant a closer look. In order to do so, I will take a brief detour into Margaret Cavendish's Convent of Pleasure to look at the space of female solidarity and community both writers create (although it is important to bear in mind that Sor Juana is here a participant, not sole creator) that promotes female agency on many different levels: utopian, erotic, ludic, satirical, and intellectual.[42]

An important place to start is with the very name of both spaces: the "Convent of Pleasure" and the "Casa del Placer." I have already addressed the similarities between Barbadillo's novel and the name of the literary academy formed by the Portuguese nuns. While there exists a possibility that the nuns may have been familiar with Barbadillo's novel, there is almost no chance that they could have heard of Margaret Cavendish and her plays and other writings. However, it is entirely probable that there existed a similarity of *intent* in the naming gesture of the Portuguese literary academy and the gesture behind Margaret Cavendish's play, *The Convent of Pleasure*. This brings us to Stephanie Merrim's highly suggestive idea of textual sorority existing between early modern women writers working in different sociocultural milieus, and how, unconsciously, elements of their writing coincide. Merrim describes these points of contact as

> a new set of possibilities for core issues that [...] constitute a blueprint of significant factors in or preoccupations of seventeenth-century women's writing. These include (in random order) fame, the esthetic of the shocking and bizarre, women's education, melancholy, revisions of the consecrated theme of love, female homoeroticism, envisioning elsewheres, the *querelle des femmes* and misogyny, women and reason, philosophical and literary syncretism, multiple self-imaging, incursions into the public domain and into masculinist genres, unstable gender ideologies and the phenomenon of the Tenth Muse. (xli)

Certain of these elements emerge in both the *Enigmas* and in Cavendish's work, and here I explore what the significance might be of this shared context.

Margaret Cavendish's *Convent of Pleasure* depicts a female protagonist, Lady Happy, who inherits a fortune on her father's death and finds herself ardently pursued by men who are anxious to gain control of her fortune. Rejecting marriage and its attendant loss of a recently won freedom, Lady Happy creates a luxurious all-female retreat in the house she inherited, which she names the Convent of Pleasure. Other than the all-female nature of the community, the Convent of Pleasure has little in common with traditional notions of the convent, being a place dedicated to sybaritic pleasures and seemingly modeled after life in Charles II's court (Shaver 13). Mulling over the formation of her retreat, Lady Happy declares: "My Cloister shall not be a Cloister of restraint, but a place for freedom, not to vex the Senses but to please them" (220). It is also to be a place where women may dedicate themselves to intellectual and aesthetic pursuits, such as the writing and performing of plays in which they themselves take on all roles, both masculine and feminine.

Lady Happy's community is not only intellectually and theatrically self-sufficient, it is also autonomous in other ways. Cavendish creates a scene in which several of Lady Happy's suitors discuss ways in which they could breach the convent's walls, perhaps disguising themselves as tradesmen or laborers who might have cause to go there. One of their company informs them, however, that this will be impossible, as women are carrying out all tasks necessary for the running of the convent. Monsieur Take-Pleasure informs his fellows: "They employ Women in all Places in their Gardens; and for Brewing, Baking and making all sorts of things; besides, some keep their Swine, and twenty such like Offices and Employments there are which we should be very proper for" (228).

Cavendish also depicts a female universe that is self-sufficient in terms of desire. Harriet Andreadis has grouped the *Convent of Pleasure* along with a handful of other early modern texts written by women that "explicitly portray female same-sex erotic behaviours" (247). She does, however, qualify her use of the word "erotic," contextualizing it within the framework of the early modern historical moment: "*Erotic* in this early modern context, then, describes that spectrum of sometimes diffuse but clearly sensuous feelings and intense emotions found in discourses of passionate engagement between women" (248). The main focus of erotic content in the *Convent of Pleasure* is the relationship between Lady Happy and the Princess (who is in fact one of Lady Happy's male suitors disguised as a woman, a fact unknown to Lady Happy). Andreadis has described the depiction of this relationship as "transgressive," placing Margaret Cavendish among a group of female writers of the time who were considered "infamous or associated with scandal" (249). In her own personage, she aimed at a "blurring of boundaries between genders similar to that produced by the *Convent of Pleasure*" (243).

Andreadis clearly locates Cavendish at the cutting edge of the spectrum of feelings she has denoted as belonging to early modern female erotics. She differentiates her from other writers whose feelings were "discursively expressed, but not explicitly acknowledged in connection with sexuality or with sexual transgression" (248). These women write under the rubric of what she terms an "erotic ellipsis." She mentions such early modern English female writers as Anne Finch and Lady Mary Chudleigh, who, while they "ignored the possibilities offered by the more explicitly sexual discourse of some of their contemporaries," did indeed write passionate poetry to other women in which such erotic ellipsis is apparent (248). A similarity of gesture can be found in the Casa del Placer and in the poems the nuns dedicate to Sor Juana. These poems reveal *textual* erotics driven by the pleasure gained from the self-sufficient all-female writing utopia in which Sor Juana is portrayed as the object of passionate love.

The Erotics of the Text: The Female Body as Utopia

The figure of Sor Juana looms large in the writings of the Casa del Placer. Not only is she, as poet, the focus of the literary academy of the Portuguese nuns, as I mentioned earlier, but her body is also the entity on which are predicated the erotics of the text. Barthes calls this presence "figuration," distinguishing it from mere "representation" (55). He describes figuration thus: "Figuration is the way in which the erotic body appears (to whatever degree and in whatever form that may be) in the profile of the text" (55–56). Reading his description of the way this trope manifests itself, we can thus understand how the body of Sor Juana *figures* in the text of the Casa del Placer:

> The author may appear in his text (Genet, Proust) but not in the guise of direct biography. [. . .] Or again: one can feel desire for a character in a novel (in fleeting impulses). Or finally: the text itself, a diagrammatic and not an imitative structure, can reveal itself in the form of a body, split into fetish objects, into erotic sites. All these movements attest to a *figure* of the text, necessary to the bliss of reading. (56)

The body, or the invoked presence of the body of Sor Juana, is the fetish object, the erotic site, upon which the nuns build the Casa del Placer.

There are four poems dedicated to Sor Juana: an *endechas endecasílabas* (hendecasyllabic quatrain)[43] by Sor Mariana de Santo Antonio from the Convent of Santa Clara, a *romance* (eight syllable verse) written by the Condesa de Paredes, another *romance* by Sor Francisca Xavier of the Convent of la Rosa, and finally another *endechas endecasílibicas* by Sor Simoa de Castilla of the Convent of Santa Ana.

In her *romance* the Condesa de Paredes writes to Sor Juana: "Amiga, este libro tuyo / es tan hijo de tu ingenio" (My friend, your book / is the child of your genius) (ll. 1–2). She employs a familiar trope of the time—the poem as offspring of the author. Her simple sentence also serves to underscore the interweaving of Sor Juana's bodily presence throughout the dedicatory poems of the text, making Sor Juana into Barthes' "figure" of the text, that which is necessary for the "bliss of reading." Sor Mariana de Santo Antonio picks up and elaborates this trope in the *endechas endecasílabas* she dedicates to Sor Juana. She invokes the physical beauty of the Mexican nun's person, referring to her "hermoso rostro" (beautiful visage) in which "las rosas y azucenas / con fecundos abriles / mejoran de estación las primaveras" (the roses and lilies / in their fertile youth / enrich the springs) (ll. 6–8). Elaborating her technique of praising the body in parts, she turns to Sor Juana's eyes, which "tanto / el sol a rayos ciega, / que ignora el occidente / amaneciendo sólo en tus estrellas" (So blind the sun with their rays / that it forgets the West / setting only in your eyes) (ll. 9–12). These somewhat conventional tropes praising Sor Juana's beauty culminate in a more unusual image in which Sor Mariana makes the association between body and book more explicit: "Tan hijo de tu musa / este libro se observa, / que están cuantos lo leen / viendo en sus hojas palpitar tu vena" (This book is your muse's true offspring / and those who read it / will see your veins palpitate within its leaves) (ll. 17–20). Those who read the book will see the lifeblood of Sor Juana coursing through its pages.

We see this image taken to its next logical elaboration in the *romance* written in homage to Sor Juana by Sor Francisca Xavier, a nun in the Convent of la Rosa. She concocts a lengthy paean to Sor Juana in which she praises her talent, highlighting the extensive geographical spread of her fame from the Americas to Europe: "Y tú, dichosa España, este tesoro / que América en sus límites esconde / cuyo discurso, de una a otra zona / ilustra a rayos, ciega a resplandores" (ll. 41–44).[44] These lines fall just before the end of the poem, and she skillfully uses the succeeding lines to bring the reader back from this trip across the ocean to the intimate setting of the Casa del Placer: "Y su nombre excelso, en letras de oro / rubrique el tiempo en nuestros corazones; / que son más perdurables las memorias / grabadas en los pechos, que en los bronces" (ll. 45–48).[45] The phrase "nuestros corazones" refers to the members of the Casa del Placer, and it is Sor Juana's pen that undertakes the intimate and almost erotic gesture of writing her name in the hearts of the nuns of the Casa del Placer, a gesture that will ensure her memory lives on with them forever.[46] The idea that this should perpetuate the fame of the poet more successfully than the traditional commemorative gesture of a bronze statue emphasizes the Casa del Placer as being a place where the talent of the female poet is nurtured and protected. Sor Francisca Xavier's mention of bronze statues places the reader firmly in a society that considers unseemly the erection of a bronze statue commemorating the literary achievements of a woman, especially a cloistered nun whose likeness could not be exhibited in a public space. Yet she discards this monument in favor of the intimate commemoration carried for the female poet in a woman's breast.

Writing as Political Solidarity: *Censuras, licenças,* **and the Enemies of Pleasure**

In a section of *The Pleasure of the Text*, entitled "*Communauté*/Community," Roland Barthes describes a "Society of the Friends of the Text":

> Its members would have nothing in common (for there is no necessary agreement on the texts of pleasure) but their enemies: fools of all kinds, who decree foreclosure of the text and its pleasure, either by cultural conformism or by intransigent rationalism (suspecting a "mystique" of literature) or by political moralism or by criticism of the signifier or by stupid pragmatism or by snide vacuity or by destruction of the discourse, loss of verbal desire. (15)

It was for reasons such as these that the nuns of the Casa del Placer sought a separate, utopian, textual space in which to seek refuge from enemies such as the infamous ecclesiastics so familiar to those of us who have studied the life of Sor Juana. From the safety of the Casa del Placer, its members could address, and even attack, those "enemies of pleasure" who opposed activities such as theirs.

Such a defensive position was nothing new for Sor Juana's partisans. In her study of the second volume of the *Obras* of Sor Juana, Margo Glantz demonstrates how Sor Juana and the Condesa de Paredes carefully planned the text's construction so that it would function as a counterattack to those ecclesiastics in Mexico who sought to halt Sor Juana's activities as a writer. The nun and the Condesa marshal their own army of churchmen, who, flagrantly contradicting their holy brothers on the other side of the Atlantic, come out in support of the nun and her activity as a writer. Glantz describes this priestly standoff: "Los escritos de la monja van protegidos por un contingente de sacerdotes [...] que pelean por ella una batalla y la defienden contra los reproches y críticas que le habían hecho en México" (161).[47] She cites a strategy of *censuras* and *aprobaciones*, which read more like a series of *panegíricos* (*La comparación* 162). Through her reading of these same defenses, Glantz comes to see the *Segundo volumen* as one more participant in a nasty intertextual, internecine war between the two sides:

> Nos permite aseverar que los argumentos expuestos por sus censores y panegiristas esbozan una polémica enconada, un debate público verbalizado como diálogo secreto, muchas veces violento entre partidarios y enemigos de la monja y una serie de estereotipos reiterados de texto en texto para ensalzar aquellas cualidades de la monja vistas por sus detractores como fallas graves. (*La comparación* 163)[48]

She asserts that this polemic becomes obvious via careful reading of "los prólogos de los tres tomos de la obra de Sor Juana publicados en España, sus propias obras, las de sus contemporáneos novohispanos, e indudablemente *La carta de Sor Filotea*" (*La comparación* 163–64).[49]

In light of Glantz's statement, I would like to take a look at how the Casa del Placer's *censuras* and *licenças* function within what she calls "un fino tramado," a network of texts "que se va tejiendo ante nuestros ojos" (woven before our eyes) (163). They possess all the qualities she outlines for those texts written in defense of Sor Juana in the *Segundo volumen*, but with certain important differences peculiar to the Casa del Placer and its virtual inhabitants. There are two *censuras*, written in prose by Sor Feliciana de Milão of the Convent of Odivelas and by Sor Maria das Saudades of the Convent of Vialonga. According to the *Grande dicionário da lingua portuguesa*, a *censura* is an "exame crítico de obras literárias feito antes da publicacão *por agentes do governo*" (a critical examination of literary works carried out before publication by *government officials*) (emphasis mine). The *censura* operated as a guarantee "com respeito ao verdade dos princípios, ao rigor da demonstração, ao solidez da doutrina, à sua influência sobre a ordem civil, política e religiosa, enfim, ao moral da composição" (with respect to the truth of principles, the rigor of example, the soundness of doctrine, its influence on the civil, political and religious spheres, in short, the morality of composition) (330). Cognizant of the wide-ranging power of the book, the author of the *censura* had to ensure that he (for it was always a he) was not jeopardizing the elements holding society and its morality together. The secrecy and intimacy of the Casa del Placer allowed the Portuguese nuns to mimic this gesture of approbation, usurping an authority given only to men and trespassing on the forbidden territory of male power—in this case, the power to authorize the word.

Both the writers of the *censuras*—Sor Feliciana and Sor Maria das Saudades—need to establish the authority that underscores their right to speak on matters of decency and propriety in literature. Sor Feliciana wastes no time in confirming the power of her position of enunciation; she begins her *censura* naming the supreme power, the monarchy, that oversees and protects all actions of the *Casa de Placer*: "Por soberano decreto li os *Enigmas* que se incluem neste breve e misterioso volume" (ll. 1–2). Sor Maria employs the same tactic. She has been commanded to approve this work by "alto preceito." The nuns follow the conventions of those who write such texts, but they tell no lies: two women at the highest levels of Iberian aristocracy have indeed sponsored this text. Both writers praise the nobility of their patrons by comparing them to goddesses. Sor Feliciana declares that only women in possession of "sagradas inteligências" (sacred intellects) can decipher enigmas such as these. At the end of her *censura* she finishes with a flourish, one that succeeds in covering all participants of the Casa del Placer in the reflected glory of Sor Juana's intelligence: "Porém tudo isto merece quem sabe reconhecer as divinidades para lhes sacrificar até o entendimento" (However, all this is worthy of the person who knows how to identify the deities, so as to make a sacrifice to understanding) (ll. 14–15).

As we know, the enigmas were intended only for the eyes of the nuns of the Casa del Placer and their female aristocratic supporters. Therefore, it is they who deserve this superior and instructive entertainment, they who are of such intelligence that they know wherein to "reconhocer as divinidades," and it is they who may be the divinities themselves, a compliment offered freely by both sides (from Mexico to Portugal and back again). Sor Maria also stresses the protection afforded by "tantas e tão superiores divinidades" (countless admirable deities) (ll. 6–7). Here, she most likely refers to the Condesa de Paredes and the Duquesa de Aveiro, but also perhaps to others of whom we are unaware. The verses are worthy of the attention of the members of that most illustrious literary community: "são dignos de que na Casa de Prazer, esfera de mais luzidos astros, se leiam e se interpretem" (they are worthy of being read and interpreted by the House of Pleasure, that sphere of brightest stars) (ll. 6–7). In this short section she has placed all the women at a remove from society and its constraints, elevating the activities of Sor Juana and the Casa del Placer to an astral plane where beauty and intelligence reign supreme.

The probity of the patrons and the audience thus established beyond any doubt, can the same be said of the verse? Does it warrant such a heavenly audience, such angelic patrons? Here we come to the principal goal of all *censura* writers: to prove beyond all doubt that what is contained in the book meets the standards of the day for decency. The Portuguese nuns must meet this goal and also go beyond it. They are writing in defense of a writer who has been dogged by charges of impropriety, and this they must address. They choose related but different strategies. Sor Feliciana cleverly links genius to decorum: "acho êstes *Enigmas* considerados e expostos com igual decôro que engenho" (I believe that these *Enigmas* have been deliberated and displayed with equal parts decorum and ingenuity) (ll. 5–6). In the next few lines, she praises the enigmas for their poetic brilliance and enigmatic quality (their true aim after all): "e observada discretamente a sua dificultosa regra de serem claros no que se diz, e escuros no que se quer dizer" (they adhere wisely to the difficult precept of being clear in what they say and obscure in what they mean) (ll. 6–7). Notwithstanding, the entertainment they provide is a decent one: "E assim me parecem dignos de ocuparem o tempo, despertando a curiosidade, porque não deixa de utilizar felizmente as horas tudo aquilo que laboriosamente apura os discursos" (ll. 7–10).[50] By this point, she has succeeded in so thoroughly intertwining the ideas of genius and decency that the two now seem inseparable. Many productive hours can be decently spent in an activity as beneficial as the deciphering of the enigmas. While she concedes that painstaking intellectual activity can weary rather than divert ("nem êste exercício tem tanto de fastidioso que no mesmo trabalho não tenha muito de divertimento") (ll. 10–11), she affirms that the instructive task of deciphering the enigmas *is* enjoyable thanks to the genius of an author who knows how to strike the perfect balance between two ideas so often deemed antithetical. Sor Feliciana refers to the "discrição de sua Autora, que soube fazer escolha de um assumpto em que não perigasse a atenção na prol[i]xidade da obra, ficando juntamente com o interesse de ver o seus *Enigmas*, venturosamente ilustrados" (ll. 11–14).[51]

In a related strategy, Sor Maria also employs the conceit of the text as instructive entertainment, claiming that the enigmas bring the reader "cortesãmente a que, entre a doméstica conversação, tenha alguma virtuosa disputa" (politely to the point that tranquil conversation may incorporate virtuous debate) (ll. 9–10). The use of the phrase "doméstica conversação" fits firmly within the theme of this second part of the *censura*, where she elaborates an image of Sor Juana and her readers as women, as well as nuns, who in no way contravene the boundaries society imposes on them. She continues this idea in the next line, where she claims ignorance in her task of *censura* writing because of the seclusion in which she lives: "Iste é o que se ofrece dizer, pois vivendo tão apartada da Côrte, só me chegam os ecos da cortesania, ainda confundidos da minha ignorância" (This is what I can offer, since living so far from the court, I only receive echoes of courtly manners which my ignorance further confuses) (ll. 11–12). In her capacity as a female religious, it was important she should be seen to be conducting herself according to the rules of her order. Moreover, her statement helps the cause of

Sor Juana, a nun so often criticized for the strength of her ties to the secular world of the court. As we see from the last lines of the *censura*, the nuns walked a fine line in their relationship with the court. The power implied by aristocratic patronage was necessary if these female religious were to indulge their passion for secular literature. Yet, as a nun, it was important to play down her familiarity with all things secular, which she does in the last line: "mas as mesmas divinidades que amparam a obra que indignamente censuro, dissimularão a rudeza com que justamente a aprovo" (the very deities who will facilitate this work which I so unworthily authorize, will cover up the coarseness with which I fittingly approve it) (ll. 13–14).

The *licenças*, written in verse, are also present to ensure that society's moral rectitude is in no way compromised. The *licença* announces that official permission has been granted a book to enter the reader's domain, and here each *licença*, written in the form of a *décima*, invokes a different authority empowered to endow *permissão* on the book in question. Sor Maria Magdalena of the Calvario Convent writes her *primeira licença* for that which "toca à fé" (regards matters of the faith); Sor Maria do Céu of the Convent of Esperança offers the *segunda* "pelo que compete à jurisdição real" (for that which pertains to the royal preserve); and finally, Sor Maria Guedes of the Convent of Santa Mónica gives us the *terceira* for that which pertains "ao bons costumes" (to good morals). The nuns are leaving nothing to chance; they are weaving a protective web of both decency and authority around Sor Juana's verses.

The author of the first *licença*, Sor Maria Magdalena, uses the first five lines of her décima to set up a series of negatives—things that the enigmas do *not* have—to drive her point home with regard to the decency of Sor Juana's verses: "Pode êste livro passar / de todo o castigo isento, / que em justo divertimiento / não é culpa adivinhar / Não tem nada que emendar" (This book is approved / deemed absent of all censure / for in righteous entertainment / no blame is foreboded / nor correction be made) (ll. 1–5). Her skillful use of antithesis powerfully eliminates any taint of sin from Sor Juana's work as she denies the necessity for "castigo" as well as the absence of "culpa"—words that place the reader squarely in the Christian duality of good versus evil. In the last four lines she mentions the enigmas by name, praising their decency ("decoro") and also finally mentioning the purpose of her *licença* to ensure that the text contains nothing that would offend the precepts of the Catholic faith. She links the two together in a quatrain that juxtaposes them, cleverly connecting Sor Juana's (secular) verses with the power of faith: "pois os *Enigmas* estão / como tanto decoro que / deixa o seguro da fé / sem escrúpulo a atenção" ("for the

Enigmas are / so decorous / that faith is secure / without need for uneasiness or vigilance)(ll. 7–10).

In the second *licença*, Sor Maria do Céu takes great pains to emphasize how Sor Juana's verses do not threaten the integrity of the *jurisdição real*, that is, the state: "Pode êste livro correr, / que não tem nenhum defeito" (This book may circulate, / no imperfection can be found) (ll. 1–2). Releasing the book into general circulation ("correr") is, in fact, something only the state has the mandate to allow. (The irony here is subtle but nonetheless apparent, as we know the book was never intended for public consumption.) In a skillful wordplay in the next couplet, the author draws a direct comparison between the state and the nuns' literary group—"pois da casa do respeito / passa à Casa do Prazer" (for from the house of respect / it moves on to the House of Pleasure) (ll. 3–4)—and thus removes any doubt that the group's activities might be judged a threat to the health of the state. Alatorre reads this as an allusion to the aristocratic protection enjoyed by the members of the Casa del Placer, both from the aristocratic families of the nuns themselves and by the patronage of the two powerful noblewomen, the Duquesa de Aveiro and the Condesa de Paredes. He defines the Casa de Respeito as "aristocracia de sangre" (aristocracy of blood) and the Casa del Placer as "aristocracia de talento" (aristocracy of talent); the limits between the two are blurred by the nuns of the Portuguese convents, who belong to both groups (*Sor Juana Inés de la Cruz* 32–33). Only Sor Juana cannot be said to belong to both circles. This seems to be of very little relevance, however, within the utopian space of the Casa del Placer. Sor Juana's close friend, the Condesa de Paredes, treats her as an equal ("Amiga, este libro tuyo / es tan hijo de tu ingenio"), and the Portuguese nuns praise her superior talent with encomiums such as "Ilustre Musa" (Illustrious Muse), "Hermosa y nueva Musa" (New and beauteous Muse), et cetera. The nuns invoke the "Casa de Respeito" and their membership therein as a political strategy to protect themselves from any attacks that might come their way, as well as to provide Sor Juana with a safe haven from which to write, something she did not have access to at home after the departure of the Condesa de Paredes from Mexico in 1688.

In the last six lines, Sor Maria do Céu draws the web of impunity more tightly around the activities of the Casa del Placer, placing its members out of reach of the criticism of even the state as she hints at the protection the group receives from an even higher authority, the monarchy: "Não acho, e meu entender / que merece correção, / pois teve tanta atenção, / que só por não fazer mal / à jurisdição real / busca real protecção" (ll. 5–10).[52] In the third and final *licença*, Sor Maria Guedes of the convent of Santa Mónica approves the enigmas based on the authority of "bons costumes," a rather vague category that is nonetheless important in a society in which every gesture must follow a strict decorum and which is, moreover, linked to the concept of "decencia."[53] Reading for pleasure was not accepted as a freewheeling activity but had to follow precepts of decency and usefulness. Although writing of *ancien régime* France, Roger Chartier's comments on the state's desire to regulate reading practices applies to the Europe of the Casa del Placer. He refers to the importance given to

> written matter and to the objects that bore writing by all the authorities who intended to regulate behaviour and fashion minds. Hence the pedagogical, acculturating and disciplining role attributed to the texts put into circulation for a wide readership; hence also the controls exercised over printed matter, which was subjected to censorship to eliminate anything that might threaten religious or moral order. (20–21)

Chartier also discusses the "various modalities for bridling the reader's interpretation, which ranged from exterior censorship—administrative, judiciary, inquisitorial, scholastic, and so forth—to constraining mechanisms within the book itself" (20–21).

We see these constraints in the *licença* of Sor Maria Guedes. Reading must be instructive, decent, and do no harm, principles the first quatrain of her *décima* forcefully affirms: "É tanta a sua atenção / e dêste livro o concêrto, / que por ditado do acêrto / o pode ser da razão" (Such respect does it offer / that the opinion about this book is unanimous / that following the dictates of discernment / it offers good judgment) (ll. 1–4). The words that end each of the four lines—"atenção," "concêrto," "acêrto," and finally "razão"—leave the reader no doubt of what she or he may gain from the perusal of Sor Juana's text. Great care ("atenção") has been employed in the review of this text, and the consensus of opinion ("concêrto") is that, following carefully the dictates of discernment ("acêrto"), the book "pode ser de razão." The word "razão" or "razón" was one charged with powerful meaning in the age of the Casa del Placer. Published in 1737, the *Diccionario de Autoridades* offers a series of different meanings, among them "la potencia intelectiva, en cuanto discurre y raciocína" (intellectual capacity, with regard to debate and reasoning) and "el acto del entendimiento o discurso" (the act of understanding or debate). The *Diccionario* also defines "razón" as "orden y método de una cosa" (order and method of something) and "justicia en las operaciones, o derecho a ejecutarlas" (judgment in actions or in the right to carry them out). Taking into account these interconnected definitions, we see how the word "razão" or "razón" acts as one among what Chartier has called "constraining mechanisms" within the text itself: a self-censorship based on a clear understanding of the differences between good and evil. Sor Maria Guedes sums up this idea in the final six lines of her *décima*: "Sem mais averiguação / nos conceitos que resume, / não acho que êste volume / possa ter impedimentos, / pois ter altos pensamentos / não é contra o bom costume" (ll. 5–10).⁵⁴ There can be no impediment to the reading of this book based on the precepts of decent and instructive pleasure, for the main attribute of the book, "ter altos pensamentos," in no way contravenes "o bom costume."

In light of the preceding analysis, I return to Margo Glantz's idea of a network of texts that stands in opposition to those written against Sor Juana. My own reading positively identifies the presence of what can be called a "rhetoric of solidarity" present in the *censuras* and *licenças* of the Casa del Placer.⁵⁵ The Portuguese nuns, like the Spanish clergymen of the *Segundo volumen*, chose their words carefully, mindful of the need to highlight the decency and beneficial nature of Sor Juana's verses. We find an important difference, however, between those texts written in support of Sor Juana's *Segundo volumen* and those that emanate from the Casa del Placer. In the *Segundo volumen*, Glantz identifies an involuntary misogyny on the part of those who praise and support Sor Juana in these *censuras* and *aprobaciones* (*La comparación* 182). The writers of these panegyrics, Glantz observes, found the singularity of Sor Juana as a writing woman somewhat unwieldy. Following the baroque love of taxonomy,⁵⁶ they attempt to classify her, to define her genius—an endeavor that is complicated by her gender.

> Se procede, entonces, a elegir los elementos fundamentales necesarios para establecer la gradación, y colocar a Sor Juana en el sitio que se merece, y con ello abarcar el genio que tanto mortifica, tanta perplejidad provoca y engendra múltiples epítetos, con los que la personalidad encomiada se cristaliza como un ser monstruoso o un milagro, una conjunción perfecta de la desmesura y lo sobrenatural. *Lo primero que se marca como evidencia es su identidad de género. Es antes que nada una mujer.* (*La comparación* 164, emphasis mine)⁵⁷

According to Glantz, the panegyrists fall back on the technique of the catalogue of worthy women, something begun with Giovanni Boccacio's *De Mulieribus Claris* (circa 1380), which drew together the biographies of illustrious and virtuous women from antiquity and the Bible. Stephanie Merrim identifies this technique as a counterbalance to misogynist attacks on women (xv–xvi), one that "patently deflated prevailing contentions that women were capable neither of learning nor of reason" (xvi). Merrim describes Sor Juana's employment of the technique in the *Respuesta* in the following terms:

> Listened to carefully, Sor Juana herself articulates an awareness that she writes in a tradition of feminist debates: in her catalog of illustrious women, Sor Juana employs the *brevitatis formula* and states that she will omit further names of women "to avoid relaying what others have said." (xiv)

It is in this particular element—the condensed catalog of worthy women—that Glantz finds Sor Juana's employment of the *brevitatis formula* particularly admirable.[58]

The nun advances the virtues of learned women, while at the same time expanding beyond the rarified domain of a few singular women to promote the more inclusive idea of unknown and unsung heroines, those "numerosas mujeres anónimas que hubiesen podido destacar en un mundo menos autoritario y patriarcalista que él de la monja" (countless anonymous women who could have made their mark in a world less authoritarian and patriarchal than that in which the nun lived)(Glantz, *La comparación* 189). Glantz contrasts Sor Juana's style, simple and direct and "jamás alambicada" (never contrived) with the "garigoleada escritura" (overembellished writing) (189) employed by those worthy men who praise her in the *Segundo volumen*. This is not their only shortcoming, however. In their hands, the cataloguing of worthy women backfires and serves inadvertently to reveal their misogyny (182). Glantz believes that by classifying the nun along with other notable women, they only underscore their belief in the freakish phenomenon that is Sor Juana, a woman so unlike her contemporaries that one must search through history and antiquity to come up with comparisons. Further compounding their misogyny, according to Glantz, is the implicit comparison with men that lies beneath each mention of a worthy woman from history or antiquity: "Mencionar a una mujer ilustre es siempre compararla con un hombre excepcional. Pareciera que sólo así fuera legítima y pudiera autorizarse y aceptarse la valía, la existencia del talento femenino y reconocer un orden" (187).[59] These women are illustrious because they have excelled at activities that are associated only with men, such as writing.[60]

There is a significant difference between the panegyrists of the *Segundo volumen* and the nuns of the Casa del Placer. The nuns avoid the trap of categorizing Sor Juana as monstrous because of her singularity. Furthermore, in the *censuras* and *licenças* and the dedicatory poems, there is no cataloguing of illustrious women—or comparisons, implicit or otherwise, with men. Instead, Sor Juana stands alone, a poet and a woman, a talent in her own right. As I have shown in my analysis of all the poems and texts included in the book, Sor Juana is praised as a brilliant poet, an "Ilustre Musa," the "Décima insigne Musa" (Exalted Tenth Muse). Not once however do the writers of the Casa del Placer raise the issue of the singularity of her gender and her occupation as a writer, thus differentiating themselves from the male panegyrists I referred to earlier. Jean Franco's point, made in reference to Sor Juana's own work, is pertinent here. She describes the creation of a destabilizing position of enunciation that takes gender differentiation "out of the rules of the game, thus untying the apparently natural association of the male with power" (29). By creating a female utopia where one is *not* obliged to justify the presence of the female writing subject, her "strangeness" no longer becomes something that must be explained and catalogued.

Muses, Goddesses, and the Love of Women

While the dedicatory poems written to Sor Juana write her body into their text, Sor Juana chooses to elaborate the poetry she presents to the Casa del Placer, a *romance* and a *soneto*, around the image of an all-female utopian space, similarly discursively eroticized (here, as above, I am following Andreadis) in its invocation of an impenetrable all-female universe. For Sor Juana, this utopian space consists of a place of beauty and safety, watched over by goddesses who expect nothing more than the offerings of artistic labor. In other words, it is the ideal place from which to write. It offers her a more sturdy protection than her convent cell, which was assailed on all sides by those who would undermine and curtail her artistic endeavors. Kate Chedgzoy reminds us that the conception of utopia in the early modern period belonged more to the idea of paradise lost than to an imaginary ideal: "In modern usage, the word utopia usually evokes a projection into a better future; but it is important to recall the importance to the mental world of early modern culture of paradises lost, whether in the form of Judeo-Christian Garden of Eden or pagan Arcadias" (67). It is the latter we see echoed in Sor Juana's two dedicatory poems to the Casa del Placer, as she evokes a stylized utopian world of beautiful and learned goddesses ("divinidades") for whom the perfect offering is the book, i.e., her enigmas.

In the *romance* she charts the journey of her book, which first presents itself as an offering to the benevolent goddesses who, like divine patrons of the arts, will assure its safe passage into the world: "A vuestros ojos se ofrece / este libro, por quedar / ilustrado a tanto sol / digno de tanta deidad" (This book is offered to your eyes / so that such a sun may enlighten it / and so that it may be worthy of such deity) (ll. 1–4). Continuing in the role of supplicant, she hopes her book may bring them a few moments of enjoyment, nothing more: "Divertiros sólo un rato / es cuanto aspirar podrá" (To amuse you for a while / is all it can but hope) (l. 5). The idea of a female Arcadia where beauty and intelligence reign supreme is echoed throughout the poem. Such is their intelligence that she can only hope to bring them a few moments of distraction: "que fuera mucho emprender / atrevérselo a ocupar" (it would be much to undertake / to dare to entertain) (ll. 7–8). Such is the importance of these women that only they can confer favor upon the book: "Tan feliz será leído / que ufano dilatará / Los instantes de atención / a siglos de vanidad" (So happy will it be to be read / that it will proudly prolong a few moments of attention / into centuries of vanity) (ll. 17–20). Sor Juana's vocabulary conjures up images of a celestial firmament where benign goddesses, patrons of the arts, look benevolently down upon those authors who bring offerings for their consideration. They are muses, both inspiring and guiding, bestowing the favor of immortality upon works of art: "Hacerse inmortal procura, / que favor tan celestial / se mide en la estimación / a precios de eternidad" (To become immortal it tries, / such a heavenly favor / is valued eternally) (ll. 21–24).

Continuing with the image of these divine patrons ("mecenas"), she describes the process by which one "submits" one's offering, one's book, to those who reside in this Arcadian artist's colony, while at the same time, writing securely under the auspices of the Casa del Placer, she obliquely addresses those critics who condemn her for her love of secular poetry: "Todo cuanto incluye en sí / por descifrado lo da, / porque no es yerro en la fe / proponer, sino dudar" (All is contained herein / and the answers are there to be deciphered / because it is no sin against the faith to suggest, / only to doubt) (ll. 25–28). To write, especially for such an audience, "no es yerro en la fe." On the contrary, she seems to imply, to waste one's talent in self-doubt would be the error. She continues this idea in the next stanza. Those who follow these divinities ("vuestro culto") learn to *think* ("creer"): "en vuestro culto, el creer / empieza por no esperar" (in worshipping you / belief starts by not waiting) (ll. 31–32). In this paradise, the female writer, watched over by female divinities, is given free rein to think and, by extension, write. The book must resign itself to the tender mercies of the divinities, but in return is rewarded with protection and, by implication, freedom from censorship: "Tan resignado el respeto / a vuestros altares va, / que la primera oblación / es no tener voluntad" (Respect goes so resignedly to your altars / that the first offering is to have no will of one's own) (ll. 33–36).

Much of the rest of the poem continues with the theme of the unworthiness of the book in comparison with the divinities to which it presents itself. Stanzas such as the following are typical: "La osadía de atreverse / no pretende disculpar,

/ que al buscaros, su razón, / elevó su indignidad" (The boldness of its daring / it does not pretend to excuse / for by seeking you out / with its judgment it elevates its indignity) (ll. 37–40). Sor Juana turns the world upside down in this *romance*, creating a place where the book, the all-powerful symbol of Western (masculine) knowledge, must go begging for approbation to a group of women. She continues in this vein: "Mas ni olvidos ni atenciones / podrá este libro lograr, / porque es de aquéllas indigno / y sois déstos incapaz" (But neither neglect nor attention / can this book attain, / because it is unworthy of them / and you are of both incapable) (ll. 49–52).

The last three stanzas focus explicitly on the power and attributes of the "deidades," something to which she has only alluded obliquely earlier in the poem: "Como deidades os cree; / pero al ver vuestra beldad, / como halla más que creer, / se excusa del ignorar" (It believes you to be goddesses; / but on seeing your beauty /it finds it beyond belief / and thus must plead ignorance) (ll. 53–56). Here she focuses on their beauty, a beauty so overwhelming it is impossible to articulate or even understand. This concept plays into the idea of a female utopian space, where beauty reigns. The idea of an indescribable beauty goes beyond the representation of an aesthetic ideal. In her analysis of beauty and its representation in art and literature, Elaine Scarry, drawing on Homer, has identified what she believes to be the three main attributes of beauty. She sees beauty as sacred, as unprecedented, and as lifesaving (23–25). These elements come together in Sor Juana's depiction of a female paradise, a sacred and singular space that protects the writer who elsewhere has been assailed on all sides. It is to this near ideal that she, with her book, will pay homage: "Tanto infiere, que creyendo / más de lo posible ya, / aun presume que es su fe / menos que su necedad" (It deduces much, believing all is possible, / it still supposes its faith / to be less than its ignorance) (ll. 57–60). The book must surrender itself to a world it may not completely understand and do so with *faith* in the beauty, goodness, and intelligence of the divinities who hold the key to all mysteries, including that of the book itself: "Y si, por naturaleza, / cuanto oculta penetráis, todo lo que es conocer / ya no será adivinar" (And if, naturally / you penetrate all that is hidden / then one will no longer have to guess / what there is to know) (ll. 61–64).

In the sonnet that follows her *romance*, Sor Juana summarizes the same ideas she charted in her longer poem, recounting the journey of her unworthy book to the celestial paradise wherein dwell the divinities for whom she is writing: "Este volumen, cuyo altivo aliento / —benévolo lector siempre invocado— / generoso presume, aspira osado / remontarse al celeste firmamento" (ll. 1–4).[61] In this poem, she makes more explicit the idea, hinted at in the previous work, of these divinities, the members of the Casa del Placer as muses, inspiring and guiding the poet's words: "a tanto Sol eleva el pensamiento / de reverente afecto apadrinado / que, a soberanas aras destinado, / pasa a ser sacrificio el rendimiento" (ll. 5–8).[62] In Greek mythology there were nine Muses, and there are nine participants, other than Sor Juana, in the endeavor of the Casa del Placer.[63] There were many sacred places associated with the Muses, including the Valley of the Muses on the eastern slopes of Mount Heraklion, where the Mouseia festival began, in which poets from all over Greece would participate. The idea of a sacred place dedicated solely to the pursuit of poetry fits with Sor Juana's conceit of this "celeste firmamento" to which she sends her book of poetry in homage. It was also customary to make sacrifices to the Muses, a fact to which she alludes in her line: "pasa a ser sacrificio el rendimiento" (l. 8).

Having appropriated the idea of the Muses to describe the members of the Casa del Placer, she then echoes the words of the writers of the *censuras* to talk about the decency ("decencia") of her poetry. As is well known, criticism dogged her throughout her writing career, so the "decencia" of her work is something that she is at pains to emphasize. She writes: "Piadoso absuelve sus indignidades, / que no son en los cultos indecencia / que profane devotas atenciones" (Piously it absolves its unworthiness / which, in worshipping, is not indecency / which itself would profane devoted adoration) (ll. 9–11). Any "indignidades" of which her book may be guilty must be forgiven, for they are not to be thought of as "indecencia" that may profane "devotas atenciones."

The phrase "devotas atenciones" could work in two registers, either as an example of her devotion to the worship of the divinities or as an assurance that her work falls in line with the devotion required of a pious woman. Although Sor Juana has continually invoked the seemingly pagan term "deidades" to describe the women of the Casa del Placer, she stresses their position as religious women whose primary devotion is to the Christian God: "Frecuentes votos hacen las deidades" (The deities make frequent vows) (l. 12). The idea of "votos" speaks to their observance of the religious life. While she does not let the reader forget their high aristocratic (and thus protected) status (they are "inmunidades de la reverencia" [immune to reverence] [l. 13]), she ends the sonnet again with an assurance of their religious piety: "No hay para el cielo cortas oblaciones" (No offering is too small for the heavens) (l. 14).

The enigmas themselves, as befits the contribution of the featured celebrity, appear last in the text the Casa del Placer produces. They are the showpiece of the literary academy's offering, for which the other texts serve as preamble and introduction. The enigmas are written in the form of twenty *redondillas*, each one forming a rhetorical question to be interpreted. According to Enrique Martínez López, the writing and deciphering of enigmas was a common pastime for the literary academies of the seventeenth century (he calls it a "pasatiempo obligatorio," 56), and it was something at which Sor Juana was already practiced. Both Martínez López and Georgina Sabat Rivers make mention of works by the nun that contain the kind of labyrinthine rhetoric found in the enigmas.[64]

The fact that these enigmas are inherently ludic is not insignificant to our conception of the clandestine nature of the Casa. The act of "play" itself holds a deeply symbolic connotation in many cultures. One of its benefits is that it draws together those who engage in it, even after the game is over. In his influential book on the concept of play, Johan Huizinga describes how play serves to form and perpetuate communities, giving these groups "the feeling of being 'apart together'" in an exceptional situation, of sharing something important, of mutually withdrawing from the rest of the world and rejecting the usual norms" (12). There is also, according to Huizinga, a special relationship between play and secrecy: "It promotes the formation of social groupings which tend to surround themselves with secrecy and to stress their difference from the common world by disguise or other means" (12). Every secret society needs a code with which to communicate its ideas between its members, and the Casa del Placer was no exception. Sor Juana's enigmas function as the clandestine message that circulates between the women, breeding involvement and trust as well as the secret power accorded by the female imagination.

The women of the Casa del Placer never intended knowledge of its activities to extend beyond its members. The nuns were extremely aware that the Church considered literary production unseemly for women, particularly for nuns; the fact that this activity was conducted in a communal fashion would only have heightened the Church's disapproval. Secrecy held an even more compelling attraction for early modern women whose clandestine writing in the period was "linked directly to society's prescription of the possibilities for women's verbal or bodily self-expression" (Graham et al. 69). Ann Rosalind Jones has described the early modern period's "ideological matrix" (7) wherein "female silence was equated with chastity, female eloquence with promiscuity" (1). Consequently, women writers often lacked confidence because there was no developed female literary tradition in which they could share and no recognition that women were capable of writing (King 74). Obviously, action in concert and the sharing of goals by the members of the Casa del Placer helped foster a sense of connectedness and confidence, something particularly relevant if we consider the timing of the Casa del Placer's output in relation to the ups and downs of

Sor Juana's literary career. The polemic surrounding Sor Juana's right to literary activity came alive with the publication of the *Carta atenagórica* in 1690. Sometime around the middle of 1693, after the success of her two volumes published in Spain, Sor Juana supposedly retired from all worldly activities. Antonio Alatorre estimates that her contribution to the Casa del Placer, the enigmas, would have arrived in Portugal at the end of 1693. Were the enigmas her swan song? Or were they a defiant reminder that she was still engaging in the indecent activity of secular literature at a time when she was supposed to have renounced such pursuits?[65] I tend to believe the latter—although the two possibilities are not unconnected.

Women had no choice other than to write using the tools of the patriarchy, albeit from a marginal locus of enunciation. In the enigmas, Sor Juana skillfully employs a highly elaborate baroque technique with which, as with other examples of her literary output, she writes herself "into the esthetic and structure of the ruling order" (Merrim 35). However, in her offerings to the Casa del Placer, she goes one step further and voids this marginality. The existence of an all-female utopia takes negative female gender differentiation out of the equation. Sor Juana's enigmas demonstrate a perfect manipulation of this genre, as she draws on disturbances, contradictions, and antithesis, among other aspects, in her adroit handling of poetic form, directing these elements in the service of that most baroque topos, love—the theme of all the enigmas. With Sor Juana's offering to the Casa del Placer, we see her fluid appropriation and imitation of patriarchal discourse—a discourse that would have preferred to exclude her as a participant. Also excluded as participants, and even as onlookers, were the women for whom she was writing. And as she posits these women as the ideal readers and decipherers of these highly baroque *redondillas*, she brings both herself and them in from the periphery and directly to the center. There is, nonetheless, an element of parody in this appropriative gesture. By so perfectly appropriating this discourse for her readers, whom she designates as being superior to it, she explodes the myth of its impenetrability for all but a select few.[66]

It is not surprising that Sor Juana chose the subject of love for her enigmas. Love, as the chief lyric discourse of the time, was, of course, that of the ruling order. It was also, as Stephanie Merrim has said, "the central site of seventeenth-century gender discourse" (39). Yet, the enigmas themselves also functioned as an elaborate private joke: Sor Juana takes this important site of gender discourse and laughs in its face. Her enigmas draw attention to the suffering love causes. Merrim believes that love is a theme that "seems to inspire true repugnance" in Sor Juana (53). Sor Juana built her poetic and intellectual universe on the principles of reason and knowledge and love, and its attendant sufferings belong instead to "the passionate world of *un*reason and *not* knowing" (40). Safely ensconced in the secret world of the Casa del Placer, Sor Juana takes the opportunity to entertain her sisters at the expense of the enemy, creating riddles that expose the torments of love, which she described in often wrenching detail in her poetry. Love, we have seen, has figured in the poems written both by the nuns to Sor Juana and from her back to them. These poems paint a tranquil portrait of love, one that is predicated on the shared intellectual and literary pursuits that have brought the women together. Looking at the images the women invoke in these poems, we see a creation of a poetic world that conjures up peace, utopia, and ultimately the triumph of reason. If we look more carefully at the enigmas, I believe we can find another more secret purpose: the parodic invocation of the miseries of *heterosexual* love.

The fact that the poems the women write to each other convey a love that is serene and rational is not surprising. Stephanie Merrim has drawn a gendered distinction between those poems that Sor Juana wrote that clearly depict heterosexual love and those that deal with the love one woman feels for another, like that expressed in her poems to the Condesa de Paredes. These particular poems have given rise to a great deal of controversy as to the exact nature of the relationship between the two women: assumptions of repressed lesbian feeling on one hand range to denials that the friendship ever actually existed because Sor Juana employs the formal rhetorical tropes of the time to express her sentiments.[67] For Merrim, what is significant is the way Sor Juana "expands on the image of women as rational beings to celebrate the rational love of one woman for another" (67). Sor Juana expresses emotion, but she does so in a controlled and contained manner. This is the same gesture we see in the poems the women of the Casa del Placer write to one another. However, it is not enough for Sor Juana and the other nuns to revel in the rational love they share for one another. They also want to draw attention to the fact that the world they have eschewed, the world of the heterosexual paradigm, is one full of torment, and worse, of irrationality. The enigmas depart from this universe of shared harmony and take the reader to a much darker and more negative place: the masculine sphere of heterosexual love. Sor Juana turns the tables on men who have always depicted women as illogical and unbalanced beings, ruled by passions of the heart rather than by the calculations of the mind. As the book reaches its climactic moment with the enigmas, it is as if the nuns, safe in the paradise of the Casa del Placer, look down mockingly on the strange and terrible maneuverings that heterosexual love drives in people.

The baroque discourse on love with its attendant sufferings that grew out of an earlier lyric tradition of courtly love is one with which the nuns of the Casa del Placer would have been thoroughly familiar. Sor Juana knew, then, that she could use certain locally recognizable elements to create her enigmas. The nuns were attuned to different shades of meaning in poetic discourse, nuances modern readers may not discern. As this code was devised to be deciphered only by initiates using a recondite vocabulary of love, I do not claim to have unraveled the enigmas. Each one deals with an aspect of love that in almost all cases mocks the travails of the lover. In the analysis that follows, I offer a close reading of each enigma that explores the nuances of the world Sor Juana creates with her heavy dose of black humor. I must leave the solutions to the riddles each poses with the members of the Casa del Placer. Their secret is safe with me.[68]

In the first enigma, Sor Juana invokes the bleak and violent universe she will repeatedly summon throughout the enigmas, in which passion cuts down all who get in its path. She employs images of struggle and death that contrast greatly with the all-female world of light and happiness the nun poets have created: "¿Cuál es aquella homicida / que, piadosamente ingrata, / siempre en cuanto vive mata / y muere cuando da vida?" (What is that homicide / that, piously ungrateful, / will always kill while it lives / and die when it gives life?).[69] Here she refers to a passion that overpowers the emotions and in the process kills reason. Love, says Sor Juana, will get you at every turn. There is no way out once it has you in its sights. The antithetical cast of the last two lines refers, I believe, to the act of loving and being loved. Neither brings happiness. Both bring devastation. In the second enigma, Sor Juana again marshals a series of uncompromising words: "¿Cuál será aquella aflicción / que es, con igual tiranía / el callarla cobardía / decirla desatención?" (What may be that affliction / that with equal cruelty / is cowardly when unmentioned / and careless when declared?). As in the first enigma, there is no respite from the suffering love imposes. Here, she refers to the double bind that declaring one's feelings to the object of one's affections will provoke. Telling one's lover of one's passion will inexorably result in misery. Conversely, keeping one's feelings to oneself only leads to a soul consumed by despair and longing.

In the third enigma, she poses the question "¿Cuál puede ser el dolor / de efecto tan desigual" (What may be that pain / whose consequences are so diverse) that it "siendo en sí el mayor mal / remedia otro mal mayor?" (is itself the greatest evil / and cures another greater still?). For Sor Juana, the experience of love leads to a chain of suffering. Perhaps this particular "dolor" of which she speaks is death—"el mayor mal"—and the "mal mayor" that it solves is perhaps lovesickness. Death, she posits, is preferable to the sufferings the tribulations of love beget.

The fourth enigma calls forth a figure from Greek mythology—the Siren. However, unlike the Muses, to whom Sor Juana compares the members of the Casa del Placer, the Siren is a destructive figure. She is a "Sirena atroz," who makes use of her "dulces ecos velozes" (sweet and swift echoes) to trick those who hear her, who "muestra el seguro en sus vozes, / guarda el peligro en su voz" (shows safety in her voices / conserves danger in her voice). The siren sings of love and its supposed delights, luring the hapless to a world of love that seems at first idyllic but wherein, perforce, lovers must abandon all reason.

In the fifth enigma, Sor Juana moves from Sirens to a deity—one who, like the Siren, wishes harm on those who fall under her spell. This unnamed deity evokes the petulant and capricious gods of Greek mythology who entertain themselves by making people suffer. Sor Juana describes the deity's "ciega ambición" (blind desire) with which it targets lovers. He succeeds in "cautivando la razón" (capturing reason)—that most prized of mental faculties. The result is that "toda se haze libertad." What is this "libertad" of which Sor Juana speaks? It is, I believe, an ironic reference with which she conjures up the world of unreason and emotional chaos that she so despises.

In the sixth enigma, she again brings up the idea of a freedom that constricts—one that plunges the mind into chaos, discarding all reason. Sor Juana writes: "¿Cuál puede ser el cuidado / que, libremente imperioso, / se hace a sí mismo dichoso / y a sí mismo desdichado?" (What may be that unease / which, liberally tyrannical, / makes itself happy / and itself unhappy too?) Love, as Sor Juana shows in her sonnets, brings torment to both oneself and to the object of one's affections. The lover may catch a glimpse of happiness, but it is fleeting and ephemeral. Moreover, joy must always come at the expense of someone else, as Sor Juana perfectly demonstrated in her sonnets that deal with the effects of "el amor no correspondido."

In the seventh enigma, Sor Juana's tone becomes more openly scornful. In the previous riddle Sor Juana's tone was more playful, but in this, the seventh, there is no room for banter. Instead, she is ruthless: "¿Cuál será aquella pasión / que no merece piedad, / pues peligra en necedad / por ser toda obstinación?" (What may be that passion / that deserves no pity / since it endangers with its stupidity / and epitomizes stubbornness?). She personifies an aspect of love that is not worthy of pity, for it brings its suffering upon itself through its "obstinación" and "necedad." If we follow this argument logically, those who suffer love's effects are also not to be pitied, for they stubbornly persist in that which makes them unhappy. In the next enigma, the eighth, Sor Juana plays again with the shadows of light and dark that love casts, recognizing that love can bring the illusion of happiness. But it is a fool's paradise, she suggests, for it is a "contento" that "con hipócrita acción, / por sendas de recreación / va caminando al tormento" (with hypocritical action, / and along paths of pleasure / heads off toward suffering). The image of the blithe lover skipping down the happy path of love only to be waylaid by misery is a powerful one, forming a stark contrast with that of the Casa del Placer—a true paradise with no nasty surprises lurking round the corner.

In the ninth enigma, Sor Juana returns to a conceit that she has employed in several of the enigmas—that of the cruel and heartless god of love. She asks "¿Cuál será la idolatría de tan alta potestad / que haze el ruego indignidad, / la esperanza grosería?" (What might be the worship of such great power / that makes begging unworthy / and makes hope vulgar?). The god of love turns away from his supplicants, offering them no hope or ease of their sufferings, unlike the one true God who would never abandon those in pain. Sor Juana's meaning is clear. Heterosexual romantic love forces its victims to turn away from the love of God and instead embrace the cult of a deity that only intensifies their pain.

The tenth enigma is quite exquisite in its rendering of one of the torments love causes. Sor Juana, someone who so prized her ability to speak and articulate her thoughts and feelings, plumbs the depths of despair where feelings control words. In other words, a world ruled by passion in which reason, words, must take a back seat: "¿Cuál será aquella expresión / que cuando el dolor provoca / antes de voz en la boca / hace eco en el corazón?" (What may be that expression / that when provoked by grief / before making a sound in the mouth / echoes in the heart?).

In enigma eleven, Sor Juana introduces the theme of the fragmented body as a manifestation of the turmoil of love. She asks: "¿Cuáles serán los despojos / que, al sentir algún despecho, / siendo tormento en el pecho / es desahogo en los ojos?" (What may be the spoils / which, upon feeling spite, / torment the breast / and find relief in the eyes?) The "despojos" of which she speaks carry the connotation of ill-gotten gains, the sense that a triumph in love can only be gained at somebody else's expense.

Enigma twelve lulls the reader into a false sense of security—much as does love, according to Sor Juana. The opening line seems to throw a positive light on love, speaking of a "favor." But winning this "favor" confers no benefits on the recipient and instead brings only distress, either real or anticipated: "si se logra es inquietud / y si se espera es temor" (if gained it brings worry / and if hoped for brings fear). In the second line, Sor Juana describes this favor as operating through "oculta virtud"—a most enigmatic phrase in a text awash in a sea of secret discourse. Hazarding an educated guess, I would say that Sor Juana's use of the modifier "oculta" neutralizes any benefits accrued to love with the use of the word "virtud." This favor has the appearance of something virtuous, but hidden from view is its power to wreak havoc, because it trails devastation in its wake. Sor Juana's tone in enigma thirteen is one of exasperation. She can no longer tolerate the vagaries of a universe where passion supplants reason. She rails at the arrogance of such an idea: "¿Cuál es la temeridad / de tan alta presunción / que, pudiendo ser razón, / pretende ser necedad?" (What is that recklessness / which presumes so much / that, instead of choosing reason, / claims foolishness instead?). Her use of the words "temeridad" and "presunción" clearly demonstrate her scorn for such a world where lovers will reject the cool light of reason for the burning darkness of a senselessness caused by love.

In enigma fourteen, Sor Juana moves away from the idea of the tortured lover as victim and instead seems to accuse the lover of complicity in his or her own misfortune: "¿Cuál el dolor puede ser / que, en repetido llorar,/ es su remedio cegar / siendo su achaque él no ver?" (What is that pain, / that, repeatedly laments, / offering blindness as a remedy / and yet complains it cannot see?). Although the question she poses situates grief as the subject, she is obviously pouring scorn on a lover who rails at the misfortunes of love but who willingly puts him- or herself in the eye of its storm. Blindness to love would be the remedy, Sor Juana says, but the masochistic lover will only complain she cannot see.

In enigma fifteen, Sor Juana does a volte-face, turning her back on the universe of unreason and briefly grabbing hold of that which she holds most dear. She praises that character trait—self-control, perhaps—that is able to withstand the ravages of love and thus fortify reason, the enemy of this kind of love: "¿Cuál es aquella atención / que, con humilde denuedo / defendido con el miedo, / da esfuerzos a la razón?" (What is that respect / that with humble valor / defends with fear, / and gives strength to reason?). Sor Juana wanted to pay homage to the members of the Casa del Placer who, favoring reason and same-sex female adoration over the agony of heterosexual love, exist on a higher plain than those to whom she refers in the other enigmas.

In the sixteenth enigma, Sor Juana returns to her negative portraits of love's miseries, albeit in a very subtle vein. In this enigma she sets up an opposition between light and dark—between love's attractions and the realities of the sufferings it causes. She writes: "¿Cuál es aquel arrebol / de jurisdicción tan bella / que, inclinando como estrella, / deslumbra como sol?" (What is that red glow / of such beautiful power / that, leaning down like a star, / dazzles like the sun?).

In this enigma she recognizes the fact that love lures its victims with its promise of beauty and splendor—hence the use of words such as "estrella." However, it also has the power to cast a terrible shadow over those who enter its domain. The shining brightness draws the victim in, but then all is darkness. The red glow ("el arrebol") turns into a darkness that is all-encompassing—like the setting sun. Love, Sor Juana says, is attractive, but once it has you in its power, it plunges you into the darkness of illogic, and perhaps even madness.

In the seventeenth enigma, Sor Juana again addresses the impudence of love and how it encourages those whom it enthralls to flout society's accepted standards of behavior. She poses the riddle: "¿Cuál es aquel atrevido / que, indecentemente osado, fuera respeto callado / y es agravio proferido?" (What is that impudence / that, indecently bold, / would be respect if it were silent / but offends once proffered?). Here she marks a distinction between the members of the Casa del Placer and those who, through the vagaries of love, speak of that which should always remain unspoken. They—the female authors of the Casa del Placer—do not have to remain silent, for nothing they say is "indecentemente osado."

In the eighteenth enigma, she resumes the scathing and ironic tone she displays in several others. The riddle she poses seems at first to allude to something positive: "¿Cuál podrá ser el portento / de tan noble calidad?" (What may be the marvel / of such nobility?) she asks. But the second half of her enigma makes clear she uses these terms of praise ironically, for the marvel she seeks is one "que es, con ojos, ceguedad, / y sin vista entendimiento" (that has eyes but is blind, / and understands without knowledge). Passion blinds those who submit to its thrall, she says. Though many have praised the exquisite sensibility of love in poetry, she instead depicts these feelings as causing blindness and voiding perception—and thus, she implies, lacking all reason.

In the penultimate enigma, she returns to a concept she has mentioned several times—that of love as a malevolent deity: "¿Cuál es aquella deidad que, / con medrosa quietud, / no conserva la virtud / sin favor de la maldad?" (What is that deity that, / with fearful stillness, / does not keep its virtue / without favoring evil?). Love here is a stealthy foe, sneaking up on its unsuspecting prey ("medrosa quietud") in order to replace virtue with wrongdoing.

In the final enigma, Sor Juana establishes one of the most dramatic of all oppositions—that of snow and fire—to heap her final scorn upon the passionate deceptions of love: "¿Cuál es el desasosiego / que traidoramente aleve, / siendo su origen nieve / es su descendencia el fuego?" (What is that unease / that traitorously perfidious, / has its origins in snow / its descendents in fire?). Once again drawing an implicit contrast between the temperate zone of the Casa del Placer where "desasosiego" will never be felt, Sor Juana invokes a topsy-turvy world where emotions start out as frozen and cold only to be plunged into the heat of the flame. These extremes of feeling are abhorrent to Sor Juana, whose poetic world favors the reason and tranquillity of the female paradise of the Casa del Placer.

In the enigmas, Sor Juana has made a mockery of heterosexual love and those who choose to put themselves in its path. This love forms part of a masculinist paradigm, a patriarchal order, that Sor Juana and the other women of the Casa del Placer have rejected in favor of an all-female love predicated on the exploration of reason. She thus stakes a claim for women's intellectual preeminence. They, and they alone, can explore the delights of rationality, for only they remain above the tyrannical fray of love and its attendant destructive emotions.

It is poignant to consider that this demonstration of Sor Juana's defiant and parodic poetic expertise was to see the light so close to her death. The *censuras* and *licenças* are dated 1695, as is the cover of the book. I believe this book was in all likelihood passed around between the Casa del Placer's members for their secret enjoyment. It is unlikely that Sor Juana herself ever saw it, although it is satisfying to consider that she might have seen it before she died, at a time when she supposedly, in the words of Núñez de Miranda, had abandoned all secular pursuits and dedicated her life completely to God: "Juana Inés no corre a la virtud, sino es que vuela" (Juana Inés did not run toward virtue, but rather she flew) (qtd. in Calleja 160).

Conclusion

The nuns of the Casa del Placer came together as a virtual community of writers. Although they lived in actual communities of women, their activities were controlled and monitored to the extent that the formation of an actual literary academy, dedicated to secular poetry, may have been impossible. Obviously, the convent space did produce writers; however, there were limits. Most wrote their *vidas* at the behest of their confessors, their texts closely monitored; Sor Juana's enterprising and creative spirit suffered as she tried to break the bonds of control. The Casa del Placer attempted to bypass this control with its creation of a virtual utopian space that speaks to the ideal of community as described by Bauman. Therein, the female collective nurtured the creative spirit, the walls of the Casa del Placer keeping all those out who wished it harm.

In her work on female friendship and solidarity, Janice Raymond has identified a historical silence with regard to female friendship that coexists with often-ignored evidence of its empowering presence:

> The constant noise about women loving women exists in tandem with the historical silence about women always loving women. The silence that prevails erases the fact that women have been each other's best friends, supportive kin, devoted lovers and constant companions. (173)

This "historical silence" of which she speaks is often countered by a criticism of denigration, often predicated on what Raymond has cited as the patriarchal adage "that women are each other's worst enemies" (174). This definitely holds true for many studies of the life and world of Sor Juana, as I discussed at the beginning of this chapter. Patriarchal histories have so often promoted the benefits of solitude over solidarity for women that this prevailing fiction has been accepted as the truth. It has been the purpose of this chapter, reading the *Carta de Serafina de Cristo* and the *Enigmas ofrecidos a la Casa del Placer*, to write the importance of female intellectual alliances and communities into the history of women in the seventeenth-century convent and to demonstrate their effectiveness as tools against the prevailing fictions of misogyny—both then and now.

Conclusion

Titles are slippery things, and I have spent quite some time—perhaps too much time—thinking about my book's. The title I finally decided on—"Convent Life in Colonial Mexico: A Tale of Two Communities"—accurately reflects what I want to communicate. I have talked about two very different communities. One is the Church's *de jure* community, which I culled from didactic, proscriptive, and prescriptive texts. The other is the nuns' *de facto* community, which I read through letters, poetry, and between the lines of male-authored official texts, such as Inquisition documents. Conflict is present as the diametrically opposing views represented by these communities clash, time and time again.

More indirectly, though, with its allusion to Charles Dickens, this title also brings a little piece of Victorian England to colonial Mexico. At some point during the trajectory of this project, I began to wonder if the reference to Dickens was as accidental as it seemed. Was there some unconscious reason why I invoked Dickens to talk about Mexican nuns? In company with all other English schoolchildren, I was force-fed Dickens from an early age, something that did not result in my lasting appreciation of his novels. A perusal of my bookshelves reveals that I don't own any of his books. So, why Dickens? And why now? I began to think about possible points of contact between that most famous of Victorian novelists and a book written about colonial Mexican nuns. I came up with a few similarities that, I believe, intriguingly shed light on some of the most important issues that frame this book.

There are two conflicting views of community at play in Dickens' work. On one hand, those of Dickens' characters who occupy positions of authority demonstrate the same desire to impose controlled and contained communities as the ecclesiastical authorities in colonial Mexico did. The forces behind such institutions as the workhouse, the orphanage, and the prison—exemplified in novels such as *Oliver Twist*, *Nicholas Nickleby*, and perhaps most strikingly,

Bleak House—strive to oppress the same people they were meant to serve, often doing so in the name of Christian community. Dickens' villains, such as Ralph Nickleby, Fagin, and Uriah Heep, are legendary; similarly, there are clerics in my study—Padre Núñez de Miranda, Bishop Fabián y Fuero, Archbishop Aguiar y Seijas—whom we may view as villainous because of the lengths they travel to impose upon others a coerced community.

A very different kind of community, a voluntary community such as the Casa del Placer mapped in my study, is also present in Dickens' novels, forming a counterpoint to the coerced communities of the institutions. The ad hoc grouping of Jo, Allan Woodcourt, Mr. George, Phil Squod, Miss Flite, and Mr. Snagsby in *Bleak House* represents the same kind of mobilization of community "on one's own terms" to counteract a threatening force as that which groups of nuns undertook in the colonial Mexican convent. My protagonists, unlike many of Dickens', are not marginalized by class or economic hardship; they are in fact almost all from the elite. They are, however, marginalized by gender, which renders their plight similar. Their deeds may not be heroic and self-sacrificing like those of a Sydney Carton in *A Tale of Two Cities*. Nevertheless, the nuns exhibit bravery in challenging the seemingly monolithic power ecclesiastic authorities wielded. They attempted to shape their own way of life in the world, while not necessarily desiring to live to shape the world.

A last point of contact between my book and Charles Dickens' work speaks to a critical and historical commonplace that helped develop this study. As far as I know, one of the only specific mentions of nuns in Dickens comes in his last, unfinished novel, *The Mystery of Edwin Drood*. It is, as the title suggests, a murder mystery. Edwin Drood is supposedly killed, and suspicion falls on his uncle. Until she comes of age, Edwin's fiancée Rosa, an orphan promised to him while she was still a child, is being educated in a boarding school run by a Miss Twinkleton in the town of Cloisterham. The school, formally a convent, is known as the Nuns' House. Dickens speculates on the former inhabitants of the Nuns' House in the following passage:

> Whether the nuns of yore, being of a submissive rather than a stiff-necked generation, habitually bent their contemplative heads to avoid collision with the beams in the low ceilings of the many chambers of their House; whether they sat in its long, low windows telling their beads for their mortification instead of making necklaces of them for their adornment; whether they were ever walled up alive in odd angles and jutting gables of the building for having some ineradicable leaven of busy Mother Nature

in them which has kept the fermenting world alive ever since; these may be matters to its haunting ghosts (if any) but constitute no item in Miss Twinkleton's half-yearly accounts. (67)

Here, Dickens sums up the sexual and somatic imagery that has attended the figure of the nun from the beginnings of the Early Church and that was most certainly pervasive in the New World cloister. The nun was either virgin or whore; she was either Eve or Mary. Dickens' picture of nuns walled up alive for having committed some "ineradicable leaven of busy Mother Nature" discloses the fear and fascination the cloistered community of women inspired—something the Church authorities themselves created. Women must be enclosed, they felt, because of their propensity to sin; but once multiple female bodies were enclosed without the normalizing male presence, did they not then have the chance to sin more?

No other body throughout history has more preoccupied the pens of society's patriarchs and its supporters than the nun's. Yet the community—so feared and controlled—was home to very different bodies than those the authorities wanted to create. This community was made up of women who mobilized the power their community gave them to fashion a different way of life for themselves. Through action in concert, they demonstrated an agency that has not always been recognized by studies of convent culture in the colonial period. By taking such texts as Núñez de Miranda's and Carlos de Sigüenza y Gongora's out of context, scholars have been able to depict the convent as a monotonous and poisonous space populated by dissatisfied and bitter women,[1] abject victims of misogynist control, or by eccentric women estranged from the community at large. Convent communities were in no way proto-feminist utopias, of course. But taking into account a more complex and layered view of convent community, we find a middle ground between these two extremes, a space where women engaged authoritarian controls and patriarchal discourse to create communities, alliances, and friendships on their own terms.

This study embraces a critical direction in the field of gender studies in the colonial period that seeks to further elucidate the significance of women in this period.[2] We can thus rethink the status of those on the margins, seeing them instead as actors with agency within their own social milieus. Signally important to this approach are the nontraditional texts I study here—sermons, letters, and official proclamations—alongside more familiar forms such as poetry. Nontraditional texts, which require a broadening of literary reading strategies and an acceptance of texts as cultural artifacts, can be approached with a view to learning what they can tell us about relationships between power and gender and how these binaries are enforced as well as challenged. Jonathan Dollimore writes of the importance of combining history and critical theory to investigate early modern texts—both literary and nontraditional—to "reveal the tenacious yet mobile forms of discrimination, sexual and otherwise" (*Sexual Dissidence* 24).[3] This methodological reciprocity, in which literary canons are opened and historical approaches extended, constitutes the often-discussed and much-acclaimed interdisciplinary approach that can only enrich the study of gender and sexuality in colonial Latin American studies.[4] Now, as we delve into archives, we can pursue investigations and reach conclusions more truly synthesized than those afforded by series of case studies (Powers 14). Theory can help us more fully understand the lived experiences and thought processes of historical actors, allowing us to discover in their texts an agency and activity that had been obscured and muted by socially imposed categories such as gender. The texts I study here, and others like them, challenge comments such as those made by Dickens' Mr. Weller who says in *The Pickwick Papers*: "A tongue: that's a very good thing when it isn't a woman's."

Appendix

"El Sr. Inquisidor Fiscal del Santo Oficio contra Tomás Roberto Barreto, aprendiz de platero en la casa de D. Eduardo Calderón, natural de Irapuato. María Ildefonsa de San Juan Bautista Álvarez, religiosa profesa de coro y velo negro del Real Convento de Jesús María, declara: 'Que con motivo de tener una mala amistad con una moza llamada María Gertrudis Rodríguez, la que determinó salirse del convento, quiso la declarante salirse también por no separarse de ella, y recurrió a Tomás, él que sabía que era mágico para lograrlo etc'" (Archivo General de la Nacion, México, Inquisición, vol. 1319, exp. 6, 1794).
[The Lord Inquisitor Fiscal of the Holy Office vs. Tomás Roberto Barreto, apprentice silversmith in the house of Don Eduardo Calderón, of Irapuato. María Ildefonsa de San Juan Bautista Álvarez, professed choir nun of the black veil of the Royal Convent of Jesús María declares: "With the intention of having what is called an illicit friendship with a servant girl named María Gertrudis Rodríguez, and the latter having resolved to leave the convent, the declarant also wanted to leave so as not to be separated from her, and appealed to Tomás, whom she knew to be a sorcerer in order to achieve this etc."]

This appendix contains selections from the Inquisition case referenced above and investigated in chapter 3. I include all correspondence written by the nun Sor María Josefa Ildefonsa de San Juan Bautista, as well as one letter from her confessor, Padre Pedro Pablo Patiño, which he sent to the Inquisition alongside a letter from the nun. I have modernized the spelling and have added punctuation for clarity where I deemed it necessary for comprehension.

⁜

Sor María Ildefonsa de San Juan Bautista Álvarez (Septiembre 1792)

María Ildefonsa de S. J. B. Álvarez religiosa profesa de Coro y velo del real Convento de Jesús María con el más debido rendimiento a los pies de VS. Ilustrísimo Digo: que hace un año y cinco meses que hallándome muy tentada del enemigo deseaba el salir y dejar la Religión, y pensando el como la ejecutaría entre los muchos y diferentes pensamientos me acordé había oído decir que un tal llamado Tomás era mágico y por saber si era cierto lo mandé convidar a una reja en la que aún sin pronunciarle el fin para convidarlo ni tan poco darme por entendida de lo que yo quería me empezó a decir que nada tenía yo por que apurarme por que todo se podía ser todo tiene remedio. Yo no entendí ninguna de estas razones, me dio un libro el que al me dijo, y encargó no saliera de mi poder y si no lo quería o no me servía se lo volviera yo. Estuvimos hablando en la dicha reja cosas indiferentes hasta que me fui a la celda que abrí el libro en el cual no había letras ningunas si no todo blanco [...] había sido burla que había hecho de mi con todo estuve registrándolo y léase entre las páginas un papel él que leí y sí digo me admiré de ver su contenido pues era como si no hubiera dicho le mi intención y los motivos, por que me contestaba a todo sin haberle dicho ni por palabra ni por escrito nada en el dicho papel; me decía que estaba pronto a sacarme sin que me vieran ni supieran nada, pues podía ser que les pareciera a las de acá que estaba yo y no faltaba y yo estar a donde quisiera sin que me vieran ni conocieran; y así que deseaba saber el día que yo quería como ya hiciera lo que me decía en cuanto estuviera yo fuera pues de lo contrario no había nada, que siempre que yo quisiera escribirle lo hiciera y metiera mi papel dentro del libro y cuando yo quisiera tener papel suyo abriera el libro y hallaría. Me contestaba a lo que quería pero que sus papeles los había de ver de noche y en parte oscura pues de lo contrario no hallaría letras ningunas sino sólo papel blanco y que así que leyera sus papeles los quemara pues si no los quemaba los metiera en el libro, pues si no guardaba estas reglas no habrá nada. Todo esto hacía yo de modo que si por curiosidad quería yo leer los papeles de día o con luz no veía más de un papel blanco pero en siendo de noche estando sin luz leía sus papeles pues las mismas letras me alumbraban por que las veía yo como luz de lucernas. También me sucedía que si no quemar el papel si me desaparecía aunque lo cargara conmigo si lo metía en el libro me sucedía el mismo y así siempre andaba yo confundida. Siempre que me antojaba escribirle y metía mi papel en el libro o este libro lo guardaba yo misma con llave y la llave no la fiaba a nadie y siempre que me antojaba tener respuesta iba al dicho libro y ya hallaba sin enviar ni papel ni el libro; y en una palabra digo que yo no entendía el como era esto ni reflejaba si era bueno o malo aunque si

nunca llegué a determinarme a la salida pues pensaba en que se había de saber y eso no quería yo después ha sido cuando he tenido algunas reflejas. El libro se lo volví al dicho Thomas; no puedo acordarme de su apellido. Habrá cosa de cuatro o seis años que estuvo en la platería de Don Eduardo Calderón después si dijo que se ha venido a Guanajuato que [. . .] a los tres o cuatro años fue cuando supe que estaba allí más no en la platería sino de músico. Después de haberle vuelto yo el libro no lo he vuelto a ver ni saber; yo me hago de esto arrepentida y para el remedio en el futuro hago la presente denuncia; suplicando a VSI se sirva determinar lo conveniente en el adjunto, cuya denuncia hago en toda forma siéndolo malicia ni encubierta alguna y por cierto y verdadero así lo juro en el Santo Convento de Jesús María de México y setiembre de 1792 años.
(ff. 1–2)

[I, María Ildefonsa de S. J. B. Álvarez professed choir nun of the black veil of the Royal Convent of Jesús María with the most befitting rendition I declare, prostrate at Your Illustriousness' feet: that a year and five months ago and finding myself greatly tempted by the enemy I desired to leave and abandon my vocation, and thinking how I would do this among the different ideas I had, I remembered having heard of a certain Tomás who was a sorcerer and to find out if this was correct I invited him to the grill where without even telling him why I had invited him nor telling him what I wanted he began to tell me that there was no need to worry, and that there was a solution for everything. I did not understand anything he said, he gave me a book which he said I should not let out of my sight, and if I did not want it or if it was no good to me, I should give it back. We spoke at the aforementioned grill about various things until I went to my cell and opened the book in which there was no writing whatsoever. [. . .] Maybe it had been a joke that he had played on me, and given all that I looked in it and found a paper among its pages, which I read, and about which I must say I marveled at its contents because it was as if I had told him of my intention and motives, because he responded to everything on the said piece of paper without me having told him anything or written anything to him. He said he was prepared to get me out of the convent without anyone either seeing me or suspecting anything, so it would seem to those here that I was still here, and not missing, and I could be where I wanted without them seeing me or knowing I was gone; and so he wanted to know the day I wanted to do it, and I was to do what he said when I was outside otherwise there would be nothing, that whenever I wanted to write to him I was to do it and put my paper inside the book, and whenever I wanted to receive a note from him, I was to open the book and

I would find it. He told me what I wanted, but he said that I had to look at his notes at night and in a dark place because if I did not there would be no letters just blank paper, and that once I had read the pages I was to burn them, and if I did not obey these rules there will be nothing. I did all this, so that if out of curiosity I wanted to read the papers during the day or with a light I only saw a blank page, but at night without light the same letters lit up for me because I saw them as if by the light of glowworms. It also happened that if I didn't burn the paper it would disappear even if I was carrying it around with me, if I put it in the book the same thing happened, and so I was always confused. Whenever I wanted to write to him, I would put my paper in the book. I locked away this book myself and I didn't entrust the key to anyone, and whenever I wanted a reply I would go to the aforementioned book and find it without having sent him a note or the book; and in a word I declare that I did not understand how this was possible nor did I consider whether this was bad or good, although I never did fix a date to leave because I thought that I would be found out, and I did not want this after having reflected somewhat. I returned the book to the said Tomás; I don't recall his last name. It was probably four or six years that he was in Don Eduardo Calderón's silver shop and afterwards it was said he has gone to Guanajuato [...] and three or four years later I found out that he was no longer in the silver shop but was instead working as a musician. After I returned the book to him I never saw nor heard of him again; I make this declaration out of repentance and to make things right for the future; I beg Your Illustriousness to make the best use of the attached, and I make the denunciation without malice nor covering up anything and I swear it is right and true here in the Holy Convent of Jesús María of Mexico, September 1792.]

Sor María Josefa Ildefonsa de San Juan Bautista (1794)

Muy Señor Mío:

Por mi mucha fragilidad y miseria y estando preocupada de la pasión del desconsuelo, vine por fin a caer en la falsedad de escribir a este Santo Tribunal diciendo que me absolviera de la falta de haber tenido comunicación con un mágico el cual me escribía que estos papeles los leyera yo en la oscuridad pues eran las letras como lucernas; siendo falso todo esto y aun que vino cierto señor enviado por orden del mismo tribunal quien me hizo jurar las dos veces que vino, le había de responder a todo lo que todo se me fuese preguntado con realidad para lo cual me hizo poner la cruz, más en todo lo engañé siendo falso este tal conocimiento,

esto es el que aunque a la dicha persona que nombré aunque no me acuerdo si nombré también el apellido por no acordarme en el día del apellido y es cierto conocí a la tal persona más no es cierto de que esta persona era mágico ni yo he tenido tal conocimiento de ningún mágico, ni es cierto tal papel y así doy cuenta para que a la dicha persona no se le siga perjuicio y si se le ha seguido no se le siga en lo adelante pues no hay nada, y sólo lo hice perturbada con la pasión como he dicho y esta es la pura verdad que a su señoría: VM
PD: estoy en que fue esto en el año de mil setecientos noventa y cuatro.
María Josefa de San Juan.
(f. 17)

[My Very Dear Sir:
Because of my great fragility and misery and being overcome with dejection, I finally fell into the falsehood of writing to the Holy Tribunal, asking them to absolve me from the error of having had contact with a sorcerer who wrote to me saying that I should read those papers in the dark since the letters lit up like glowworms; all of this being false, and although a certain gentleman came, sent by command of the same tribunal who made me swear on the two occasions he was here, and I was to answer truthfully all he might ask of me for which purpose he made me make the sign of the cross, but I completely deceived him as all of this information is false, although I don't remember if I said what this person's surname was because I didn't remember his surname that day, and it is true I met the person in question but it is not true that this person was a sorcerer and nor have I heard of any sorcerers nor is it true that such a thing exists, and thus I declare so that said person will not continue to be in trouble, and if he has been then let him not in the future because he did nothing, and I only did it as my emotions were disturbed as I have said, and this is that whole truth for Your Worship.
PS. I believe this happened in 1794.
María Josefa de San Juan]

Padre Pedro Pablo Patiño (Abril 25, 1797)

Muy Ilustre Señor:

El papel adjunto es de esa religiosa del convento de Jesús María. Días ha que se lo hice escribir como era justo informado de la falsedad de la denuncia que había practicado contra el inocente de quien depuso diciendo que era mágico. No obstante lo he reservado dando tiempo para reconocer si estaba constante en la retractación por ser mujer joven, y sumamente apasionada, y melancólica. Pero viendo que está firme en ella, asegurando que todo fue falso, me pareció debía ya noticiarlo a VSM Ilustre, lo que pongo por obra remitiendo su propia esquela, con esta otra denuncia de una niña que confieso pocos días ha en Santa Inés. Dios nuestro señor guarde a VSM Ilustre en su mayor grandeza. Convento de Descalzos de San Diego, y Abril veinte y cinco de mil setecientos noventa y siete. (f. 18)

[Father Pedro Pablo Patiño (April 25, 1797)

Most Illustrious Sir:

The attached letter is from this nun of the convent of Jesús María. A few days ago I made her write it as it was only proper to bring to light the falsity of the denunciation, which she had levied against the innocent man, whom she had claimed was a sorcerer. Nevertheless, I have held it back allowing time to pass in order to confirm if her retraction was consistent as she is a young woman who is highly emotional and melancholic. But seeing as she is firm in this, assuring me that what she said before was false, it seemed to me that I should inform Your Illustriousness of this, which I enclose here separately, along with another denunciation of a girl I confessed a few days ago in Santa Inés.

May God our Father in his greatness keep Your Illustriousness.

The Discalced Convent of San Diego, April 25th, 1797]

Sor María Josefa Ildefonsa de San Juan Bautista (Octubre 24, 1799)

Muy Reverendo Padre Pedro Pablo Patiño:

Mi muy venerado Padre me alegraré no tenga novedad en su apreciable salud. Estimado Padre pensará VM que el no haberle escrito antes ha sido de desidia o cosa semejante. Más no ha sido así sino que quería darle razón de todo pero esto no me es posible por causa de la falta de memoria la que aunque nunca la he tenido muy bien pero desde que me echaron el cáustico en el cerebro enteramente la he perdido y aunque he procurado acordarme no puedo darle enteramente razón de todo. Lo que sí puedo asegurar es que el hombre es ciertamente el mismo que le dije el Viernes—del apellido no me acuerdo pero espero me den razón pues lo he solicitado y luego que lo sepa le avisaré. Lo que no me parece conseguir es el saber a dónde está, sólo puedo asegurarme que era de Irapuato y que estaba de oficial en la platería de Don Eduardo Calderón, Calle de Nuestro Padre San Francisco enfrente del vivaque, que de lo más no sé cómo estuvo. Pues sólo por obedecer a VM escribo éste y lo hago con bastante mortificación por no poder acordar pero no me parece que entonces tenía confesor y por esto me confesé varias ocasiones con un padre con quien no quería yo quedarme no sé si por esto o por otra cosa y hice confesión general con el mismo, pero no me acuerdo aunque me parece fue así que, le dije deseaba tener comunicación con un mágico por mis desconsuelos pero él se entendió que la tenía y así ya después sí dije que la tenía y esto fue por que como lo entendió. Así por esto me parece que no quise después decir que eran solos deseos pero dudo de si le dije con certeza el que tenía yo la dicha comunicación que de esto no me acuerdo, pero aunque fuera que le hubiera dicho el que deseaba el tener el tal conocimiento pero ya después sí dije que lo tenía este Sr. lo consultó aunque le costó bastante [...] por que no quería yo. Batalló mucho para que diera el aviso a el Santo Oficio pero por fin lo hice y el coger el nombre del sujeto que he dicho no me acuerdo ni fue por pensar que si vivía estaría muy lejos o si por haberle visto algunos lugares cuando estaba yo en la calle, pues no tengo presente por qué ni tampoco sé si dije del dicho sujeto otra cosa o sólo que era mágico, pues tengo mil dudas no obstante que [...] ver si me acuerdo bien para darle razón; y porque me mandó le diera razón de mi madre lo hago diciéndole se llama María Antonia Gálvez y Estrada que vive en la Segunda calle de la Verónica numero cuatro. Quien también puede dar razón de todo es mi tía la Madre María Brígida de la Santísima Trinidad religiosa profesa del convento de Nuestra señora de Balvanera ya cuanto puedo decirle pues no tengo presente nada mas y con esto a Dios que me guarde la vida de [...] Su hija LSMB

Octubre 24

María Josefa Ildefonsa de San Juan Bautista.

(f. 25)

[Most Reverend Father Pedro Pablo Patiño:

My most esteemed Father: I am glad to hear there has been no change in your estimable good health. Dear Father, Your Worship will most likely think that I have not written to you out of idleness or some such thing. But this is not the case. Instead, I had wanted to give you a full account of everything but this is not possible for my memory fails me. It has never been good but since they applied the *cáustico* to my brain I have lost it entirely, and although I have tried to remember I cannot give a full account of everything. What I can confirm is that the man is definitely the same one I named on Friday—of whose last name I do not remember but I hope they believe me, because I have asked for it and when I find out I will let you know. What I don't think I can find out is where he is, I can only confirm that he was from Irapuato and worked in the silver shop of Don Eduardo Calderón, on Our Father San Francisco Street, in front of the jail, and more I do not know. I write this only out of obedience to Your Worship and I do it with quite some embarrassment because I cannot remember but it seems that at that time I did not have a confessor and that is why I made confession on several occasions with a priest with whom I did not want to be, and I don't know if for this or another reason I made a general confession with the same, but I don't remember although it seems to me that it was so, I told him I wanted to make contact with a sorcerer because I was unhappy but he understood me to mean I already had, and so afterwards I did say that I had had such contact and this was how he understood it. It seems to me that this was the reason why I did not want to say afterwards that these were only wishes, but I doubt that I said with certainty that I had had this contact—that I don't recall, but although it might have been that I had said that I wanted to have such information but afterwards I did say that I had it, and this gentleman gave advice although it took him a great deal of effort [illegible] because I did not want to. He strove to make me inform the Holy Office, which I finally did. I don't remember how I came up with the name of the person I did, and if it was because he probably lived far away or because I had seen him around before entering the convent, I am not clear if I said anything else about this person or just that he was a sorcerer. I have a thousand doubts however [illegible] I want to see if I can remember so as to inform you; and because I was told to give information about my mother I do so with the information that her name is María Antonia Gálvez y Estrada and she lives in the second Veronica Street, at number 4. My aunt, Mother María Brígida de la Santísimia Trinidad, a professed nun of Our Lady of Balvanera convent can also give a full account. As to what else there might be to say I have nothing to add, and with this may God keep you for me.

Your Daughter [untranslatable]

October 24

María Josefa Ildefonsa de San Juan Bautista]

Notes

Chapter 1. Introduction: A Tale of Two Communities

1. Construction of the Catedral Metropolitana first began in 1573.

2. Jo Ann McNamara traces the evolution of these prejudices in the Early Church in the first three chapters of her book *Sisters in Arms: Catholic Nuns through Two Millennia*.

3. On the subject of the origins of enclosure for women, Makowski writes that modern historians agree that "some form of enclosure has been part of the monastic ideal for nuns in the West from a very early date" (9).

4. "Periculoso et detestabili quarandum monialum statui, quae, honestatis laxatis habenis et monachali modestia sexusque verecundia impudentur abiectis, extra sua monasteria personas supectas admittunt, in illius, cui suam integritatem voluntate spontanea devoverunt gravamen, offensam, in religionis opprobrium et scandalum plurimorum" (qtd. in Makowski 133–34).

5. Makowski points out that *Periculoso* had the effect of diminishing the importance of female monastic houses as the rules of enclosure jeopardized the convents' financial stability (3).

6. The Church authorities only valued chastity when it stayed firmly within their control. As McNamara points out, "uncontrolled virginity" was perceived to be as dangerous as "uncontrolled sexuality." She cites the case of early fourteenth-century Beguines who were persecuted and burned by the Church for having "embraced vows of chastity without ecclesiastical approval and supervision" (*Sisters* 379).

7. In *Medieval Misogyny and the Invention of Western Romantic Love*, Howard Bloch defines misogyny as "any essentialist definition of woman, whether negative or positive, whether made by a man or woman" (6).

8. "Active enclosure" referred to the egress from the cloister of nuns. "Passive enclosure" indicated the entrance of strangers into the convent.

9. During the fourteenth and fifteenth centuries, *Periculoso* was the subject of commentary by some of the most important jurists and intellectuals of the time (Makowski 1). This sustained legal interest over nearly two centuries helped ensure its reenactment at Trent in 1563 (Makowski 2).

10. McNamara characterizes the session in which enclosure was mandated as almost an afterthought: "On December 3rd, 1563, as they were leaving the final meeting, the prelates hastily decreed that nuns were universally to observe strict enclosure" (*Sisters* 461).

11. Sampson Vera Tudela describes Mexico City in the colonial period as "a place where the presence of the Counter-Reformation Church in every sphere of life was hard to ignore" (40).

12. The term is Foucault's from *Discipline and Punish: The Birth of the Prison*.

13. For a detailed description of the activities engaged in by male religious—both sanctioned and not—see Antonio Rubial, "Varones en comunidad."

14. Jo Ann McNamara calls for an awareness of how women's experiences documented throughout history are "fractured by hostile sources." She writes: "This is the history we were all trained not to write: a history in confrontation with our sources rather than in conformity with them" (239).

15. In seventeenth-century Spanish America, tensions were also present between criolla nuns and those born in Spain, *gachupinas* (Elisa Sampson Vera Tudela 14–34). However, by the late seventeenth century and eighteenth century, this particular difference was less marked. A convent for Indian women was not established until the foundation of Corpus Christi in 1728.

16. There are, of course, exceptions. Some abbesses did manage to influence events both within and without the convent community. For an example of this, see Chowning's depiction of certain of the abbesses in the eighteenth-century convent of La Purísima in San Miguel de Allende (for instance, chapter 3 of her book *Rebellious Nuns*).

17. Phelan analyzes the concept of "being-in-common" in the following terms: "Being-in-common means being with others, but this is the opposite of 'being common.' Being common is the continual denial of community in favor of oneness. Community in fact works to destabilize identity, as our being with others brings us face to face with multiplicity and its differences" (241).

18. *The Doctrinal Sermon That Father Núñez of the Company of Jesus Gave on the Day of Profession of a Nun in the Convent of San Lorenzo* (1697) and *Primer on Religious Doctrine Offered by One of the Company of Jesus for Two of His Spiritual Daughters, Who Were Brought Up to Be Nuns and Desire to Be So in All Perfection* (1698).

Chapter 2. Death and the Maiden: Buried Alive in the New World Cloister

1. "The convent was a place of refuge and protection for women whose birth into elite colonial society had not been accompanied by sufficient family wealth to forestall

an unequal marriage. The figure of woman, as represented in pedagogical and legal texts of the period, was weak and subject to all types of dangers. She should retire, if not into her own home, then into an institution created specifically for this purpose."

2. "The convent functions as a substitution mechanism: the nuns, feeble, innocent beings, practitioners of theological virtues, are charitable, humble, obedient, chaste, and unselfish. They mortify their own bodies in order to help wipe away the sins of the world."

3. "The submission of the body to the spirit is constantly emphasized and symbolized through the individual gestures and activities forbidden to all those who constitute the convent family. The role of the confessor, the regime of punishments and penances, as well as the ever-present obligation to negate the self through submission to doctrinal repression and self-censorship are inevitable aspects of religious life, which contribute to explain the terms in which the colonial period's intellectual and ecclesiastic image has become formalized as the expression and transgression of a subalternity in throes to a power which has been thought out down to the last minute detail."

4. "The purpose of his works was to persuade nuns to live the life they had professed according to their vows, emphasizing the rules that he knew were most often broken and which produced laxity in the convent, even adversely affecting the most observant nuns."

5. See translation, n. 18 to chapter 1 above.

6. "He sent off a little notebook to the printing press with the title of *Primer* in which by way of a dialogue of questions and answers, he facilitates, with admirable method, clarity and brevity, an understanding of all the difficult obstacles facing nuns [...] and he does so without the encumbrance of ponderous declarations and citations and with a great clarity and simplicity of style."

7. "Most beloved Father [...] tell us now what are the obligations of its very lofty state [the state of being a nun], and show us the way to fulfill them, effortlessly and efficiently; and most of all show us to what end and with what purpose have we to desire and try to be nuns?"

8. "What does it mean to sacrifice to God a virgin in her entirety—all her body, soul, powers, feelings, assets and desires, one who keeps nothing of or for herself, nor for the world, neither flesh nor blood; instead who sacrifices everything to God in the sacred fire of his compassion."

9. "They are virgins offered in holocaust, as in ancient times, not unlike the sacrificial victims burnt alive by a priest during a ritual ceremony. Moreover, the nun's body itself becomes a sacred space, when on offering up herself, the victims and priests become as one on the altar. In other words, in their embodiment the nuns bring together all the elements of both sacrifice and sacrificial victim."

10. "By way of the solemn profession of the four vows of poverty, chastity, obedience, and enclosure, together with an adherence to the rules and constitutions of the order, and the holy customs of the convent."

11. "To neither give nor receive, nor lend, nor spend, nor possess in any form an object of value, without the general or specific, formal or interpretative license given by a legitimate superior."

12. "And it [particular friendship] creates other most disreputable affronts to the community; because from here stems the problem of not loving all equally, of feeling aggrieved because of a certain person's behavior, of desiring to give a certain person a gift, and of finding the time to speak with a certain person."

13. "Each time she gives or receives, lends or bestows, without the permission of the legitimate superior, she breaks the vow of poverty by owning something, which is serious if it is something substantial for it is a mortal sin, and if it is something negligible then it is a venial sin, because the object is meager or paltry."

14. "In respect of all things, jewels, clothing and underclothing, food, expenses, cells and servants etc; because everything should be modest and unpresumptuous as befits poor nuns. And if at the grill, or gatherings, or with gifts, you spend money superfluously or excessively, or if you decorate your cell or person with precious and costly adornments that reek of secular profanity, or greatly distance themselves from poverty and religious modesty then I, at least, do not see how this can be free of serious blame, according to the extent of the profanity and exorbitance."

15. "And so the pure souls and chaste bodies of the brides of Christ are unsullied vessels, consecrated through their vows to the divine worship and service of God; and to permit or allow them to experience any kind of human love or profane enjoyment would be to sully the sacred vessels with worthless and shamefaced abuse."

16. "I believe that being a bride of Christ greatly raises a woman's standing, as well as the responsibilities of her sacred state, that, in my considered opinion, what we might consider unimportant in a secular woman would be a grave sin in a nun."

17. "A strange and widespread custom; just as nowadays there are fans of actresses, singers, and dancers or tennis champions, there were those then who paid court to nuns."

18. Octavio Paz quotes Antonio Robles' *Diario de sucesos notables* of the 5th of January 1682, in which he records a "Notificación a las monjas de la Concepción y San Jerónimo no tengan ni consientan devotos en las rejas y porterías" (165) (Notification to the nuns of La Concepción and of San Jerónimo that they do not have nor allow the presence of followers at the grill or in the porter's lodge). Archbishop Aguiar y Seijas ordered an edict affixed to all convent doors in Mexico City in May of 1693 in which he banned these types of relationships (Archivo Histórico de la Secretaría de Salud, Fondo Jesús María, Sección Legajos, exp. 17).

19. "Faced with the choice of convent or hymen, doubtlessly a greater percentage of Spanish women would tend to opt for the latter. However, unfortunately, one person rules and one obeys, and although this supposed greater percentage preferred matrimony, it was their parents who ruled and thus it was that many of these innocent young ladies—with more than one not likely to be young or innocent—were forced to accept

the other possibility, which of course does not necessarily mean that for these this was the best option."

20. Further evidence of the conflation of nun and prostitute can be found in the "burlerías de monjas" as they satirize *why* nuns in the convent sought out such suitors. Ferrer Chivite quotes several satire authors who claimed that women sold their affections to men in the most cynical ways so as to receive gifts and sustenance (56).

21. Baudot and Águeda Méndez, 196–97.

22. The prefatory remark to this poem in Baudot and Águeda Méndez's collection of censured and confiscated texts in viceregal Mexico reads: "Soneto erótico burlesco, incluído entre unos papeles sueltos recogidos en 1701. Se atribuye al bachiller Pedro Muñoz de Castro, dominico. Acompaña otros poemas de corte satírico que hacen burla del virrey y de su esposa y que tienen por tema las vicisitudes de la Nao de China" (196). (Erotic and satirical sonnet found among loose papers from 1701. It is attributed to the graduate Pedro Muñoz de Castro, Dominican monk. It accompanies other poems of a satirical bent which mock the viceroy and his wife and take as their theme the tribulations of the Manila galleon.)

23. "Says Don Juan with all his gall
He will not be happy 'til he finishes them off
And may God not kill me 'til I extinguish them all.

Fathers, I want them to make great haste
And marry their daughters off
And if not, less harm than making them nuns
Would be to let them be whores.

To reach the stars with one's hand
Will be easier than locking up the hens
Without the cock in the pen, Oh *Jaramillas*!

Though you call yourselves maidens
Finery, I know, and fuss you'd rather have
And husbands and suitors, than rough old habits."

24. The author uses the third person only once, in the second line, to identify the speaker for the reader ("Dice Don Juan").

25. Águeda Méndez and Baudot define "cogullas" as "el hábito o ropa que visten los monjes basilios, benitos y bernardos, la cual es muy ancha y la traen sin ceñir, llena de pliegues de arriba a bajo, con unas mangas muy anchas, que caen en punta, como también la capilla que está pegada al mismo hábito" (the habit or garment that the Basilian, Benedictine and Bernardine monks wore. It was wide and worn without a belt, full of

folds from top to bottom, with wide sleeves that fell to a point, as did the short cape which was attached to the habit) (197).

26. "O how many fell and how hard, solely because, reassured in vain, they thought they could not fall! Be very modest, my daughters, and God will keep you very chaste."

27. "In obeying the male and female superiors in every way, with the goodwill and good sense that are the initial and most important components of submission."

28. "Just as in secular life, it is the male figure that appropriates the ultimate authority over all the consciences over which he holds sway. In this way a patriarchal society is configured. The mother only plays the supporting role of mediator, arbitrator between the unquestionable word of the Father and the offspring. The same situation occurs in the female convent, and although the Abbess or Mother Superior indisputably rules the limited space of the cloister, the male Prelate or Inspector of the appropriate male religious order ultimately wields full spiritual jurisdiction."

29. "To the letter of the law, inviolately, without doubt, alteration, or discussion. And if you do not overcome this with heroic resolve, your spirit will be forever troubled and imperiled."

30. The online version of the *Catholic Encyclopedia* describes the Divine Office—*oficio divino*—as comprising "certain prayers to be recited at fixed hours of the day or night by priests, religious, or clerics, and in general by all those obliged by their vocation to fulfill this duty." (See http://www.newadvent.org/cathen/11219a.htm.)

31. "Matins is by tradition prayed from four o'clock the previous afternoon, or a little before, until twelve at night of the following day. Once this time has passed it is not possible to pray the previous day's matins, because its time has passed. It is possible to begin half an hour before four, because it is acceptable at the time, and it is even possible with just cause to begin to pray them at four."

32. "I believe that if there is [a reason], it has been proven through many examples; because of the brain's weakness, the individual's frailty, the curious ignorance of the Latin language, the difficulty and discomfort with the readings and instructions, and a lack of responsibility. [. . .] It seems to open the door to inconstancy and to persuade nuns to excuse themselves from their obligations with much less cause than male ecclesiastics, whose qualifications and adherence to these rules are unquestioned. They in turn possess greater strength, ability and dispatch in both Latin and prayer. Thus, what we would find hard to forgive in a monk or cleric we must quite often reasonably excuse in a nun; but in cases of doubt, you must always consult with a learned confessor and heed his advice."

33. "the embroilments, contingents, groups, favoritism, illicit circles, which exist only to foment discord, antipathies, gossip, complaints, emotions, insults, allegations, reporting of serious offenses, invective and turmoil."

34. "To be hidden away, abandoned and silent in your corner, whilst the strictest obligation compels you not to leave. To attend only to yourself: and ignore others: to not know, see, hear, like or touch, or even smell something from afar [. . .] to have supreme independence and holy disregard for everything and everyone created. Will a true bride

of Christ allow herself to take a fancy to or even depend on someone else? Oh, what an indignity so worthy of even dreaming of loathing! You must only associate with heavenly angels, and with your Husband, other beings do not exist for you. God and you. God and you, and nothing else in the entire world."

35. "Come from Libanus, my spouse, come from Libanus, come: thou shalt be crowned Queen from the lofty peaks and high summits of the soaring mountains of Amana, Sanir and Hermon. Come away from the menacing dens of the lions, from the craggy caverns of the leopards."

36. According to Landy, it is ambiguous as to whether this unification is imagined or real (318).

37. "Whosoever gives a diamond of the highest stock and incredible value, while believing it to be only a despicable piece of glass, offends with her vileness, as if in reality she were only offering this; but if supposing that by way of an understandable error believing it to be a majestic jewel she in fact offers an ordinary piece of glass, she deserves without doubt the gracious acceptance of he who receives it."

38. "The profession of a female religious means to marry Christ; and to marry as a Queen means to hand oneself over completely with all one's being, body and soul to the Husband's will: it means for everything to belong to Christ, including all relationships, desires and assets; and to keep nothing for herself, not even her free will; because the profession dictates everything must be offered in holocaust."

39. "In the first ceremony the entire community, holding lights, takes she who is to profess, dead with love as if they were taking her to her funeral, by foot to the sepulcher in the lower choir; where before reaching the Communion rail which is to be her nuptial bed, they recite for her the litany of the dying as she lies prostrate as if she were dead."

40. "To profess is to die to the world and to self-love and to love of all created things, in order to live alone with one's Husband. For all this the nun must be dead and buried without parents, relatives, friends, dependents, niceties, visits, and in a word without the love of any creature, fulfilling this completely: the dead do not pay or receive visits; they know nothing of etiquette or niceties. Who gives gifts to the dead or wants the dead in turn to give gifts?"

41. "are not content with simply not loving a man; instead they also want to be despised by all, and that men should flee from them as if from a dead body. Because of this they abhor their beauty and nice clothes, and so they wish to be dead so as to be rendered ugly and so repellent that everyone will run from them."

42. *Imitatio Christi* by Thomas à Kempis (1379–1471), a guide to penitence, was widely read at the time. According to Ibsen, it underscored that the progress toward salvation was not possible "until you look upon yourself as inferior to all others" (*Women's Spiritual Autobiography* 71).

43. Acts of self-mortification have been interpreted by some scholars as subversive of masculine power structures. See Bordo for a discussion and critique of such analyses.

44. "May this earthly beauty that men look upon with unchaste eyes perish and die,

and so that they will not desire me I want to die, ripped to shreds and rotting away so as to strike them with horror." Santa Inés (St. Agnes) was a young and beautiful aristocrat who eschewed marriage, desiring to dedicate her life to God. A group of her frustrated suitors denounced her, as a Christian, to the Roman governor, who threatened and tortured her so she would renounce Christ. This she refused to do, and so the governor decided to send her to a brothel where the youth of the city were to enjoy her body. However, as they set off for the brothel God thwarted their attempt; the girl's purity so amazed them that they were unable to touch her. The governor then ordered her execution and she was beheaded.

45. "always becoming more virtuous, hour by hour, until the last magnificent half day of her coronation, and with temporal finery and continual perfection repaying that immediate and excellent providence with which the King of Heaven chose them as his eternal brides."

46. "What disgust and anger would it cause God and his angels to see that a queen of heaven, the king's wife, so prizes and shows off disgusting rags befitting the slavish prisoners of hell or the world?"

47. "The veil extends and covers not only the head and neck but also the face and the entire chest, so that no one can see it nor take a fancy to it. She must always live thus, all hidden away in her veil, where her Husband favors her."

48. "and it is called crown, not only because it crowns the ring finger and thus the heart, which are connected by an artery [...] but also because by making her truly the King of Heaven's wife it crowns her Queen, since to marry the King is to become Queen."

49. "Here she owes the gratitude worthy of such favor: the respect which corresponds to such an honor. [...] Withdrawn from all, like she who has been freed from the worldly fire and Babylonian oven of her scorching affiliations, she gives grateful thanks to her Husband and Lord Jesus Christ's Father, through whose offices she was freed from such a voracious fire, and from such grimy and noxious heat, and raised up to a heavenly state of angelic purity."

50. "Here, take my heart and my will; possess me body and soul; take my strength and my emotions; dispose of it all as if it were your own; control and countermand, do and undo, everything I am is at your command and bidding etc. Oh and let it be so! And let it be forever, without end or interruption. Amen."

51. According to Josefina Muriel, Núñez's texts were popular well into the eighteenth century (72).

Chapter 3. The Community of Lovers: *Mala amistad* in the Convent

Author's Note: I borrow this chapter's name from a section of Maurice Blanchot's *The Unavowable Community*, where he describes the community of lovers as a defense against the "arid solitude" of society (33). This alliance does not guard against danger, however. It can, in some cases, constitute "the lethal leap toward death" (33). As I point out in this chapter, the community of lovers exemplified by a young nun and a servant girl is one such alliance fraught with peril.

1. "Tomás was prepared to get me out of the convent without anyone either seeing me or suspecting anything, so it would seem to those here that I was still here, and not missing, and I could be where I wanted without them seeing me or knowing I was gone."

The fact that Sor María Josefa believed that such a maneuver was possible is not as preposterous as it may seem. She would have been aware of the Catholic phenomenon of bilocation, perhaps from the case of the seventeenth-century Spanish nun Sor María de Agreda (1602–1665), who became famous for her claims that she had brought the gospel to the indigenous people of New Mexico and Texas without once having left her convent in the Spanish province of Soria. (See Clark Colahan's *The Visions of Sor María de Agreda: Writing Knowledge and Power*.)

2. *Mala amistad*, sometimes more generously called *amistad particular*, refers, in this case, to an intimate and proscribed relationship between women in the convent.

3. I use the word "same-sex" to describe the relationship between the two women in this study. As both Lillian Faderman and Carroll Smith-Rosenberg have pointed out, it is important to view these types of relationships in the cultural and social setting in which they took place rather than *avant la lettre* manifestations of individual psychosexual behavior approached from a post-Freudian perspective (Smith-Rosenberg 2). Therefore we should not be concerned necessarily as to the exact form these relationships took, as to whether they were "genital" or not (Faderman, *Surpassing* 80). Nor should we try to make them fit neatly within our present-day, and often rigid, conceptions of what constitutes lesbianism.

4. The set of documents describes the case brought against Sor María Josefa Ildefonsa de San Juan Bautista, of the convent of Jesús María, Mexico City (Inquisición, vol. 1319, exp. 6, ff. 1–29).

5. Following rulings made at the Council of Trent (1543–1560), a novice could not, in theory, profess before her fifteenth birthday or take the veil before she was sixteen (Lavrin, "La celda" 145).

6. "with the intention of having what is called an illicit friendship with a servant girl named María Gertrudis Rodríguez (the latter having resolved to leave the convent), the declarant also wanted to leave so as not to be separated from her."

7. "She is asked if she suffered from hysteria or what is commonly called *latido* or if she has some sort of condition which afflicts her sometimes, or if she suffers from hypochondria or another condition."

I have not been able to find any substantive information regarding the origins of the term "latido" as a synonym for "histeria." The only reference I have found is in José Antonio López Espinosa's article "La primera revista médica de América" (*ACIMED* 8, no. 2 (2000), 133–39), which discusses the circulation in the eighteenth century of the Mexican medical journal *Mercurio volante*. Espinosa lists the contents of the sixteen published editions, including number 6, which contains "Avisos acerca del mal histérico, que llaman latido" (Warnings about the acute hysteric, called "latido") (*Mercurio volante* 1772, no. 6, noviembre 25, miércoles) and "Se sugiere la aplicación de ciertas medidas en la dieta, en el vestuario, en los hábitos higiénicos y a la hora del reposo, como alternativa para combatir y curar la histeria" (recommends certain measures in terms of diet, clothing, hygiene, and rest as alternative means to fight and cure hysteria) (136).

8. "the deceit brought on by a mind damaged by illness or by the vehemence of the desire she had to leave the cloister so as to improperly be with the servant girl with whom she had an illicit relationship."

9. There are ten cases in all in which the phrase "*mala amistad*" is mentioned. Apart from the case of Sor María Josefa, the only other case involving two women is from 1780. The complaint reads as follows: "El Sr. Inquisidor Fiscal de este Santo Oficio contra María Gertrudis de la Zerda, española, dueña de la chocolatería de la calle de San Lorenzo, denunciada por María Josefa de Ita, española, por haber tirado el rosario y decir que no había de rezar y solicitándola de tener mala amistad con ella" ("The Inquisitor Fiscal of this Holy Office vs. María Gertrudis de Zerda, Spaniard, owner of the chocolate shop on San Lorenzo Street, who has been denounced by María Josefa de Ita, Spaniard, for having thrown a rosary to the ground and for saying she had no need of prayer and for inviting her to engage in an illicit friendship with her") (AGN, Inquisición, vol. 1203, exp. 16, 1780).

10. Of this projection of perversity onto the body of the nun, Janice Raymond has written: "Lust, carnal attachments, harlotry—all vices reputed to reside in convents from the very beginning of their existence—were said to derive from the loose condition of religious women, that is, their state of being independent and unattached to men" (73).

11. Mary Elizabeth Perry also offers evidence of lesbian practices using "artificial male genitalia" (84) in prisons in Seville in the sixteenth century. She cites a contemporary commentator who described women who "appeared to want to be men, strutting about and crowing like roosters" (84). The punishment for those who were discovered was two hundred lashes and permanent banishment from Seville (84).

12. Having studied the records of the three Inquisition tribunals that prosecuted sodomy (other cases were prosecuted by the State), Carrasco was unable to find any evidence of women being burned alive for sodomy in Valencia, unlike men convicted of the same crime. However, both Francisco Tomás y Valiente and Louis Crompton cite the writings of the sixteenth-century Spanish jurist Antonio Gómez, who, in claiming that sodomy between women with the use of a prosthetic device was as sinful as the act between men, refers to the case of two Spanish nuns who were burned at the stake for the crime of sodomy with the use of a material instrument (Tomás y Valiente 48; Crompton 19). Traub cites the example of France, where a distinction was drawn between "sinful *desires*," which were not criminal, and acts of penetration, which were ("(In)significance" 66).

13. Commenting on Traub's article in regard to a study on same-sex female relationships in the work of María de Zayas, Mary Gossy writes: "The lack of an outcry or pun-

ishment of this feminine erotic experience does not mean that it was not a source of gender trouble. Sometimes very troubling facts produce little outcry, and the lack of outcry in fact frequently signals big trouble; this whole process is called repression" (20).

14. In this regard, see Serge Gruzinski's essay "Las cenizas del deseo," which includes an analysis of a case study of a mass prosecution in Puebla of men accused of sodomy, including clergy.

15. See David Higgs' essay "Tales of Two Carmelites: Inquisitorial Narratives from Portugal and Brazil."

16. Male bonding was actively encouraged among Jesuits. Basing his opinion on Eve Sedgwick's theory of the homosocial, Dušan Bjelic describes how Jesuits used abstention from sexual activity with women to "collectively mobilize and redirect their desire away from women and towards each other in order to advance male power/knowledge" (66). He describes this in more detail, suggesting that "born out of a Christian military ethos and its imperfect homoerotic discourse, the Society of Jesus inherited homosocial structures of power and homoerotics as a semi-concealed discursive pleasure, from which their scientific inquiries never broke away, though they were transformed into a discourse on scientific rationality" (67).

17. For a detailed analysis of this issue and its origins, see the introduction to this study.

18. In Hispanic texts of the early modern period warning against intimate relationships in the convent, both the terms *mala amistad* and *amistad particular* are used to refer to the same behaviors.

19. "It seems that too much affection between us cannot be a bad thing; but it brings so many imperfections with it that I don't think anyone would believe it unless they had seen it with their own eyes. The devil makes mischief here—those who try boorishly to please God don't really notice it, and it seems virtuous to them. But those who aim for perfection understand the danger very well, because little by little it drains the strength that should be spent in completely loving God."

20. "And restrain yourself, for the love of God, from these relationships, however pious they may be. They are even poisonous between sisters and I see no benefit in them. Among relatives it is even worse; it's a plague."

21. "wanting to have something to give her, finding time to speak with her, and many other times to tell her she is loved rather than loving God."

22. "'my love,' 'my dearest,' or other things like this that women call one another. Leave these compliments for God. It's such a female thing, and I don't want my sisters to seem like anything other than powerful men."

23. "forgetting the fidelity they promised to their husband on the day of profession, waste their time and efforts in idle pursuits, which even among women outside the convent are deplorable."

24. "They spend months and even years involved in such activities, without attend-

ing to the needs of their jealous husband. Their conscience does not even prick them. Instead they live as if there were no God, or as if eternity were but a lie."

25. "Although Petronila was well, she could not resolve to stop communicating with her [the nun] because such an undertaking seemed impossible to her."

26. "She best displayed the excellence of her fervor and the perfection of her virtue in her role as teacher and novice mistress, which she carried out for eleven years."

27. "Her most common piece of advice was that they try to detach themselves from the worldly contact and conversation, and to instead try to love each other through God, which is the most powerful weapon against these predilections that so undermine discipline in the convent."

28. Edicto de Aguiar y Seijas, Archivo Histórico de la Secretaría de Salud, Fondo Jesús María, Sección Legajos, exp. 17.

29. "If he found out a woman had entered his house he would command that the bricks she had stepped on be ripped up. [...] He did not want women to touch anything in his house, he did not want them to prepare food nor did he want to hear them sing, nor even speak."

30. "The Illustrious Dr. don Francisco de Aguiar y Seijas, Archbishop of Mexico, has been given notice that in the convents of this city exists the practice of devotions, both in and outside of the cloister. Accordingly, he is notifying the prelates of the convents and the nuns that they refrain from outrageous and unsettling illicit friendships, known as devotions, with anybody."

31. "The most disgraceful devotions are those that take place within the convent and that the nuns have with each other, and with the secular young ladies and with servant girls, and they in turn with each other. These occasion serious problems, significant indignity and spiritual downfall. And so that these devotions come to an end, together with the serious damage they cause, and so that from now on these do not occur as they are offensive to God, His Illustriousness orders that the Mother Abbesses, prioresses, and vicaresses of said convents take special care to ensure that these devotions be avoided and to punish those who contravene and break the tenets of this decree."

32. The situation culminated in the *cédula real* of 1774 that restricted the number of servants only to those truly necessary for the efficient running of the convents, although again many exceptions were made on an individual basis. Salazar calls these reforms "drásticas pero no definitivas ya que un análisis exhaustivo trae a la luz múltiples excepciones" (drastic but not definitive in that a detailed analysis brings multiple exceptions to light) ("Niñas" 179).

33. "where none of the aforementioned nuns, young ladies, or servant girls may dare to remove it or tear it up under threat of complete excommunication."

34. Borda was a Franciscan friar, university professor, and official of the Inquisition. He died at some point in the early eighteenth century (Águeda Méndez, "La palabra" 104).

35. See chapter 2 for an analysis of the appropriation of the female voice in this type of dialogic "encounter."

36. "These relationships may be innocent, such as when the servant takes care of the nun, cooking for her, but if it comes to pass that the maid is allowed to engage in indecent and iniquitous actions, if she keeps her secrets and acts as a go-between in her problems, then this, for me, constitutes a mortal sin, the downfall of all nuns, and the undermining of discipline."

37. Fernando Benítez includes a description of these *amistades particulares* between nuns and these so-called "madres de amor" in his book *Los demonios en el convento*. His description is highly explicit, if not salacious:

> Las criadas [. . .] eran peligrosas y se las llamaban significativamente "madres de amor." [. . .] Estas mujeres venían de otro mundo en que el sexo no producía miedo ni sentimientos de pecado sino placer. Una monja desnuda dejaba de ser monja y se convertía en una mujer de hermosos pechos, de muslos redondos tapizados de un vello muy fino y con un sexo cubierto del pelo rizado y espeso del que las esclavas carecían. Las metían suavemente en el agua tibia perfumada con hierbas y enjabonaban sus cuerpos y les daban masajes y acariciaban sus partes mas intimas. (48)

> [The maidservants [...] were dangerous and were known, significantly, as "mothers of love." [...] These women came from another world, one in which sex did not produce fear nor feelings of guilt but instead was something pleasurable. A naked nun ceased to be a nun and became a woman with beautiful breasts, rounded thighs covered in fine fuzz and with genitals covered in thick curly hair that the slaves did not possess. They would put them gently into the warm water fragrant with herbs and would soap their bodies, giving them massages and caressing their most intimate areas.]

It is not clear what Benítez's primary sources are for these details. It is hard to imagine that any document of the period would contain such unambiguous details. I have no knowledge of any such text.

38. I am not suggesting here that María Josefa possessed, for herself or for the Inquisitors, a sexual identity or orientation in the modern sense of the term, but rather that the convergence of the charges of *mala amistad* and "una enfermedad propia de su sexo" (an illness typical of her sex) contributed to the view of her, which emerges from the documents, as an aberrant body. My goal is to interrogate, through this case study, what David Halperin calls "the multiplicity of possible historical connections between sex and identity" (109).

39. "Because of my great fragility and misery and being overcome with dejection, I finally fell into the falsehood of writing to the Holy Tribunal."

40. "although I don't remember if I said what this person's surname was because I didn't remember his surname that day, and it's true I met the person in question but it is not true that this person was a sorcerer and nor have I heard of any sorcerers nor is it true that such a thing exists."

41. "A few days ago I made her write it as it was only proper to bring to light the falsity of the denunciation, which she had levied against the innocent man, whom she had claimed was a sorcerer."

42. See translation, n. 8 to chapter 3 above.

43. It is possible to see this conflation or confusion of illness and "aberrant" affections between women as an example of what Lillian Faderman has called "the morbidification" of same-sex female relationships in the nineteenth century. She claims that during this time, "medical science and psychology have morbidified intense love relationships between women by inventing a syndrome of ills (which has changed from era to era) that supposedly accompany such affection" ("The Morbidification of Love" 76).

44. Rousseau gives particular credit for this rethinking of the disease to the English physician Thomas Sydenham (1624–1689), whose work in the seventeenth century served to "demystify hysteria by rendering it an authentic medical affliction, neither diabolical nor fanciful," as well as forming part of a process that "demystified the reproductive organs of the female body" (141).

45. In a study of same-sex love between women in England from the seventeenth to the nineteenth century, Emma Donoghue describes how the term "passion" held multiple meanings, all of which, however, had intensity of feeling in common. She identifies passion as referring to "connotations of strong feeling, interest, anger, grief, enthusiasm, sexless as well as sexual love" (1–2).

46. According to Stanley W. Jackson in his study *Melancholy and Depression: From Hippocratic Times to Modern Times*, the term "love-melancholy" was brought into prominence by Robert Burton in his *Anatomy of Melancholy* (1632). Jackson lists the different, and often interchangeable, names with which this illness has been described: "love-sickness, love, and others" (352). Interestingly, Burton dedicated a subsection of his famous work to a discussion of melancholy in celibate women, including "nuns and maids" whom he believed could be cured by being "well-placed and married to good husbands in due time" (355), as sexual activity would remedy the buildup of "the torrent of inward humors" (356).

47. From Graub's 1763 essay *De regimine mentis* (qtd. in Jackson, 367).

48. See n. 8 to chapter 3 above.

49. "She was shown and given the letter pertinent in these matters so she could read it and identify it, and having read it and looked it over to her satisfaction she said that it was all in her hand and that she supposes by the context that she wrote it to send to the Holy Inquisitors but she does not recall if this was indeed the case, nor does she remember to whom she sent it."

50. "This nun suffers greatly from hysteria, to the extent that her mind is weak and full of the strangest things and it is impossible to make her see sense: once she got it into her head that a servant girl climbed through a window into her cell, with the shutters of this same window being closed; on another occasion she claims she had seen a man in a

red cape in a passageway at four in the morning; and thus with the greatest certainty she makes similar assertions and affirmations: suffering as she does with this illness they have just finished applying a *cáustico* which they had put on her brain, as she had an attack. Perhaps this weakened her or affected the nerves of a delicate area. The Abbess made all this known so that all she has said can be taken with a grain of salt, including the original accusation she made."

51. The "cáustico" mentioned here was most likely some sort of plaster or medical dressing, made of caustic potash, which would have been applied to the temple area.

52. "The conflict between moral obligations and physical needs was always resolved in favor of the soul's salvation to the detriment of the body's well-being."

53. "typical of a disturbed mind, and in this regard I consider this nun to be entirely free of malice and guilt and worthy of compassion."

54. "I don't remember how I came up with the name of the person I did and if it was because he probably lived far away or because I had seen him around before entering the convent."

55. "A protective and tyrannical father figure, the image of an authority that represented religion and repression, salvation and condemnation, beginning and end. We can locate the confessor in that dark and impenetrable zone of intimacy, in the shadowy border that separates sin and sanctity."

56. "In such an atmosphere, the guardians of souls meddled in the nuns' lives and controlled their behavior, but, more seriously still, they also controlled their minds, taking over both their physical and mental freedom."

57. "she made the denunciation because her confessor at the time, Fernando Martínez de Soria Esq., told her to do so."

58. "having spoken with her confessor she is now sure that she can truthfully say and without any fear that actually her accusation was false."

59. "My most esteemed Father: I am glad to hear there has been no change in your estimable good health. Dear Father, Your Worship will most likely think that I have not written to you out of idleness or some such thing. But this is not the case. Instead, I had wanted to give you a full account of everything but this is not possible for my memory fails me."

60. "I write this only out of obedience to Your Worship and I do it with quite some embarrassment because I cannot remember but it seems that at that time I did not have a confessor."

Chapter 4. Mobilizing Community: The Fight against *vida común*

1. According to the *Catholic Encyclopedia*, "vida común" means "common life."
2. Luis Sierra Nava-Lasa has documented the existence of 20 convents of nuns in Mexico City of which 11 were of *calzada* nuns, as well as 11 convents in Puebla of which 5 were *calzado* (195).

3. This insistence on the particularity of each convent's constitutions was something the nuns used to challenge the Church's imposition of *vida común*.

4. Although debated and discussed, the *vida común* was never enshrined in the Canons of Trent. Writes Chowning: "In Europe the *vida común* was resisted so strenuously by nuns and their families that the papacy backed down on imposing it across the board and it was never made a requirement for all convents" (*Rebellious Nuns* 221).

5. The Bourbon reforms vested more power in the secular clergy, weakening the power of the mendicant orders. In 1749 the Crown decreed that all parishes administered by the Franciscans, Dominicans, and Augustinians were to be handed over to the control of the secular clergy (Brading, *The First America* 492). The expulsion of the Jesuits from Spain and all its dominions must also be considered as part of this reform of the Church. However, this event must be viewed in the larger context of the order's suppression throughout Europe (1759–1767) and the events that led up to the curtailment of its power.

6. Convents founded after 1747 were either orders strictly observant of the vow of poverty or were convents of teaching orders. Of the latter, the French order the Compañía de María founded three convents after mid-century (Chowning, *Rebellious Nuns* 154).

7. Chowning herself admits that the two main proponents of reform in New Spain, the Archbishop of Mexico and the Bishop of Puebla, were perhaps more interested in "individual piety" rather than in the Enlightenment focus on the individual ("Convent Reform" 31).

8. Brading characterizes the broad reform movement in the Spanish Church as a diverse one, "united only by a repudiation of the spiritual and intellectual culture of Baroque post-Tridentine Catholicism" (*The First America* 500).

9. For a discussion of Church reform in Spain, see Loreto López (87).

10. The council, set up by Archbishop Lorenzana, was intended to combat the relaxation of the convents and focused mainly on the reform of female religious houses. Chowning does, however, cite it as an example of the New Spanish Church's reforming bent, as it did take up "many other issues of broad consequence" ("Convent Reform" 14).

11. There can be no doubt that there was a philosophical division between Peninsular and creole ecclesiastics regarding the reform of the Church in New Spain. The most powerful prelates were, almost without exception, born in Spain, and many held the inhabitants of the colonies—both creole and Indian—in very low esteem. The "enlightened" prelates who arrived in New Spain implemented their reforms "without first acquiring any knowledge of the social realities of the country and people whom they came to govern" (Brading, *The First America* 497).

12. These comments notwithstanding, Sánchez de Tagle does not waste his sympathy on the nuns, deeming them to have long enjoyed their "privilegiado nicho" as "hijas predilectas" (favorite daughters) and as having fed parasitically off a city that threatened

to be "devorada ella misma por estas ingentes criaturas suyas" (itself devoured by its own colossal children [the convents]) (149).

13. Salazar, *La vida común* 10.

14. *Bienes Nacionales* 77 (1729–1778), exp. 20, ff. 56–85, AGN Mexico.

15. "Not all the nuns who receive these annual money advances always spend it on what they need. Instead sometimes, and without any favorable advice or forethought they waste it and spend it badly, showering their friends outside the convent with gifts and donations, which without doubt provokes eventual disaster and then the ultimate destruction of the convent."

16. The text was originally published in Amsterdam in 1771 as *La Nymphomanie ou traité de la fureur utérine*.

17. María Águeda Méndez has detailed the prominence the consumption of chocolate held in the attribution of decadence to Mexican society. In an essay entitled "Una relación conflictiva: La Inquisición novohispana y el chocolate," she claims how, with the arrival of the Spaniards, the once-revered consumption of chocolate acquired "tintes sesgados y visos de sexualidad" (perverse sexual overtones and appearance) ("La palabra" 113). She details many cases from the files of the Inquisition that demonstrate the use of chocolate in, among other heterodox uses, the propagation of love magic. In a similar vein, and in specific reference to the reformed Carmelite order, Manuel Ramos Medina points out that although the consumption of chocolate was initially deemed to be nutritious, by the eighteenth century it was considered a vice and was outlawed. Each nun who professed was to sign a paper claiming "hago voto de no beber chocolate, ni ser causa de que otra lo beba" (I swear to not drink chocolate, nor cause anyone else to drink it) (162).

18. While Grosz accepts that this comparison has usually been made between the body and the state, rather than the city, she believes it is operational in a comparison between the latter and the body as well: "clearly there is a conceptual and historical linkage between the state [the domain of politics] and the city [polis]" (106).

19. For a detailed description of the presence of "niñas" in the convents, see Loreto López 94–96.

20. Sierra Nava-Lasa calls this lack "el *handicap* de la inexistencia de colegios para niñas" (the handicap of the nonexistence of girls' schools) (197). This, he claims, was made even more serious by the prolonged absence of the father from the home due to the exigencies of colonial society, as well as the dangers posed by what he calls "la plebeyez del ambiente callejero" (the vulgarity of the city streets) (197). All these things made the convent a convenient and desirable place for girls to live and receive education (197).

21. The fact that girls who found themselves in these circumstances turned to the convents for help was not surprising. One of the social functions of convents "was to provide security for girls who had lost parental protection" (*Rebellious Nuns* 44).

22. According to Chowning, many did indeed stay on to profess (*Rebellious Nuns* 160).

23. Licenses for lay women to reside in the convent were, according to Chowning, "relatively easy to obtain" (*Rebellious Nuns* 160).

24. "Each one of the [convents'] larger cells housed a nun, the young girl or girls entrusted to her care, the maids in her service, and her favorites."

25. The institution of the *peculio* circumvented restrictions against nuns' owning personal property. Known euphemistically as "the fund for chocolate," the money did not strictly belong to the nun, but instead she used the income from the monies deposited by her family until her death, when it would be incorporated into the convent's general coffers (Chowning, *Rebellious Nuns* 195).

26. All excerpts from the Bishop of Puebla's letter appear in Salazar, *La vida común*, 99–106, to which the parenthetical page references herein point.

27. "Each nun must prepare her soul to not repudiate nor place obstacles in the way of the common life when their [male] superiors show this to be their will."

28. "intends not to destroy but instead better the religious life in accordance with the holy rule and with indescribable benefits to the community."

29. "leaving only the number of servants which corresponds to the number of nuns, and food should be prepared communally for the healthy and the sick according to what their needs dictate."

30. "The necessary rooms will be constructed and designated for the appropriate offices."

Architectural requirements were designed to increase vigilance over the convent population. According to Chowning, the new dormitories were to be positioned so as to make it easy for the abbess to keep a watchful eye on the nuns (*Rebellious Nuns* 32).

31. "It is not our desire to make homeless or throw onto the street any of the poor secular women who live in our convent, for whom we all have a great deal of compassion, and we will take the necessary measures to ensure they do not suffer or go astray."

32. "We, the superior and the female prelates are obligated to try to introduce the observance of the common life, and we will not act in this way unless we are sure in our minds it is right."

33. "In light of what [. . .] is laid out, how could we not hope that our suggestions would not have a positive effect, when accepting the rule of the common life implies the avoidance of all kinds of distractions of the mind, cares of the spirit, and anxieties of the heart? It is so, and in this knowledge and in the relief we can now offer—which perhaps may not be available to us in the future—we find consolation. In the same way your happiness and that of all your daughters is to be found in your willing acceptance."

34. "The union of possessions greatly facilitates the union and community of hearts which constitutes charity, which is itself the bond and tie of perfection as well as the purpose of whatever God orders us to do."

Shortly after Fabián y Fuero issued his first set of instructions, his former colleague from the metropolis Archbishop Lorenzana also entered the debate. In December 1766 he circulated a printed pastoral letter in which he sharply criticized the convents in

Mexico City for the same reasons Fabián y Fuero had accused the convents in Puebla (Sierra Nava-Lasa 202). Brading describes his foray as being more "cautious" after seeing the initial reaction to his colleague's actions (*The First America* 496).

35. All excerpts from this poem appear in Salazar, *La vida común*, 107–10, to which the parenthetical page references herein point.

36. "Our Mother Church established in all communities of both sexes a venerable account of the way of life of the apostles, bishops, priests, deacons, and other faithful members of the Early Church."

37. "Let the satirist know that you are with your Husband, / Imitating and portending a special love, / And you know how to carry out your talent / In copying such a holy model."

38. Arendt herself makes a distinction between power and violence, claiming that the latter can destroy the former, and declares them opposites—with power being "action in concert," and violence as constituting domination over others. Hartsock indicates a weakness in this distinction, referring to Arendt's claim that power and violence are often found together. Hartsock believes that power can be wielded through violence and is not always a force for good ("Community" 33–34).

39. According to Allen, Foucault rejects the resistance to power via community or solidarity. Allen claims Foucault's conception of resistance is strategic, and this commits him to "a wholesale rejection of any sort of understanding of the power that is generated through reciprocal, collective, social action" (56).

40. See for example, Marilyn Friedman, "Feminism and Modern Friendship: Dislocating the Community," and Janice Raymond, *A Passion for Friends*.

41. All excerpts from the nuns' letter to the viceroy appear in Salazar, *La vida común*, 119–47, to which the parenthetical page references herein point. All references to the nuns' letter are cited in Salazar, *La vida común*, 119–47.

42. "Your Excellency: The below signed nuns of this convent throw themselves most humbly at your feet secure in the knowledge of your Excellency's charity and saintly actions, since this has been made known to the world and is the solace of these kingdoms. We present ourselves to you the most afflicted and helpless who have ever lived or who will ever live on earth."

43. The nuns also show themselves here to be astute political actors, conscious of the changes being wrought in society due to the Bourbon Reforms. In this ambiguous time, appealing to the viceroy against the Church authorities was a canny move, owing to the movement of secularization of which the viceroy was in charge. Although Fabián y Fuero was a regalist, the nuns here are exploiting the Crown's resentment of the Church's power (see Chowning's "Convent Reform," 14–21, for an astute analysis of the contradictory issues at play in the relationship between Crown and Church in the eighteenth century).

44. "We first must tell you that when he arrived in this city we expected to find a loving father and priest, like his predecessors. On the day when he came to the visiting room,

where we all came to pay our respects, having already presented him in a daughterly fashion with some gifts befitting his holy state, we suffered shame when he refused to accept anything, and having been in said visiting room for only a very short time, which did not exceed a quarter of an hour, and without more ado than taking the necessary leave of the Mother Superior, he left us inconsolable and has never honored us with another visit."

45. "This destruction and the violence associated with the news, took the life of a nun who had had no other illness other than sadness and shock at seeking such lamentable destruction."

46. "Your Excellency must be told how we have suffered the worst indignity before we entered into the common life, which was the inventory that his Illustriousness ordered be carried out, making lists of all the clothes we possessed, both outer and underwear, so that each of us had to tell him what we had. The embarrassment was so great imagining that our misfortunes would be made public and read in the Accounting Office of the Bishopric, so public was the humiliation that some oafs wrote some verses on the subject."

47. "Afterwards he began to take away our confessors, suspending the licenses of most if not all of those who directed us, and having carried this out, he ordered that in all the sacristies of our convents printed letters of warning should be placed, so that the few who did come to confess us must sign and write down the names of those whom they confessed, without any of us knowing why such a change was taking place."

48. "As he did not permit those nuns who were dying the support of their confessors during the night, thus inflicting pain on them so they had not a minute's peace, the confessors were obliged to abandon the dying, who expired greatly afflicted. We saw one who begged for her confessor to make peace with God and whilst they went to get him she died, suffering greatly, and many nuns have ended their lives this way."

49. "So that as our true father and earthly lord you listen to us, console and help us; we doubt not, knowing of your holy heart, that if you had known before of the misfortunes, trials and tribulations we your loving daughters, your loyal servants, have suffered, we truly believe we would not be in the terrible position of which your Excellency will soon be aware."

50. "knocking down the novice's rooms as well as our dormitories and many costly cells with pickaxes, and with such violence that we did not even have time to take out what we needed from there, and to such an extent that it was incredibly difficult to take out a poor sick nun from one of the cells."

51. "The girls' company was such a boon and comfort. When we were ill they would take care of us and carefully attend to us, and we could be at choir without having to worry about household tasks, and this, without any great fuss, was always done."

52. "When they began to leave this and other convents it was the saddest thing that could make you cry forever, for many of them were orphans with nowhere else to go who had grown up in the cloister. The violence took them by surprise and, there in the street, they bewailed their helplessness."

53. "We swear to your Excellency that many we know of were forced through necessity to sin against God and some have died in childbirth and others have been obliged to marry without wanting to; some have died and others are homeless and although some have enrolled in schools as his Illustriousness promised all would be able to, these were few in number and they were only given four pesos a month."

Certain "niñas" also petitioned on their own behalf. One such text puts their case in the following terms:

> Hemos vivido desde nuestros tiernos años, y otras que ya grandes nos venimos a retirar por vivir aquí escondidas de las olas del mar tempestuoso y estar en la religión porque nos hallábamos en total desamparo [. . .] y lo que es más pensar que hemos de salir de nuestra amada clausura se nos acaba la vida y aun eso nos sirve de consuelo porque nos es más fácil morir que salir del convento. (qtd. in Loreto López 97)

> [Since our most tender years we have lived here, and others of us now old came here to live quietly away from the waves of the tempestuous sea, and to live the religious life because we were totally helpless [. . .] and to consider we might have to leave our beloved cloister makes us feel our lives are over, but even this is comforting because it is easier to die than leave the convent.]

54. "His Illustriousness found out and sent out another decree ordering the nuns to stop helping them, neither giving alms nor even a bite to eat, nor even the littlest piece of bread, or anything else."

55. In her detailed case study of the impact of the *vida común* reforms on the convent of La Purísima in San Miguel Allende, Chowning has shown that despite the reformers' claims that the *vida común* would curb excessive expenditure, the modifications it mandated actually resulted in greater outlays due to its "inherent inefficiencies" (*Rebellious Nuns* 197).

56. "We began to miss the food we used to have, which was well cooked and seasoned. Now with the cauldrons that feed more than a hundred people it is not possible to cook and season individual portions."

57. "Coming through the door which led to the quarters of the twelve nuns who lived separately, they began to unlock the interior convent doors and those of the dormitories. A great group of men came in and began to pass out hatchets and torches, going up even onto the convent's roof; they broke down the doors to the rooms in which they [the nuns] were sleeping for which they used ropes, chains, bolts and padlocks. So outrageous was their behavior that the Vicar hit one nun so hard that the next day she had to be bled twice because he had so badly injured her face; Sr. Redondo pulled so hard on the arm of another nun simply because she was going to help another who was terribly ill that he dislocated her shoulder [. . .] so she is now disabled. Another of the men hit a nun so hard in the chest that she was unconscious for several hours."

58. "We intend to tell Your Excellency as much as possible so as not to tire you, [but] looking first toward the greatest honor and glory of Our Lord God and so as not to put so many souls in jeopardy, we ask that you please inform our King and natural lord, whom God preserve for us."

59. "They have made many nuns believe that they as obedient daughters must embrace the common life and all its precepts and constitutions and that she who does not is guilty of mortal sin, and they not only harass us in the confessional but also from the pulpit and in private homilies."

60. "There are nuns who so regret having entered the convent that they can be heard constantly cursing the moment they took the veil; and we swear to Your Excellency, as above, that most of us have lost the pleasure and comfort of our vocation; and that perhaps we would be better off in bad marriages rather than desperate nuns living with the monster that this has become."

61. "until we were even deprived of seeing our relatives because they run from us in great horror, having seen what some have suffered."

62. "Following the fact that they did not allow any convent to elect the prelates we wanted, as the Holy Council in fact mandates, they instead harshly ordered us to elect those who his Illustriousness favored, and on the day of the elections he delivered such an outrageous sermon, in which he threatened those of us who neither wanted nor want the common life with the greatest retribution."

63. See María Justina Sarabia Viejo, "Controversias sobre la 'vida común' ante la reforma monacal femenina en México" (586).

64. "Let them [the bishop and his followers] leave us in peace to follow the religious life that we professed, wherein much virtue flourished and of which the whole world recognized the union of peace and charity that reigned in all the calced convents; and now our reputation is the opposite, so that no one wishes to become a nun seeing how dreadful the convents have become."

65. Jones is very careful to point out that this "female" authority is constructed according to a female "experience" that arises not from essential gender differences, but from the different ways men and women have been socialized throughout history. She claims that by studying gender differences from a "non-essentialist standpoint," we will come upon what she calls "different ways of knowing and seeing." She urges an examination of manifestations of "female experience" that "will provide us with such a model" ("On Authority" 127).

66. *Bandos 8* (1771–1774), exp. 8, ff. 263–66, AGN Mexico.

67. "I desire and wish that in all of the convents of my American dominions the rule of common life is kept and observed such as the same Holy Council and Sacred Canons ordered and enjoined."

68. "In order to be fully informed in the matter each and every one of the nuns will be permitted to discuss it with their confessors, directors, and with all persons of virtue, learning and counsel."

69. "Likewise the respective prelates must take great care to ensure that in the convents of their jurisdictions great peace and fraternal charity reigns amongst the nuns, ensuring the temporal well-being and spiritual solace of all with complete impartiality."

70. "experience having shown how harmful and dangerous it is to religion itself that secular persons converse and communicate with the Brides of Christ."

71. *Correspondencia de Virreyes* 13 (1774), exp. 1319, ff. 25–37, AGN Mexico.

72. "Asked the same question [. . .] she responded [. . .] that she doesn't accept the common life and that with regard to everything else, in both her name and that of the holy community, she is prepared to accept all of our sovereign's precepts (may God keep him) and this she declared and signed."

73. *Correspondencia de Virreyes* 8 (1774), exp. 1817, ff. 362–410.

74. "We, the nuns of the convent of Our Mother Santa Inés of the city of Puebla, sign this document on behalf of the others who chose to maintain the way of life they were observing when they professed."

75. "In the Royal Decree of the 21st of May of last year, 1774, in which it was stipulated that the nuns might choose, it was also laid down that the prelates kindly accept too those nuns who might choose to stay in the former way of life, and that they take great care to ensure the maintenance of great peace and charity between both groups for the temporal well-being and spiritual solace of all, with complete impartiality both for those observing the common life as well as those remaining in the former way of life."

76. "This has not been carried out here or in the other calced convents in this city. Both the Mother Superiors and those who observe the common life, who enjoy the favor of our Prelate, have treated us with the greatest disregard. They make us suffer, which we tolerate with resignation so as not to increase the discord caused by the division. And although we would never officially complain about the above stated because it has always been our desire to make up for these adversities as far as we can, we also are suffering in another way—in spiritual matters—which affects our salvation and our souls, which we cannot abandon."

77. "Many confessors have begun to hint to us that we are in a state of mortal sin and not in a state of absolution, terrifying and harassing us to such a degree that although we still believe the contrary, as your Highness pointed out in your Royal Decree, because as far as sin is concerned you would not have allowed us the freedom to choose to stay in the old way of life."

78. "Having been insulted and repeatedly fearing they would attack her, the Chaplain Don Antonio Romero came to confess her who we swear pressured her in this matter because the next day she accepted the common life."

79. "They gave her the sacrament and anointed her as she had been dangerously ill. Her confessor, Father Don Ildefonso Fuentes, attended her and comforted her, upon which observing that said confessor had not carried out what others had done [pressured her to accept *vida común*], on two occasions they deviously brought in Padre Don Joachim Castro without her requesting him, so that he could persuade her. The patient

did not bow to their wishes and instead requested that they bring back her confessor because this other one had pressured her."

80. "She always indicated that God had not called her for this change of life as proven by the serenity of her conscience before death, she again refused when the aforementioned priest urged her to die in the common life, which caused amazement because she had not spoken that day for many hours and it was proven she died in the way of life she had originally professed on the 23rd of this the month of March."

81. "Now we find ourselves faced with the dilemma that Holy Week is upon us and it will be necessary to fulfill the Church's obligations with the fact that there are no confessors, apart from those who do not want to give absolution because the others have excused themselves as we have already mentioned. We have no other recourse than to appeal to your Excellency's defense and patronage."

82. "As they fear punishment if their names were to be revealed and that they would be in greater trouble, we humbly beg your benign and paternal heart that you do not disclose the names and convent of those of us who make this complaint."

83. "Look into yourselves and take notice that the devil tempts you to move away from perfection and deprives you of the imponderable benefits offered by His superior intention. Reflect upon the eternal goods and with this good fortune you may happily carry His cross and follow in the footsteps of Jesus your husband, who suffered sorrows on His cross crowned not with flowers but with thorns."

84. An ongoing debate that kept male ecclesiastical authorities from imposing the *vida común* concerned whether the reforms actually helped or hindered the observation of the vow of poverty, which had been one of the main reasons for its original imposition (Chowning, "Convent Reform" 26).

Chapter 5. Sor Juana, Serafina de Cristo, and the Nuns of the Casa del Placer: Intellectual Alliance and Learned Community

1. "I will be studying and two servants will come to me to arbitrate their dispute; I will be writing and a friend will come to visit me, making a bad job of a good intention. [...] And this goes on continually, because the moments I dedicate to studies are those that are left over from my regular community duties, and others use these same moments to come and bother me."

2. Here I refer to Paz's monumental study *Sor Juana Inés de la Cruz o las trampas de la fe* and Puccini's *Una mujer en soledad: Una excepción en la cultura y la literatura barroca*.

3. Even feminist critics such as Stephanie Merrim have claimed solitude as the only recourse for the female scholar. In *Early Modern Women's Writing and Sor Juana Inés de la Cruz*, Merrim describes the solitude of the female writer thus: "Isolation, one must note, was often their means of negotiating a separate peace" (xxviiii).

4. "Anecdotal Self-Invention in Sor Juana's *Respuesta a Sor Filotea de la Cruz*," *CLAR* 4, no. 2 (1995): 73–83.

5. "The investigations of the last few years have revealed the existence of thousands of women who throughout the centuries, at times in communities, stimulated cultural creativity and thought, at the same time as they participated in its development."

6. Kathleen Ross has discussed the importance of the *vidas* written by nuns to the writing of the history of the colonial period. She advocates a "consideration of how these women's histories intersect with the dominant rhetorical patterns of their era—and especially with the *relación*. [. . .] The life stories of colonial nuns should be read in the context of the changing discourse of New World historical narrative. [. . .] Just as life within the convent walls reflected the complexity of the world outside, so do these nuns' narratives participate in the dramatic developments taking place in the world of history" ("Historians" 134).

7. *Letter of Serafina de Cristo* and *Engimas Offered to the House of Pleasure*. Marie-Cécile Bénassy-Berling cites both of these texts as examples of the fact that "el sorjuanismo va avanzando" (Sor Juana studies are advancing). She also celebrates the fact that they "han aclarado un elemento importante del sorjuanismo, el terreno biográfico" (have cleared up an important element in Sor Juana studies, her biography), helping to shed light on the mysterious end to Sor Juana's writing life, the so-called "conversión" that has so preoccupied critics ("Actualidad" 290).

8. María Luisa Manrique de Lara y Gonzaga, Condesa de Paredes de Nava and Marquesa de la Laguna, Vicereine of Mexico, 1680–1686.

9. According to Sor Juana, the greatest gift given to us by Jesus was in fact that he gave us no gift, in that he left us in full possession of free will. Vieira's hypothesis included a refutation of three of the greatest of the Church Fathers: St. Augustine, St. Thomas Aquinas, and St. John Chrysostom. After challenging their theories, he went on to claim that the greatest "fineza" of Jesus Christ was that he did not demand our love in exchange for his own, but rather wanted us to love one another instead as a proof of the love he had for us.

10. The letter was printed with the title *Carta atenagórica de la madre Juana Inés de la Cruz, religiosa profesa de velo y coro en el muy religioso convento de San Jerónimo [. . .] Que imprime y dedica a la misma sor Philotea de la Cruz, su estudiosa aficionada en el convento de la Santísima Trinidad de la Puebla de los Ángeles* (*Athenagorian letter written by Mother Juana Inés de la Cruz, professed choir nun of the black veil in the most religious convent of San Jerónimo [. . .] Which she prints and dedicates to the very same sister Philotea de la Cruz, her studious admirer in the convent of La Santísima Trinidad in Puebla de los Ángeles*). The Bishop of Puebla, masquerading as Sor Philotea, thus entitled the text, attaching to it his own *Carta de Sor Philotea*. However, Sor Juana gave her own text the title *Crisis de un sermón de un orador grande entre los mayores* (*Crisis of a sermon of a great orator among the greatest*).

11. According to Francisco Vidargas (*La Jornada*, September 24, 1996), the letter was eventually placed in the collection of the Biblioteca Francisco Xavier Clavijero at the Universidad Iberoamericana in Mexico City, where it was first exhibited in 1982.

12. *Carta de Serafina de Cristo, 1691*, facsimile edition, introduction and paleographic transcription by Elías Trabulse (Toluca, México: Instituto Mexiquense de Cultura, 1996).

13. In his various articles on the subject, Trabulse asserts that in the *Carta atenagórica* Sor Juana not only refutes an old sermon of Vieira's, but a more current work by Núñez de Miranda, *Comulgador penitente de la purísima* (1690), in which he maintained that the greatest "fineza" of Christ was the Eucharist. It is Trabulse's belief that with her assertion that the greatest proof of Jesus' love was to leave us in complete freedom, she was secretly censuring Núñez for having attempted to curtail her literary pursuits.

14. A main source of the scandal that ensued after the publication of Sor Juana's text was the sermon given by Spanish cleric Francisco Xavier Palavicino in the very convent where she lived, San Jerónimo, on March 10, 1691, ten days after Sor Juana dated her *Respuesta a Sor Filotea*. Although praising both Sor Juana and Vieira, Palavicino offers his own interpretation of the greatest proof of Jesus' love for humankind. More importantly, Palavicino refers directly to the furor caused by Sor Juana's *Carta atenagórica* and to a certain anonymous document critical of her that was circulating in Mexico (Alatorre and Tenorio 35). It is Palavicino who dubs the anonymous critic "el Soldado," a name that is taken up and used by Serafina.

15. One of the elements in the letter on which they disagree is the inconsistency in the gender of the addressee. Serafina begins the letter "Mi señor," but ends it "Mi señora." Alatorre and Tenorio, believing the letter is addressed to Sor Juana, regard this discrepancy as a copyist's error (79). Trabulse, believing the text to be addressed to Fernández de Santa Cruz, decides it is Serafina's way of letting him know she is aware of his transvestism in his self-styling as Sor Filotea ("La guerra" 206). Trabulse's analysis fits with the game of cross-gendering carried out by many participants in this intertextual debate, including Sor Margarida Ignácia, whose 1727 *Apología a favor de R. P. Antonio Vieira* (Lisbon) criticizing Sor Juana was supposedly written by her brother, Luis Gonçalves Pinheiro.

16. This claim from Alatorre and Tenorio's book sums up their argument for Castorena's authorship. They do attempt a more detailed textual analysis (140–46), but in my opinion fail to deliver more convincing proof than that suggested by shared elaborate styles.

17. *Proceso*, December 29, 1996, 65.

18. *Prophessiones que hazen las Religiosas de el Monasterio de Sancta Paula* (1586–1713).

19. It is important to note the difference in register of the pseudonym used by Serafina de Cristo and that used by some of the early modern English writers mentioned by Wayne and others. In England, pseudonyms with obvious political and satirical intent were commonly used in this period. Diane Purkiss cites this phenomenon with regard

to authors such as "Mary Stiff," "Virgin Want," and "John Satisfie" (83). Serafina's pseudonym is different. There appears to be no apparent play on words, although Antonio Marquet holds a different opinion. Following Elías Trabulse, he believes Serafina to be a pseudonym for Sor Juana and that the name was deliberately selected to "esconderse mostrándose" (hide in plain sight) (113). For him, "sera" stands for "será" (to be), which implies the future ("una fuerza que tiende hacia el futuro" [a force which looks to the future]), while "fina" refers back to the *Carta atenagórica* and its discussion of the "finezas de Cristo."

20. See chapter 2 for a discussion of Harvey's theory in relation to Núñez de Miranda's appropriation of the female voice in his *Cartilla de la doctrina religiosa*.

21. "For the criollo oligarchy of the seventeenth century and its intellectuals, the baroque is, as we said, a model of expression, the image of language and power, to be either venerated or subverted, according to the degree of understanding attained. In it we perceive the voice of scholasticism, Aristotelian poetics, and gongoresque ways of writing. The appropriation of this model is, to a large degree, symbolic, as well as retaliatory. This appropriation takes on political connotations when these dominant models become, let's say, opaque, calling attention to themselves, showing that what is important here is not just the appropriation of the canon, but also the values that this canon institutionalizes, values that are judged by a group of people highly aware of themselves."

22. "Having seen the Athenagorian accounts that Your Worship settled with the most perfect orator among the greatest in the world, kindly take a look at the sum of this bountiful letter in the *Epítome platónico de doña María de Ataide*." (All citations from this letter are taken from Alatorre and Tenorio's transcription included in their book *Serafina y Sor Juana*.)

23. "The truth is that on the always flowering plain of genius, he could never be a dead cypress, instead his glory lives forever, immortal."

24. The figure of the "disorderly woman" is invoked by Wayne to refer to one who openly challenges, in print, the tenets of the patriarchal order.

25. Serafina's use of Camilla as Amazonian figure has been received differently by Alatorre and Tenorio, who dismiss it as "un estereotipo": "Así como toda mujer que se distingue en la poesía (comenzando con Safo) es una 'décima Musa,' así toda mujer que ejecuta viriles acciones es una amazona" (Thus just as every woman who makes a mark in poetry (beginning with Sappho) is a "Tenth Muse," every woman who engages in virile activities is an Amazon) (52).

26. Similar to the figurative "widow's weeds," though of different hue, the Latin *in albis* (*vestibus*) refers to "white women" or the white garments traditionally worn by neophytes in the early Catholic Church between the time of their baptism on Holy Saturday (Easter eve) and "Sunday *in albis*," the first Sunday after Easter. These garments were an emblem of innocence and of the meekness of the Lamb of God. Not the most flattering image for a soldier and therefore an arch, ironic usage.

27. Alatorre and Tenorio refer to Serafina's somewhat heavy-handed style, mentioning her "afán de torcer el lenguaje para sacarle todo el jugo posible, sus alusiones y elusiones, sus metáforas, su conceptismo *à outrance*" (enthusiasm in twisting language to squeeze out all the juice, her allusions and elusions, her metaphors, her excessive conceptualizing)(62).

28. "That which was legitimately born of a fecund ingenuity in writing could not tarnish, but instead, printed, gives honorable credit to the Fathers."

29. Alatorre and Tenorio also draw attention to the repetition of the words "guerra" and "juicio" in the *quintillas*. "Guerra" is repeated four times and "juicio" fourteen. I have already drawn attention to some of the different uses to which Serafina puts the word "juicio," and it is worth commenting on another wordplay involving both words. Serafina, with her love of baroque intertextuality, is hinting at the existence of yet another text that impugned Vieira, the *Sermón del juicio*, written by the preacher Fray Manuel Guerra (59). Never one to miss a trick, Serafina strengthens her arsenal with yet another weapon that puts Sor Juana's text in company with others.

30. "In this convent of our Holy Father San Gerónimo, on February 1st 1691, she kisses the hand of Your Worship whom she loves in the Lord and for whom she desires and hopes all good things."

31. "Enigmas Offered to the Discreet Intelligence / of the Sovereign Assembly of the House of Pleasure / by their most Humble Follower / Sor Juana Inés de la Cruz, the Tenth Muse."

32. Only two known copies of the text exist. Both were located by Enrique Martínez López in Lisbon in the 1960s. There is no evidence that the manuscript ever made it to Mexico or even to Spain. See Martínez López's article "Sor Juana Inés de la Cruz en Portugal: Un desconocido homenaje y versos inéditos."

33. María Guadalupe de Lancaster y Cárdenas, Duquesa de Aveiro, 1630–1715. Sor Juana dedicated a *romance* to her, "Grande Duquesa de Aveyro" (*Obras Completas*, 1:100). Sor Juana also includes her in the list of great female intellects in the *Respuesta a Sor Filotea*. She was married in 1665 to Manuel Ponce de León, Duque de Arcos. She was a highly cultured and intelligent woman, as well as extremely devout (Sabat Rivers 121–26).

34. "the most important proof of the recognition of Sor Juana's fame, and of the solidarity that existed between lettered nuns and noble women."

35. This section of the book is in Portuguese.

36. I use *Enigmas* to refer to *all* material collected in the book produced by the Casa del Placer, including all dedicatory poems *and* Sor Juana's *redondillas*. I use "enigmas" solely to talk about the *redondillas*.

37. According to José Sánchez, literary academies did not appear in Mexico until later on in the eighteenth century, owing to the fact that the "condiciones sociales de esa época no eran propias para el desenvolvimiento y estímulo en el campo intelectual" (social conditions of the period were not suitable for the development and encourage-

ment of intellectual life) (*Academias y sociedades* 72). There were, however, *certámenes* or contests celebrating events of religious or political importance, in which different poets would participate.

38. "For social and psychological reasons man associates with others like him in order to share his interests and feelings; the coming together of the cultured class, and the expressions of feeling takes the shape of aesthetic pleasures derived from compositions written with love and inspiration. It is natural to seek refuge in a friend's company to both recount and to listen to something that gives us pleasure or pain."

39. The case of Peru was different from that of Mexico. Literary academies such as the Academia Antártica were in existence from the seventeenth century. Moreover, a woman member, known to some as Clarinda and to others as La Anónima, wrote the famous "Discurso en loor de la poesía." Another famous woman poet was Amarilis, also a pseudonym, famous for her verse correspondence with Lope de Vega, "Epístola a Belardo" (see Raquel Chang-Rodríguez's "Clarinda, Amarilis y la 'fruta nueva' del Parnaso peruano," as well as her *Poesía hispanoamericana colonial: Historia y antología*).

40. Jean Franco has identified the palace, to which milieu belong both the Condesa de Paredes and the Duquesa de Aveiro, as being one of the predominant domains of discourse during Sor Juana's day. Franco refers to "two broad discursive domains in which the symbolic repertoires of New Spain were at work. In colonial New Spain, the domains of discourse were constituted around the viceregal court and the Church" (25). The Condesa de Paredes was no longer the center of the viceregal court during the compilation of the *Enigmas*, but rather was located in Madrid at the Spanish court. I have extended Franco's "discursive domains" to include the Spanish court, which could be considered to be the "master domain" of the time.

41. In his article on the *Enigmas*, Enrique Martínez López suggests the possibility of a connection between the names of the two literary academies (55).

42. This is not the first time that a parallel has been drawn between Margaret Cavendish, Duchess of Newcastle, and Sor Juana. Stephanie Merrim included Cavendish in her book *Early Modern Women's Writing and Sor Juana Inés de la Cruz*, citing her as an example of a female writer with whom Sor Juana shared, unwittingly, "certain signal features" (xiii). Merrim analyzes both writers' interest in the complexities of fame—their reflections on their anomalous condition as published female writers of the seventeenth century—as well as their pioneering autodidactic work in the field of scientific inquiry.

43. I have used the version of the poems found in Antonio Alatorre's edition. The Martínez López edition differs slightly.

44. "And you, O fortunate Spain / this treasure that America hides within its borders / whose discourse passes from one zone to another / instructing with lightening, blinding with brilliance."

45. "And your lofty name [America, functioning metonymically for Sor Juana] in golden letters / marks time in our hearts; / memories engraved on the breast / last longer than those carved on bronze."

46. This image is reminiscent of the mystical discourse of the time, which foregrounded a bodily—almost erotic—connection with the divine. Used to suggest a strong connection between the divine realm and the Casa del Placer, it echoes throughout the women's texts and accentuates the erotic connection between the nuns of the Casa del Placer and Sor Juana.

47. "A phalanx of clergymen protect the nun's writings [...] they wage war for her and defend her against the criticisms and accusation leveled against her in Mexico."

48. "It is arguable that the arguments her advocates and panegyrists lay out outline a bitter dispute, a public debate articulated as a very often violent secret dialogue between the nuns' enemies and her supporters, and as a series of stereotypes repeated from text to text so as to praise the very qualities the nuns' detractors consider to be serious flaws."

49. "the prologues of the three volumes of Sor Juana's work published in Spain, her own works, those of her New Spanish contemporaries, and doubtlessly the letter of Sister Filotea."

Glantz also asserts, quite rightly, that her reading is supported further by the recent discovery of other texts written by Sor Juana and/or her supporters: the *Carta de Monterrey*, the *Carta de Serafina de Cristo*, and the *Enigmas ofrecidos a la Casa del Placer*.

50. "And thus they seem to me worthy of occupying one's time and awakening one's curiosity, because they do not overlook the felicitous employment of that which with effort perfects debates."

51. "discretion of an author who knows how to choose a subject matter that does not threaten the attention with its prolixity, and who is equally interested in seeing her *Enigmas* felicitously interpreted."

52. "I do not believe, in my opinion / that it needs correction, / since it possesses such respect / that only so as not to harm the royal preserve / does it seek royal protection."

53. Writing of the concept of decorum or decency ("decencia"), Margo Glantz comments, "tal pareciera que cometer una indecencia además de caer en un acto deshonesto fuese transgredir una regla social, una conducta sancionada, romper el decoro" (it would seem that to commit an indecorous act as well as to commit a dishonest one, would be to transgress a social norm, a sanctioned mode of conduct, as well as a break with decorum) (*La comparación* 237).

54. "Without further investigation / of the ideas it contains / I do not believe this book contains any impediment / since to possess high-flown thoughts / does not contravene good morals."

55. Alison Weber uses this phrase to describe Teresa of Ávila's tactic when writing *Camino de la perfección* for the nuns of her newly founded convent of San José.

56. See Michel Foucault's *The Order of Things: An Archaeology of the Human Sciences*.

57. "They thus begin to select the fundamental elements necessary to establish a ranking, and situate Sor Juana in her rightful place therein, and so get a handle on this genius that has caused so much upset, provoked so much confusion, and given rise to multiple epithets, with which the person so dubbed has been transformed into monster

or miracle, a perfect marriage of exorbitance and the bizarre. *The first thing that sets her apart is her gender. More than anything, she is a woman.*"

58. It is important to point out that other critics have designated the cataloguing of illustrious women as a pro-female gesture. I have already cited Merrim's analysis. Raquel Chang-Rodríguez comes to a similar conclusion in her discussion of the use of this technique by the seventeenth-century Peruvian poet, Clarinda, in her article "Clarinda's Catalogue of Worthy Women in Her *Discurso en Loor de la Poesía*." Both critics, however, deal with the use of the technique by women writers, a distinction Glantz herself draws with her mention of Sor Juana's *Respuesta a Sor Filotea de la Cruz*.

59. "To mention a famous woman is always to compare her with an exceptional man. It would seem that only thus could she be legitimate and only thus could her merit and the existence of feminine talent and the recognition of a category be endorsed and accepted."

60. Glantz quotes one of the panegyrists of the *Segundo volumen* who, in his praise of Sor Juana, likens her to Santa Teresa, describing them as two women who picked up the pen, eschewing more typical and less intellectual female pursuits: "pasaron al empleo de la pluma, los primorosos entretenimientos del aguja" (they moved on to the pen, leaving behind the delicate pastime of needlework) (*La comparación* 183).

61. "This volume, whose arrogant breath / O benevolent reader forever invoked! / —greatly presumes, daringly aspires— / to climb up to the celestial firmament."

62. "so much sun elevates thought / which reverent affection sponsors / where—destined for sovereign altars— / surrender becomes sacrifice."

63. There are several legends of the Muses, with differing statements as to where they lived, who they were, and how many they were in number. From the classical period in ancient history, it was generally accepted that they were nine (Grimal 298–99).

64. Both critics cite the *loa* that precedes Sor Juana's *auto sacramental San Hermenegildo* and the *Carta atenagórica* (see Martínez López 63 and Sabat Rivers 220).

65. The texts in which Sor Juana abjured worldly pursuits and excoriated herself for less-than-perfect religious observance are dated 1693, *Petición causídica*, and March 5, 1694, *Protesta que rubrica con su sangre*. In 1694 Sor Juana also returned to the spiritual guidance of Antonio Núñez de Miranda.

66. Stephanie Merrim has likened this double-sided gesture of appropriation and explosion, which she views as typical of early modern women writers, to feminist literary criticism of the 1980s. She writes: "Both are operating within an orbit still essentially dominated by the masculine (masculine theory and/or masculine literature) and are attempting to articulate spaces of feminine/feminist resistance. To *voler* or steal paternal discourse, to explode it, describes both the basically thematic and formalist thrust of 1980s feminist criticism and the erudite, intertextual baroque culture in which writers such as Sor Juana moved" (53).

67. For a detailed discussion of this topic, see Nina Scott's excellent article "'Ser mujer

ni ser ausente / no es de amarte impedimento': Los poemas de Sor Juana Inés de la Cruz a la Condesa de Paredes."

68. Few critics have written on Sor Juana's enigmas. Other than Martínez López's article following his discovery of the text, Alatorre's book-length study, and a couple of short articles by Georgina Sabat Rivers and Elias Rivers, very little mention has been made of this particular aspect of Sor Juana's poetic production. These critics disagree slightly on the interpretation of the enigmas. Martínez López considers them "perfiles del amor" (portraits of love) typical of the age, in which the writer sets up rhetorical questions designed to offer "un placer dialéctico" (dialectical delight) (64). He himself does not offer solutions to the enigmas; instead, he draws parallels with Sor Juana's other poetry to remove any doubt that the manuscript he found is genuine (64–67). Sabat Rivers and Alatorre, on the other hand, do interpret some of the riddles. The former believes that although the answer to each riddle may not necessarily be love, each one deals with related aspects of love, such as jealousy (222). Sabat Rivers offers parallels with Sor Juana's other works, believing the poet intended her readers to find the answers in her poetry, "la cual, por supuesto, las monjas conocían muy bien" (which, of course, the nuns were well aware of) (222). Alatorre believes that Sor Juana intended more than one plausible answer to each enigma (*Sor Juana Inés de la Cruz* 52).

69. I have modernized the spelling for the ease of the reader.

Conclusion

1. In this vein, Octavio Paz has written of convent life: "Lo primero que sorprende es la monotonía de este régimen. Lo extraordinario, con este género de vida, no es que unas cuantas monjas se abandonasen a piadosas o crueles excentricidades sino que no se hayan enloquecido todas. Para ciertas naturalezas poco sólidas, el tedio y las largas horas de ocio fomentaban delirios mórbidos, fantasmagóricas y no pocas veces el disgusto y horror por sus hermanas y por ellas mismas" (169). (The first surprise is the monotony of this regime. Given this way of life, it is not unusual that many nuns indulged in pious or cruel eccentricities, but rather that they did not all go mad. For certain characters of a weak nature, the tedium and long leisure hours promoted morbid and illusory fantasies and, frequently, distaste and horror of both their sisters and themselves.) See also Fernando Benítez's *Los demonios en el convento*.

2. See, for example, works by Karen Vieira Powers, Pete Sigal, and Kristine Ibsen.

3. For an interesting discussion of the role of theory in colonial Latin American studies, especially in the area of eighteenth-century studies, see Mariselle Meléndez's "Eighteenth Century Spanish America: Historical Dimensions and New Theoretical Approaches."

4. Much controversy surrounds the term "interdisciplinary" nowadays. Recent unfavorable comments in a review of new books in the field that take interdisciplinary

approaches to the study of gender and sexuality in the colonial period are not uncommon. The reviewer cautions the reader that these texts are only for "specialists with a strong stomach for theory," as they "push the boundaries of theory to an almost painful extreme" (Lipsett-Rivera 149).

Bibliography

Manuscript Sources

Archivo General de la Nación, Mexico City, Mexico:

Bandos 8 (1771–1174). Exp. 68, fojas 263–66. "El Rey: Mi Virrey, Gobernador y Capitán General del Reino de la Nueva España y Presidente de mi Real Audiencia de la Ciudad de México. Como Protector que soy de los Sagrados Cañones, y del Santo Concilio de Trento, deseo y quiero que en todos los conventos de mis dominios de América se observe y guarde la vida común. La Real Cédula dada en Aranjuez a veinte dos de mayo de mil setecientos setenta y cuatro."

Bienes Nacionales 77 (1729–1778). Exp. 20, fojas 56–85. "Doctrina cerca de la vida común de las monjas que para mejor y más acertado gobierno de los prelados eclesiásticos que intentan introducirla en los monasterios donde no se observa estampada. El patrono y maestro de las letras Benedicto XIV, Pontífice Máximo, en el tomo que escribió el Sínodo Diocesano, Lib. 13, Cap. 12, Núms. 18, 19, 20 y 21, de donde se sacó fielmente traducido a este papel. México."

Bienes Nacionales 1005 (1774). Exp. 10, fojas 12–19. "Declaraciones de las religiosas del convento de Santa Catarina sobre la vida común que guardan. México."

Correspondencia de Virreyes 8 (1774). Exp. 1817, fojas 362–92. "Las religiosas del convento de Nuestra Madre Santa Inés de la ciudad de Puebla que firmaron este escrito en consorcio de las demás que eligieron permanecer en el método de vida que se observaba cuando profesaron."

Correspondencia de Virreyes 13 (1774). Exp. 1319, fojas 25–37. "En el coro bajo de estos conventos se les leyere el referido testimonio con este su decreto y que practicada esta diligencia en el modo que se ha expresado mandó a mí su infrascripto secretario dé razón en forma del obedecimiento de la religiosas a continuación de este su decreto. Fray Isidoro Murillo. Convento de Santa Clara, Puebla."

Inquisición. Vol. 1319, exp. 6 (1794). "El Sr. Inquisidor Fiscal del Santo Oficio contra Tomás Roberto Barreto, aprendiz de platero en la casa de D. Eduardo Calderón, natural de Irapuato. María Ildefonsa de San Juan Bautista Álvarez, religiosa profesa de coro y velo negro del Real Convento de Jesús María, declara: 'Que con motivo de tener una mala amistad con una moza llamada María Gertrudis Rodríguez, la que determinó salirse del convento, quiso la declarante salirse también por no separarse de ella, y recurrió a Tomás, él que sabía que era mágico para lograrlo etc.'"

Printed Works

Águeda Méndez, Maria. "La palabra persuasiva: El poder de los confesores sobre las monjas." *Nictimene . . . sacrílega: Estudios coloniales en homenaje a Georgina Sabat-Rivers*. Ed. Mabel Moraña and Yolanda Martínez-San Miguel. Mexico City: Universidad del Claustro de Sor Juana, 2003. 101–10.

———. *Secretos del oficio: Avatares de la Inquisición Novohispana*. Mexico City: Colegio de México, 2001.

Alatorre, Antonio. "La carta de Sor Juana al Padre Núñez (1682)." *Nueva Revista de Filología Hispánica* 35, no. 2 (1987): 591–673.

———. *Sor Juana Inés de la Cruz: Enigmas ofrecidos a la Casa del Placer*. Ed. A. Alatorre. Mexico City: El Colegio de México, 1994.

Alatorre, Antonio, and Martha Lilia Tenorio. *Serafina y Sor Juana*. Mexico City: El Colegio de México, 1998.

Allen, Amy. *The Power of Feminist Theory: Domination, Resistance, Solidarity*. Boulder, Colo.: Westview Press, 1999.

Andreadis, Harriet. "The Erotics of Female Friendship in Early-Modern England." *Maids and Mistresses, Cousins and Queens: Women's Alliances in Early Modern England*. Ed. Susan Frye and Karen Robertson. Oxford: Oxford University Press, 1999. 241–58.

Arenal, Electa, and Stacey Schlau. "Escribiendo yo, escribiendo ella, escribiendo nosotras: On Co-Laboring." *Journal of Hispanic Philology* 17, no. 3 (Spring 1989): 214–29.

———. "'Leyendo yo y escribiendo ella': The Convent as Intellectual Community." *Tulsa Studies in Women's Literature*, no. 1 (1995): 39–49.

———. *Untold Sisters: Hispanic Nuns in Their Own Works*. Albuquerque: University of New Mexico Press, 1989.

Auerbach, Nina. *Communities of Women: An Idea in Fiction*. Cambridge, Mass.: Harvard University Press, 1978.

Bachelard, Gaston. *The Poetics of Space*. Trans. Maria Jolas. Boston: Beacon Press, 1994.

Barthes, Roland. *The Pleasure of the Text*. Trans. Richard Miller. New York: Hill and Wang, 1975.

Bassein, Beth Ann. *Women and Death: Linkages in Western Thought and Literature*. Westport, Conn.: Greenwood Press, 1984.

Baudot, George, and María Águeda Méndez, eds. *Amores prohibidos: La palabra condenada en el México de los Virreyes. Antología de coplas y versos censurados por la Inquisición de México*. Mexico City: Siglo Veintiuno, 1997.

Bauman, Zygmunt. *Community: Seeking Safety in an Insecure World*. Cambridge: Polity Press, 2001.

Behar, Ruth. "Sex and Sin, Witchcraft and the Devil in Late Colonial Mexico." *American Ethnologist* 14, no. 1 (February 1987): 34–54.

———. "Sexual Witchcraft: Colonialism and Women's Powers: Views from the Mexican Inquisition." *Sexuality and Marriage in Colonial Latin America*. Ed. Asunción Lavrin. Lincoln: University of Nebraska Press, 1989. 178–206.

Bénassy-Berling, Marie-Cécile. "Actualidad del sorjuanismo (1994–1999)." *Colonial Latin American Review* 9, no. 2 (2000): 277–92.

———. *Humanismo y religión en Sor Juana Inés de la Cruz*. Mexico City: UNAM, 1983.

Benítez, Fernando. *Los demonios en el convento: Sexo y religión en la Nueva España*. Mexico City: Ediciones Era, 1985.

Bernstein, Marcelle. *The Nuns*. Philadelphia: Lippincott, 1976.

Bjelic, Dušan. *Galileo's Pendulum: Science, Sexuality, and the Body-Instrument Link*. Albany: State University of New York Press, 2003.

Blanchot, Maurice. *The Unavowable Community*. Trans. Pierre Joris. Barrytown, N.Y.: Station Hill Press, 1988.

Bloch, Howard. *Medieval Misogyny and the Invention of Western Romantic Love*. Chicago: University of Chicago Press, 1991.

Bobb, Bernard E. *The Viceregency of Antonio María Bucareli in New Spain, 1771–1779*. Austin: University of Texas Press, 1962.

Borda, Andrés de. *Práctica de confesores de monjas, en que se explican los quatro votos de obedencia, pobreza, casstidad* [sic]*, y clausura, por modo de diálogo*. Mexico City: F. de Ribera Calderón, 1708.

Bordo, Susan. "The Body and the Reproduction of Femininity." *Writing on the Body: Female Embodiment and Feminist Theory*. Ed. Kate Conboy et al. New York: Columbia University Press, 1997. 90–110.

Brading, D. A. *Church and State in Bourbon Mexico: The Diocese of Michoacán, 1749–1810*. Cambridge: Cambridge University Press, 1994.

———. *The First America: The Spanish Monarchy, Creole Patriots, and the Liberal State, 1492–1867*. Cambridge: Cambridge University Press, 1991.

Bravo, María Dolores. "El costumbrero del Real Convento de Jesús María de Mexico." *Mujer y cultura en la colonia Hispanoamericana*. Ed. Mabel Moraña. Pittsburgh: Instituto Internacional de Literatura Iberoamericana, 1996. 159–68.

———. "Erotismo y represión en un texto del Padre Antonio Núñez de Miranda." *Literatura mexicana* 1 (1990): 127–34.

———. "La excepción y la regla: Una monja según el discurso oficial y según Sor Juana." *Y diversa de mí misma entre vuestras plumas ando: Homenaje internacional a Sor Juana Inés de la Cruz*. Ed. Sara Poot Herrera. Mexico City: El Colegio de México, 1993. 35–42.

Brooks, Peter. *Troubling Confessions: Speaking Guilt in Law and Literature*. Chicago: University of Chicago Press, 2000.

Brown, Judith C. *Immodest Acts: The Life of a Lesbian Nun in Renaissance Italy*. New York: Oxford University Press, 1986.

Bullough, Vern. "Homosexuality and Catholic Priests." *Free Inquiry Magazine* 22, no. 3 (2002): 18–20.

Burns, Kathryn. *Colonial Habits: Convents and the Spiritual Economy of Cuzco*. Durham, N.C.: Duke University Press, 1999.

Burton, Robert. *The Anatomy of Melancholy*. Ed. Floyd Dell and Paul Jordan-Smith. New York: Farrar and Rinehart, 1927.

Butler, Judith. "Performative Acts and Gender Constitution: An Essay in Phenomenology and Feminist Theory." *Theatre Journal* 49, no. 1 (December 1988): 519–31.

Calleja, Diego. *Vida de Sor Juana Inés de la Cruz*. Toluca, Mexico: Instituto Mexiquense de la Cultura, 1996.

Carrasco, Rafael. *Inquisición y represión sexual en Valencia: Historia de los sodomitas, 1565–1785*. Barcelona: Laertes, 1985.

Catholic Encyclopedia Online. February 2003. <http://www.newadvent.org/cathen>.

Chang-Rodríguez, Raquel. "Clarinda, Amarilis, y la 'fruta nueva' del Parnaso peruano." *Colonial Latin American Review* 4, no. 2 (1998): 181–96.

———. "Clarinda's Catalogue of Worthy Women in Her *Discurso en Loor de la Poesía* (1608)." *Calíope* 4, no. 1–2 (1998): 94–106.

Chang-Rodríguez, Raquel, and Antonio R. de la Campa, eds. *Poesía hispanoamericana colonial: Historia y antología*. Madrid: Alhambra, 1985.

Chartier, Roger. *The Order of Books: Readers, Authors, and Libraries in Europe between the Fourteenth and Eighteenth Centuries*. Trans. Lydia Cochrane. Palo Alto, Calif.: Stanford University Press, 1994.

Chedgzoy, Kate. "'For Virgin Buildings Oft Brought Forth': Fantasies of Convent Sexuality." Ed. Rebecca D'Monté and Nicole Pohl. *Female Communities, 1600–1800: Literary Visions and Cultural Realities*. London: Macmillan Press Ltd., 2000. 53–75.

Chowning, Margaret. "Convent Reform, Catholic Reform, and Bourbon Reform in Eighteenth Century New Spain: The View from the Nunnery." *Hispanic American Historical Review* 85, no. 1 (February 2005): 1–36.

———. *Rebellious Nuns: The Troubled History of a Mexican Convent, 1752–1863*. New York: Oxford University Press, 2006.

Cohen, Sherrill. *The Evolution of Women's Asylums since 1500: From Refuges for Ex-Prostitutes to Shelters for Battered Women*. New York: Oxford University Press, 1992.

Colahan, Clark. *The Visions of Sor María de Agreda: Writing Knowledge and Power*. Tucson: University of Arizona Press, 1994.

Crompton, Louis. "The Myth of Lesbian Impunity: Capital Laws from 1270–1791." *Journal of Homosexuality* 6, no. 1–2 (1980/1981): 11–25.

Davis, Natalie Zemon. Foreword. *The Book of the City of Ladies*. Trans. Earl Jeffrey Richards. [1982] N.Y.: Persea Books, 1998. xv–xxiii.

Dickens, Charles. *The Mystery of Edwin Drood*. [1870] London: Collins, 1956.

———. *Pickwick Papers*. Oxford and New York: Oxford University Press, 1988.

D'Monté, Rebecca. "Mirroring Female Power: Separatist Spaces in the Plays of Margaret

Cavendish, Duchess of Newcastle." Ed. Rebecca D'Monté and Nicole Pohl. *Female Communities, 1600–1800: Literary Visions and Cultural Realities*. London: Macmillan Press Ltd., 2000. 93–110.

D'Monté, Rebecca, and Nicole Pohl, eds. Introduction. *Female Communities, 1600–1800: Literary Visions and Cultural Realities*. London: Macmillan Press Ltd., 2000. 1–27.

Dollimore, Jonathan. *Death, Desire and Loss in Western Culture*. New York: Routledge, 1998.

———. *Sexual Dissidence: Augustine to Wilde, Freud to Foucault*. Oxford: Oxford University Press, 1991.

Domínguez Ortiz, Antonio. *Sociedad y estado en el siglo XVIII*. Madrid: Editorial Ariel, 1990.

Donoghue, Emma. *Passions between Women: British Lesbian Culture, 1668–1801*. London: Scarlet Press, 1993.

Dopico-Black, Georgina. *Perfect Wives, Other Women: Adultery and Inquisition in Early Modern Spain*. Durham, N.C., and London: Duke University Press, 2001.

Easton, Martha. "Pain, Torture, and Death in the Huntington Library's *Legenda aurea*." *Gender and Holiness: Men, Women and Saints in Late Medieval Europe*. Ed. Samantha Riches and Sarah Salih. London: Routledge, 2002. 49–64.

Enright, D. J., and David Rawlinson, eds. *The Oxford Book of Friendship*. Oxford and New York: Oxford University Press, 1991.

Faderman, Lillian. "The Morbidification of Love between Women by Nineteenth-Century Sexologists." *Journal of Homosexuality* 4, no. 1 (1978): 73–90.

———. *Surpassing the Love of Men: Romantic Friendship and Love between Women from the Renaissance to the Present*. New York: Morrow, 1981.

Ferrer Chivite, Manuel. "Sustratos sociológicos de la literatura burlesca: Burlerías monjiles." *Tiempo de Burlas: En torno a la literatura burlesca del Siglo de Oro*. Ed. Javier Huerta Calvo et al. Madrid: Editorial Verbum. 37–65.

Foucault, Michel. *Discipline and Punish: The Birth of the Prison*. Trans. Alan J. Sheridan. New York: Vintage Books, 1979.

———. *The History of Sexuality*. Trans. Robert Hurley. New York: Pantheon Books, 1978.

———. *Madness and Civilization: A History of Insanity in the Age of Reason*. Trans. Richard Howard. New York: Vintage, 1973.

———. *The Order of Things: An Archaeology of the Human Sciences*. New York: Vintage Books, 1994.

Franco, Jean. *Plotting Women: Gender and Representation in Mexico*. New York: Columbia University Press, 1989.

Friedman, Marilyn. "Feminism and Modern Friendship: Dislocating the Community." *Ethics* 99, no. 2 (January 1989): 275–90.

Frye, Susan, and Karen Robertson, eds. Introduction. *Maids and Mistresses, Cousins and Queens: Women's Alliances in Early Modern England*. Oxford: Oxford University Press, 1999. 3–17.

Gage, Thomas. *Travels in the New World: The English-American or A New Survey of the West Indies*. Ed. and introduction J. Eric S. Thompson. Westport, Conn.: Greenwood Press, 1981.

Giles, Mary E., ed. Introduction. *Women in the Inquisition: Spain and the New World*. Baltimore: Johns Hopkins University Press, 1999. 1–15.

Glantz, Margo. "El cuerpo monacal y sus vestiduras." *Mujer y cultura en la colonia Hispanoamericana*. Ed. Mabel Moraña. Pittsburgh: Instituto Internacional de Literatura Iberoamericana, 1996. 171–82.

———."La ascesis y las rateras noticias de la tierra: Manuel Fernández de Santa Cruz, Obispo de Puebla." *Sor Juana Inés de la Cruz y sus contemporáneos*. Ed. Margo Glantz. Mexico City: CONDUMEX, 1998. 271–90.

———. *La comparación y la hipérbole*. Mexico City: Conaculta, 1999.

Gossy, Mary. "Skirting the Question: Lesbians and María de Zayas." *Hispanisms and Homosexualities*. Ed. Sylvia Molloy and Robert McKee Irwin. Durham, N.C., and London: Duke University Press, 1998. 19–28.

Graham, Elspeth et al. "Pondering All These Things in Her Heart: Aspects of Secrecy in the Autobiographical Writings of Seventeenth-Century Women." *Women's Lives/Women's Times: New Essays on Auto/Biography*. Ed. Trev Lynn Broughton and Linda Anderson. Albany: State University of New York Press, 1997. 51–72.

Greenleaf, Richard. "Historiography of the Mexican Inquisition: Evolution of Interpretations and Methodologies." *Cultural Encounters: The Impact of the Inquisition on Spain and the New World*. Ed. Mary Elizabeth Perry and Anne J. Cruz. Berkeley: University of California Press, 1991. 248–76.

Grimal, Pierre. *The Dictionary of Classical Mythology*. Trans. A. R. Maxwell-Hyslop. Oxford: Blackwell Publishers, Ltd., 1986.

Grosz, Elizabeth. *Space, Time, and Perversion: Essays on the Politics of Bodies*. New York and London: Routledge, 1995.

Gruzinski, Serge. "Las cenizas del deseo: Homosexuales novohispanos a mediados del siglo XVII." *De la santidad a la perversión o porqué no se cumplía la ley de Dios en la sociedad novohispana*. Ed. Sergio Ortega. Mexico City: Editorial Grijalbo, 1986. 255–81.

Halperin, David. "Forgetting Foucault: Acts, Identities, and the History of Sexuality." *Representations* 63 (Summer 1998): 94–120.

Harbison, Craig. *The Art of the Northern Renaissance*. London: Calman and King, 1995.

Harrington Becker, Trudy. "Ambiguity and the Female Warrior: Vergil's Camilla." *Electronic Antiquity* 4, no. 1 (August 1997). 15 December 2002 <http://scholar.lib.vt.edu/ejournals/ElAnt>.

Hartsock, Nancy. "Community/Sexuality/Gender: Rethinking Power." *Revisioning the Political: Feminist Reconstructions of Traditional Concepts in Western Political Thought*. Ed. Nancy J. Hirschmann and Christine Di Stefano. Boulder, Colo.: Westview Press, 1996. 27–49.

———. "Foucault on Power: A Theory for Women?" *Feminism/Postmodernism*. Ed. Linda Nicholson. New York and London: Routledge, 1990. 157–75.

Harvey, Elizabeth. *Ventriloquized Voices: Feminist Theory and English Renaissance Texts.* London and New York: Routledge, 1992.

Higgs, David. "Tales of Two Carmelites: Inquisitorial Narratives from Portugal and Brazil." *Infamous Desire: Male Homosexuality in Colonial Latin America.* Ed. Pete Sigal. Chicago: University of Chicago Press, 2003.

Hodgkin, Katharine. "Dionys Fitzherbert and the Anatomy of Madness." *Voicing Women: Gender and Sexuality in Early Modern Writing.* Ed. Kate Chedgzoy, Melanie Hansen, and Suzanne Trill. Keele, Staffordshire: Keele University Press, 1996. 69–92.

Holler, Jacqueline. *"Escogidas Plantas": Nuns and Beatas in Mexico City, 1531–1601.* New York: Columbia University Press, 2002.

Huizinga, Johan. *Homo Ludens: A Study of the Element of Play in Culture.* New York: Roy Publishers, 1950.

Ibsen, Kristine. "The Hiding Places of My Power: Sebastiana Josefa de la Santísima Trinidad and the Hagiographic Representation of the Body in Colonial Spanish America." *Colonial Latin American Review* 7, no. 2 (1998): 251–70.

———. *Women's Spiritual Autobiography in Colonial Spanish America.* Gainesville: University Press of Florida, 1999.

Ilarione da Bergamo, Fra. *Daily Life in Colonial Mexico: The Journey of Friar Ilarione da Bergamo, 1761–1768.* Trans. William J. Orr. Ed. W. J. Orr and Robert Miller. Norman: University of Oklahoma Press, 2000.

Jackson, Stanley W. *Melancholia and Depression: From Hippocratic Times to Modern Times.* New Haven: Yale University Press, 1986.

Johnson, Penelope. *Equal in Monastic Profession: Religious Women in Medieval France.* Chicago: University of Chicago Press, 1991.

Jones, Ann Rosalind. *The Currency of Eros: Women's Love Lyric in Europe, 1540–1620.* Bloomington: Indiana University Press, 1990.

Jones, Kathleen B. "On Authority: Or, Why Women Are Not Entitled to Speak." *Feminism and Foucault: Reflections on Resistance.* Ed. Irene Diamond and Lee Quinley. Boston: Northeastern University Press, 1988. 119–33.

———. "What Is Authority's Gender?" *Revisioning the Political: Feminist Reconstructions of Traditional Concepts in Western Political Thought.* Ed. Nancy J. Hirschmann and Christine Di Stefano. Boulder, Colo.: Westview Press, 1996. 61–79.

King, Margaret. "Book-Lined Cells: Women and Humanism in the Early Italian Renaissance." *Beyond Their Sex: Learned Women of the European Past.* Ed. Patricia Labalme. New York: New York University Press, 1980. 66–90.

Kuznesof, Elizabeth Ann. "Ethnic and Gender Influences on 'Spanish' Creole Society." *Colonial Latin American Review* 4, no. 1 (1995): 153–76.

Landy, Francis. "The Song of Songs." *The Literary Guide to the Bible.* Ed. Robert Alter and Frank Kermode. Cambridge, Mass: Harvard University Press, 1987. 305–19.

Lavrin, Asunción. "Ecclesiastical Reform of Nunneries in New Spain in the Eighteenth Century." *The Americas* 22 (1965): 182–203.

———. "La celda y el siglo: Epístolas conventuales." *Mujer y cultura en la colonia Hispanoamericana*. Ed. Mabel Moraña. Pittsburgh: Instituto Internacional de Literatura Iberoamericana, 1996. 139–60.

———. "Value and Meaning of Monastic Life for Nuns in Colonial Mexico." *The Catholic Historical Review* 58, no. 3 (1972): 367–87.

Lehfeldt, Elizabeth. "Sacred and Secular Spaces: The Role of Religious Women in Golden Age Valladolid." Diss. Indiana University, 1996.

Lipsett-Rivera, Sonya. "Many 'Others': The Colonial Project, Women, and Sexuality." *Colonial Latin American Review* 11, no. 1 (2002): 147–50.

Loreto López, Rosalva. *Los conventos femeninos y el mundo urbano de la Puebla de los Ángeles del siglo XVIII*. Mexico City: Colegio de México, 2000.

Luciani, Frederick. "Anecdotal Self-Invention in Sor Juana's *Respuesta a Sor Filotea*." *Colonial Latin American Review*, no. 2 (1995): 73–83.

Lynch, John. *Bourbon Spain, 1700–1808*. London: Blackwell, 1989.

Makowski, Elizabeth. *Canon Law and Cloistered Women: Periculoso and Its Commentators, 1298–1545*. Washington, D.C.: The Catholic University of America Press, 1997.

Marquet, Antonio. "Para atravesar el espejo: De Sor Juana a Serafina de Cristo." *Sor Juana y Vieira: Trescientos años después*. Ed. K. Josu Bijuesca and Pablo A. J. Brescia. Santa Barbara, Calif.: Center for Portuguese Studies, Dept. of Spanish and Portuguese, UC Santa Barbara, 1998. 113–26.

Martínez López, Enrique. "Sor Juana Inés de la Cruz en Portugal: Un desconocido homenaje y versos inéditos." *Revista de Literatura*, no. 33 (1968): 33–54.

McKnight, Kathryn. *The Mystic of Tunja: The Writings of Madre Castillo, 1671–1742*. Amherst: University of Massachusetts Press, 1997.

McNamara, Jo Ann. "*De Quibusdam Mulieribus*: Reading Women's History from Hostile Sources." *Medieval Women and the Sources of Medieval History*. Ed. Joel T. Rosenthal. Athens, Ga.: University of Georgia Press, 1990. 237–58.

———. *Sisters in Arms: Catholic Nuns through Two Millennia*. Cambridge, Mass.: Harvard University Press, 1996.

Meléndez, Mariselle. "Eighteenth Century Spanish America: Historical Dimensions and New Theoretical Approaches." *Revista de Estudios Hispánicos* 34, no. 3 (2001): 615–32.

Merrim, Stephanie. *Early Modern Women's Writing and Sor Juana Inés de la Cruz*. Nashville, Tenn.: Vanderbilt University Press, 1999.

Mignolo, Walter. *The Darker Side of the Renaissance: Literacy, Territoriality, and Colonization*. Ann Arbor: University of Michigan Press, 1995.

Moraes e Silva, Antonio de (1755–1824). *Grande dicionário da lingua portuguesa*. Lisbon: Editorial Confluência, 1949–59.

Moraña, Mabel. *Viaje al silencio: Exploraciones del discurso barroco*. México, D.F: UNAM, 1998.

———, ed. Introduction. *Mujer y cultura en la colonia Hispanoamericana*. Pittsburgh: Instituto Internacional de Literatura Iberoamericana, 1996. 7–22.

Muriel, Josefina. "Sor Juana Inés de la Cruz y los escritos del Padre Antonio Núñez de Miranda." *Y diversa de mí misma entre vuestras plumas ando: Homenaje internacional a Sor Juana Inés de la Cruz*. Ed. Sara Poot Herrera. Mexico City: El Colegio de México, 1993. 71–84.

Myers, Kathleen Ann. "Crossing Boundaries: Defining the Field of Female Religious Writing in Colonial Latin America." *Colonial Latin American Review* 9, no. 2 (2000): 151–65.

———. "The Mystic Triad in Colonial Mexican Nuns' Discourse: Divine Author, Visionary Scribe, and Clerical Mediator." *Colonial Latin American Historical Review* 6, no. 4 (Fall 1997): 479–524.

Nancy, Jean-Luc. *The Inoperative Community*. Ed. Peter Connor et al. Trans. Peter Connor. Minneapolis: University of Minnesota Press, 1991.

Newcastle, Margaret Cavendish, Duchess of. *The Convent of Pleasure and Other Plays*. Ed. Anne Shaver. Baltimore: Johns Hopkins University Press, 1999.

New International Version Study Bible. Grand Rapids, Mich.: Zondervan, 2001.

Núñez de Miranda, Antonio. *Cartilla de la doctrina religiosa y Plática doctrinal*. Mexico City: A. Valdés, 1831.

Parker, Alan Michael, and Mark Willhardt. "The Cross-Gendered Poem." *The Routledge Anthology of Cross-Gendered Verse*. Ed. Alan Michael Parker and Mark Willhardt. London and New York: Routledge, 1996. 193–210.

Paz, Octavio. *Sor Juana Inés de la Cruz o las trampas de la fe*. 1982. Mexico City: Fondo de Cultura Económica, 1998.

Peace, Mary. "The Economy of Nymphomania: Luxury, Virtue, Sentiment, and Desire in Mid-Eighteenth-Century Medical Discourse." *At the Borders of the Human: Beasts, Bodies, and Natural Philosophy in the Early Modern Period*. Ed. Erica Fudge et al. New York: Palgrave, 2002. 240–62.

Perelmuter, Rosa. "La estructura retórica de la *Respuesta a Sor Filotea de la Cruz*." *Hispanic Review* 51, no. 2 (Spring 1983): 147–58.

Perry, Mary Elizabeth. *Gender and Disorder in Early Modern Seville*. Princeton, N.J.: Princeton University Press, 1990.

Petroff, Elizabeth A., ed. *Medieval Women's Visionary Literature*. New York: Oxford University Press, 1986.

Phelan, Shane. "All the Comforts of Home: The Genealogy of Community." *Revisioning the Political: Feminist Reconstructions of Traditional Concepts in Western Political Thought*. Ed. Nancy J. Hirschmann and Christine Di Stefano. Boulder, Colo.: Westview Press, 1996. 235–50.

Pisan, Christine de. *The Book of the City of Ladies*. Trans. Earl Jeffrey Richards. New York: Persea Books, 1998.

Powers, Karen Vieira. "Conquering Discourses of 'Sexual Conquest': Of Women, Language, and *Mestizaje*." *Colonial Latin American Review* 11, no. 1 (2002): 7–31.

Puccini, Darío. *Una mujer en soledad: Una excepción en la cultura y la literatura barroca*. Trans. Esther Benítez. Mexico City: Fondo de Cultura Económica, 1997.

Purkiss, Diane. "Material Girls: The Seventeenth-Century Woman Debate." Ed. Clare Brant and Diane Purkiss. *Women, Texts and Histories, 1575–1760*. London: Routledge, 1992. 69–101.
Ramos Medina, Manuel. *Imagen de santidad en un mundo profano*. Mexico City: Universidad Iberoamericana, 1980.
Raymond, Janice. *A Passion for Friends: Toward a Philosophy of Female Affection*. Boston: Beacon Press, 1986.
Real Academia Española. *Diccionario de Autoridades*. Madrid: Imprenta de Francisco del Hierro, 1737.
Ross, Kathleen. *The Baroque Narrative of Carlos de Sigüenza y Góngora: A New World Paradise*. New York: Cambridge University Press, 1993.
———. "Historians of the Conquest and Colonization of the New World, 1550–1620." *Cambridge History of Latin American Literature*, vol. 1. Ed. Roberto González Echevarría and Enrique Pupo-Walker. Cambridge: Cambridge University Press, 1996. 101–42.
Rousseau, G. S. "'A Strange Pathology': Hysteria in the Early Modern World, 1500–1800." *Hysteria beyond Freud*. Ed. Sander L. Gilman et al. Berkeley and Los Angeles: University of California Press, 1993. 91–221.
Rubial, Antonio. *Los libros del deseo*. Mexico City: Instituto Nacional de Antropología e Historia, 1996.
———. "Varones en comunidad: Los conventos urbanos de los mendicantes en el siglo XVII novohispano. *Tepotzotlán y la Nueva España*. Ed. María del Consuelo Maquívar. Mexico City: Instituto Nacional de Antropología e Historia, 1994. 162–74.
Sabat Rivers, Georgina. *En busca de Sor Juana*. Mexico City: UNAM, 1998.
Sabat Rivers, Georgina, and Elias L. Rivers. "Sor Juana Inés de la Cruz: *Los enigmas* y sus ediciones." *Revista Iberoamericana*, no. 172–73 (July–December 1995): 677–84.
Salazar, Nuria. "Niñas, viudas, mozas y esclavas en la clausura monjil." *La América abundante de Sor Juana*. Ed. María del Consuelo Maquívar. Mexico City: Instituto Nacional de Antropología e Historia, 1995. 161–88.
———. *La vida común en los conventos de monjas de la ciudad de Puebla*. Puebla, Mexico: Biblioteca Ángelopolitana, 1990.
Sampson Vera Tudela, Elisa. *Colonial Angels: Narratives of Gender and Spirituality in Mexico, 1580–1750*. Austin: University of Texas Press, 2000.
Sánchez, José. *Academias literarias del Siglo de Oro español*. Madrid: Gredos, 1961.
———. *Academias y sociedades literarias de México*. Chapel Hill: University of North Carolina Press, 1951.
Sarabia Viejo, María Justina. "Controversias sobre la 'vida común' ante la reforma monacal femenina en México." *El monacato femenino en el imperio español: Monasterios, beaterios, recogimientos y colegios*. Ed. Manuel Ramos Medina. Mexico City: Condumex, 1995. 583–92.
Scarry, Elaine. *On Beauty and Being Just*. Princeton, N.J.: Princeton University Press, 1999.

Schlau, Stacey. *Spanish American Women's Use of the Word: Colonial through Contemporary Narratives*. Tucson: University of Arizona Press, 2001.

Schroeder, H. J. *The Canons and Decrees of the Council of Trent*. Rockford, Ill.: TAN Books and Publications, 1994.

Scott, Joan Wallach. "Gender: A Useful Category of Historical Analysis." *American Historical Review* 91 (1986): 1053–1073.

Scott, Nina M. "'Ser mujer ni ser ausente / no es de amarte impedimento': Los poemas de Sor Juana Inés de la Cruz a la Condesa de Paredes." *Y diversa de mí misma entre vuestras plumas ando: Homenaje a Sor Juana Inés de la Cruz*. Ed. Sara Poot Herrera. Mexico City: El Colegio de México, 1993. 159–70.

Segel, Harold B. *The Baroque Poem: A Comparative Survey*. New York: E. F. Dutton & Co., 1974.

Sharp, Ronald A. *Friendship and Literature: Spirit and Form*. Durham, N.C.: Duke University Press, 1986.

Shaver, Anne, ed. Introduction. *The Convent of Pleasure and Other Plays*. Baltimore: Johns Hopkins University Press, 1999. 1–21.

Sierra Nava-Lasa, Luis. *El Cardenal Lorenzana y la Ilustración*. Madrid: Fundación Universitaria Española, 1975.

Sigal, Pete. *From Moon Goddesses to Virgins: The Colonization of Yucatecan Maya Sexual Desire*. Austin: University of Texas Press, 2000.

Sigüenza y Góngora, Carlos. *Paraíso Occidental*. Mexico City: CONACULTA, 1995.

Simón Palmer, María del Carmen. "La higiene y la medicina de la mujer española a través de los libros (s. XVI–XIX)." *La mujer en la historia de España (Siglos XVI–XX): Actas de la II Jornada de Investigaciones Interdisciplinarias*. Madrid: Universidad Autónoma, 1983. 71–84.

Smith-Rosenberg, Carroll. "The Female World of Love and Ritual: Relations Between Women in Nineteenth-Century America." *Signs* 1, no. 1 (1975): 1–29.

Sor Juana Inés de la Cruz. *The Answer/La respuesta*. Ed. and trans. Electa Arenal and Amanda Powell. New York: The Feminist Press at the City University of New York, 1994.

———. *Enigmas ofrecidos a la Casa del Placer*. Ed. Antonio Alatorre. Mexico City: El Colegio de México, 1994.

———. *Obras completas I: Lírica personal*. Ed. Alfonso Méndez Plancarte. Mexico City: Fondo de Cultura Económica, 1951.

Stallybrass, Peter. "Patriarchal Territories: The Body Enclosed." *Rewriting the Renaissance: The Discourses of Sexual Difference in Early Modern Europe*. Ed. Margaret Ferguson, Maureen Quilligan, and Nancy J. Vickers. Chicago: University of Chicago Press, 1986. 123–44.

Starobinski, Jean. *History of the Treatment of Melancholy from the Earliest Times to 1900*. Basel, Switzerland: J. R. Geigy, 1962.

Teresa of Ávila, Saint. *El camino de perfección*. Madrid: Espasa-Calpe, 1969.

Tomás y Valiente, Francisco. "El crimen y pecado contra natura." *Sexo barroco y otras trans-*

gresiones premodernas. Ed. Tomás y Valiente et al. Madrid: Alianza Editorial, 1990. 33–56.

Trabulse, Elías. *Los años finales de Sor Juana: Una interpretación (1688–1695)*. Mexico City: Condumex, 1995.

———. *El enigma de Serafina de Cristo: Acerca de un manuscrito inédito de Sor Juana Inés de la Cruz, 1691*. Toluca, Mexico: Instituto Mexiquense de Cultura, 1995.

———. "La guerra de las finezas: La otra respuesta a Sor Filotea en un manuscrito inédito de 1691." *Mujer y cultura en la colonia Hispanoamericana*. Ed. Mabel Moraña. Pittsburgh: Instituto Internacional de Literatura Iberoamericana, 1996. 203–16.

Traub, Valerie. *Desire and Anxiety: Circulations of Anxiety in Shakespearean Drama*. New York: Routledge, 1992.

———. "The (In)significance of 'Lesbian' Desire in Early Modern England." *Queering the Renaissance*. Ed. Jonathan Goldberg. Durham, N.C., and London: Duke University Press, 1994. 62–83.

Trill, Suzanne. "Engendering Penitence: Nicholas Breton and 'The Countesse of Penbrooke.'" *Voicing Women: Gender and Sexuality in Early Modern Writing*. Ed. Kate Chedgzoy et al. Keele, Staffordshire: Keele University Press, 1996. 25–44.

Wayne, Valerie. "The Dearth of the Author: Anonymity's Allies and *Swetnam the Womanhater*." *Maids and Mistresses, Cousins and Queens: Women's Alliances in Early Modern England*. Ed. Susan Frye and Karen Robertson. Oxford: Oxford University Press, 1999. 221–40.

Weber, Alison. *Teresa of Avila and the Rhetoric of Femininity*. Princeton, N.J.: Princeton University Press, 1990.

Index

Abbess, 32–36, 55, 63, 82, 190n16, 203n50, 206n30; females as, 2; Heloise, 2; as mother, 12, 27, 194n28; power of, 11; of Sor María Josefa, 72, 79. *See also* Mother Superior
Active enclosure, 189n8
Aeneid (Virgil), 137, 138
Aguiar y Seijas, Francisco, 58, 64–65, 131, 200n30
Alatorre, Antonio, 132, 137, 158, 167, 214n16, 215n25, 216n27
Allen, Amy, 13–14
Amazon women, 138–39, 215n25
Ambrose of Milan, 7
Amistad particular, 59, 199n18, 201n37. *See also* Mala amistad
Ana María de los Dolores, 124
Andreadis, Harriet, 150–51
Arenal, Electa, 128–29
Arendt, Hannah, 13–14, 103, 207n38
Auerbach, Nina, 129
Authority, 146; compassionate, 116–17; women challenging ecclesiastic, 13

Bachelard, Gaston, 144
Baglivi, Georgio, 70
Baldung-Grien, Hans, 45
Baroque wordplay, 139

Barreto, Joseph Tomás Roberto, 51–80, 181, 197n1
Barthes, Roland, 153
Bassein, Beth Ann, 42, 44
Bauman, Zygmunt, 144, 174
Beauty, 164
Becker, Trudy Harrington, 138
Behar, Ruth, 75
Benedict XIV (Pope), 87
Bernstein, Marcelle, 67
Bienville, M. D. T., 88
Bjelic, Dušan, 199n16
Blazing World (Cavendish), 148
Bleak House (Dickens), 176–77
Bloch, Howard, 189n7
Bobb, Bernard E., 95
Boccacio, Giovanni, 160
Body: mortification of, 44; Núñez on nun's, 41–46; relinquished to God, 40–41; sacrificing, 23, 24; submission of, 191n3. *See also* Female body
Boniface VIII (Pope), 3, 58; decree influence on women, 5
The Book of the City of Ladies (de Pisan), 89
Borda, Andrés de, 58, 65, 66, 200n34
Borromeo, Carlo, 101
Bourbon reforms, 85–87
Brading, David, 85, 95, 204n8

Bravo, María Dolores, 32; on *Plática doctrinal*, 49
Bride of Christ, 36–37, 38, 100, 194–95n34, 211n70
Brooks, Peter, 77, 78, 79
Brothels, convents compared to, 7, 26–27, 31, 193n20
Bullough, Vern, 57

Calderón, Don Eduardo, 52, 181
Camino de perfección (Teresa of Ávila), 59
Carrasco, Rafael, 56–57
Carta atenagórica (Letter Worthy of Athena), 130, 132, 140
Carta de Serafina de Cristo (Letter of Serafina de Cristo), 16, 130–32
Carta de Sor Filotea, 130–31
Cartilla de la doctrina religiosa (Núñez de Miranda), 17–50
Casa del Placer: aristocracy and, 158; clandestine nature of, 147–48; convent of pleasure and, 148–51; imitating male literary academy, 147; nuns writing, 145; Serafina, Sor Juana and, 136–43; Sor Juana and, 127–79, 143–48, 151
La casa del placer honesto (Salas de Barbadillo), 148
Catalog of worthy women, 160–61
Catholic Church, 8; masculinist reform of, 5–6; women suppressed by, 1, 3, 7
Cavendish, Margaret, 145, 148–51, 217n42
Censorship theme, 163
Censuras, 153–57
Charity, 66
Chartier, Roger, 159
Chastity, 189n6; Fabián y Fuero undermining vow of, 106–7; silence as sign of, 102, 166; as source of empowerment, 4; vow of, 21, 28–32, 55, 66, 191n10
Chedgzoy, Kate, 162

Chivite, Manuel Ferrer, 29
Chocolate, 88–89, 206n25
Chowning, Margaret, 83, 85, 86, 204n7, 205n22, 209n55
Christ: bride of, 36–27, 38, 100, 194–95n34, 211n70; nuns as slaves to, 46–49
Chudleigh, Mary, 151
Citation, use of, 135
City of ladies, 89–92; inhabiting, 92–94; King not in favor of, 118; tearing down, 94–95
Clement of Rome, 7
Cloister, 19–20; female empowerment and, 9; to protect female religious, 2
Cohen, Sherrill, 19
Collective solitude, 37, 52
Community, 120–21, 190n17, 207n39; of collective solitude, 37, 52; defining, 12–13; disharmony in, 10; gaining strength through, 36; mobilization of, 177; perfect, 18; power in, 103–4
Compassionate authority, 116–17
Condesa de Paredes, 34, 130, 139, 143–45, 151–53, 155, 158, 168, 213n8, 217n40, 220n67
Confession, 77–80; withholding, 122–23
Confessor, 191n3, 203n55; lack of access to, 107; nun's relationship with, 32–33, 51–80, 107–8; of Sor María Josefa, 51–80
Control: of female body, 7; of men, 7–9; self-, 172; silencing tactics for, 11–12
Convent of Pleasure (Cavendish), 148–51
Convents, 6, 21–24, 190n1, 191n2; boarding school function of, 92–93; brothels compared to, 7, 26–27, 31, 193n20; chocolate consumption at, 88–89, 206n25; economic activity in, 93–94; education in, 9–10; friendships in, 52; Gage targeting, 81; inquiry into matters of, 117–20; intellectual solidarity in, 16;

mala amistad in, 51–80; male reforms of female, 83–84; men visiting, 28–32; prison similarities to, 12; race in, 10; reform of, 85–87; removing private spaces in, 93–94; Santa Inés, 120–24; space manipulation of, 35–36; as utopian feminist space, 10; violence in, 109–11, 208n52, 209n57; as voluntary communities, 120. *See also* Community

Council of Trent, 5, 46, 86, 99, 101, 109, 197n5; on vida común, 83–84

Cromwell, Oliver, 82

da Bergamo, Ilarione, 94
Davis, Natalie Zemon, 90
Death: /desire relationship, 42–43; female utopian space contrasting, 169; living, of nuns, 36–37, 38, 41–46, 48, 49, 125, 195n40
de Bucareli, Antonio, 104
De Mulieribus Claris (Boccacio), 160
Diccionario de Autoridades, 159
Dickens, Charles, 176–79
Dollimore, Jonathan, 179
Dopico-Black, Georgina, 42
Double monastery, 2, 3

Easton, Martha, 45–46
Empowerment, from chastity, 4
Enclosure, vow of, 21, 33–34, 191n10
Enigmas ofrecidos a la Casa del Placer (Enigmas Offered to the House of Pleasure), 16, 130, 147, 213n7, 217n41, 220n68; Cavendish work compared to, 149; as centerpiece of Casa del Placer, 145; described, 169–74; written as redondillas, 165–66
Eroticism, 46, 151–53
Eulalia del Sacramento, 122–23

Fabián y Fuero, Francisco de, 95–102

Factionalism, 35–36
Feliciana de Milão, 154–55
Female body, 42; control of, 7; dangers of, 60–61; enclosed garden likened to, 99; fear attached to, 58; importance of, 40–41; symbols of, 91–92; of utopia, 151–53
Female eloquence, and promiscuity, 166
Female imagination, power of, 166
Female network, communication and, 144
Female religious, 195n38; cloistering of, 2; confessor of, 32–33; cult of admiration for, 28; discord among, 11; patronage, writing and, 157; providing base for political mobilization, 126; restrictions of, 18–19
Female utopian space, 10, 162–64, 167; death and struggle contrasting, 169
Female virgin martyr, 45–46
Fernández de Santa Cruz, Manuel, 130–31
Figuration, 151
Finch, Anne, 151
Foucault, Michel, 12, 14, 69, 102, 103, 104, 190n12, 218n56
Francisca Xavier, 145, 151–52
Friedman, Marilyn, 120, 207n40
Friendships, 63–65, 192n12; difference male and female, 11, 142; female, in history, 58; harm of, 24–26; psychosexual fears of, 52; sensuality and, 65–67; Sigüenza warning against, 62. *See also* Same-sex relationships
Frye, Susan, 142

Gage, Thomas, 81, 87
Gender, 210n65; biases, 23, 34–35, 85–87; differences between monks and nuns, 3; religious reform and, 83–85; stereotypes in writing, 140; studies, 178; writing and, 133–34, 162
Gift-giving, 205n15; anti, 25–26
Giles, Mary E., 80

Glantz, Margo, 17, 24, 53, 153–54, 218n49, 219n60; on female body, 42; on nuns, 18; on *Segundo volumen*, 160; on Sor Juana, 141
Goddesses: muses, love of women and, 162–74; patrons compared to, 155, 157
Graub, Jerome, 70
Greek mythology, 165, 170
Greenleaf, Richard, 75
Grosz, Elizabeth, 91

Hartsock, Nancy, 102, 103, 207n38
Harvey, Elizabeth, 22, 133–34
Heterosexual love, 168–71, 174
Hodgkin, Katharine, 70
Holocausto, 23, 24
Homer, 164
Huizanga, Johan, 166
Hysteria, 68–70, 84, 197n7, 202n44, 202n50

Ibsen, Kristine, 11, 33, 44, 89, 195n42, 220n2
Inquisition case. *See* Mexican Inquisition
Intellectual solidarity: in convent, 16; importance of, 129, 136–43
Inundación castálida (Sor Juana), 143, 147

Johnson, Penelope, 8; on monastic life, 10
Jones, Ann Rosalind, 166
Jones, Kathleen B., 105, 109, 116
Juana Inés de la Cruz, 14, 16, 20, 34, 93; Casa del Placer and, 143–48, 151; depictions of life of, 142; female paradise description of, 164; nuns of Casa del Placer and, 127–79, 136–43, 218–19n57, 219n65; poems dedicated to, 151–52, 162; reply to Sister Filotea, 127; *Segundo volumen* of, 141, 147, 160; vocabulary of, 163

Ladrón de Guevara, Baltasar, 93
Landy, Francis, 39
La Santísma Trinidad, 104–26
Last Rites, nuns denied, 108
Lavrin, Asunción, 17, 27, 126
León, Fray Luis de, 38–39
Lesbianism. *See* Same-sex relationships
Lezamis, José de, 64
Licenças, 157–62
Literary academies, 147
López, Victoriano, 114
Love, 162–74, 170, 220n68; heterosexual, 168–71, 174; illusion of happiness and, 171; negative aspects of, 172–73
Luciani, Frederick, 128
Luxury, 88–89, 95

Mala amistad (illicit relationship), 15, 198n9, 199n18, 201n38; Aguiar y Seijas on, 65; in convents, 51–80
Maldonado y Paz, Doña Juana de, 82
Male body, city parallels with, 91, 205n18
Male religious, freedoms of, 18–19
Marcela de San Felipe Neri, 122
María Ana de la Encarnación, 88
María Antonia de Santo Domingo, 93
Maria das Saudades, 154–56
María de Ataide, 137
Maria de Guedes, 145, 157, 159–60
Maria do Céu, 145, 158
María Josefa Ildefonsa de San Juan Bautista, 181, 198n9; illness and discredit of, 71–74; investigation of, 53–55; letters concerning Tomás, 51–80; Patiño correspondence with, 182–88; retraction and humiliation, 67–71
Maria Magdalena, 145, 157
Mariana de Santo Antonio, 145, 151–52
Marina de la Cruz, 62
Martínez López, Enrique, 166, 216n32
Masculine power, vida común and, 95–102

Masculinist reform, 5–6
Matriarchial power, battle of, 96
McNamara, Jo Ann, 5, 189n1, 190n14
Melancholy, 70, 202n46
Men: control of women by, 7–9; convents visited by, 28–32; nuns inaccessibility and, 29; vida común and, 95–102
Merrim, Stephanie, 135, 146, 212n3, 217n42, 219n66; on love, 167–68; on technique of catalog of worthy women, 160–61
Mexican Inquisition, vii, 15, 20, 51–57, 67–80, 75, 176, 181, 198n12, 200n34, 205n17
Mignolo, Walter, 146
Misogyny, 134–36
Monastery, double, 2, 3
Monks, 3; homosexual relationships of, 57; nuns visited by, 81–82. *See also* Male religious, freedoms of
Moraña, Mabel, 19, 76, 77, 134
Mortal sins, 34–36
Mortification, 11, 41, 44, 128, 177, 195n43
Mother-daughter bond, 62
Mother Superior, 48, 95–96, 98, 208n44, 211n76
Muñoz, Pedro, 30, 193n22
Muses: in poetry, 165; women and, 162–74
The Mystery of Edwin Drood (Dickens), 177

Nancy, Jean-Luc, 13, 120–21
Nava-Lasa, Luis Sierra, 88, 92, 93, 203n2, 205n20
New World city of ladies. *See* City of ladies
Nicholas Nickleby (Dickens), 176
Nuestra Señora de la Concepción, 6
Núñez de Haro, Alonso, 117
Núñez de Miranda, Antonio, 12, 15, 20, 52, 65, 87, 107, 127, 178, 215n20; *Cartilla de la doctrina religiosa* of, 17–50; convent life vision of, 21–24; gender roles and, 23, 34–35; on mortal sins, 34–36; on nuns as Christ's slave, 46–49; nun's body to, 41–46; on nun's primary obligation, 36–37; *Plática doctrinal* of, 17–50; on vow of chastity, 28–32; on vow of enclosure, 33–34; on vow of obedience, 32–33; on vow of poverty, 24–27
Nuns, 3, 18, 194n32; accusing bishops group, 113–14; adornment of, 27; bishop undermined by, 105; body of, sexualized, 30–31; calzada, 203n2; of Casa del Placer, 127–29, 136–43, 218–19n57, 219n65; Casa del Placer writing, 145; as Christ's slave, 46–49; confessor relationships with, 32–33, 51–80, 107–8; denied Last Rites, 108; devotions between, 200n31; with dowry, 93; fight against vida común, 81–126; four vows of, 21; imprisoning disobedient, 112; of La Santísma Trinidad, 104–17; living death of, 36–37, 38, 41–46, 48, 49, 125, 195n40; men drawn to inaccessibility of, 29; monks visiting, 81–82; Núñez on, 21–24, 41–46; obligations of, 36–37; parental role to servants, 111; prostitutes associated with, 7, 26–27, 31, 193n20; as scapegoats, 87; as seducers, 28–29; servant relationships with, 65–66, 92, 94; silencing tactics to control, 11–12; sleeping together forbidden, 56; society elite as, 89; writing, 129, 145, 147, 157. *See also* Convents; Female religious
The Nuns (Bernstein), 67

Obedience, vow of, 21, 32–33, 44, 191n10
Oficio divino, 34
Oliver Twist (Dickens), 176
Ortiz, Antonio Domínguez, 84
Oviedo, Juan de, 22

Paraíso Occidental (de Sigüenza y Góngora), 60–64
Passion, 173–74, 202n45
Passive enclosure, 189n8
Patiño, Pedro, 51–80, 181; Sor María Josefa correspondence with, 182–88
Patrons, 158; goddesses compared to, 155, 157
Paz, Octavio, 27, 82, 93, 127, 130, 192n18, 220n1; on nuns' visits from men, 28–29
Perelmuter, Rosa, 128
Periculoso (Boniface VIII), 3, 5, 8, 190n9
Peter of Abelard, 2
Petroff, Elizabeth, 46
Phelan, Shane, 12–13
The Pickwick Papers (Dickens), 179
Pisan, Christine de, 89–91, 135
Plática doctrinal, 17–50
Play, concept of, 166
The Pleasure of the Text (Barthes), 153
Poetry, 151, 217n43; dedicated to Sor Juana, 151–52, 162; female, 151–53; love in, 167–68; muses in, 165; of nuns, 129, 147; on same-sex relationships, 168
Poverty, 100; from vida común, 115; vow of, 21, 24–27, 87, 191n10, 192n13, 204n6, 212n84
Power, 35, 96, 103–4, 164; from chastity, 4; danger of women in, 3; of female imagination, 166; hierarchy of, 113; as idea, 142–43; masculine, 95–102; violence and, 103–4, 111, 112, 207n38; of written word, 146
Prostitutes, nuns associated with, 7, 26–27, 31, 193n20
Puccini, Dario, 127
Purity: eroticism of, 46; women as guardians of, 4
Purkiss, Diane, 135, 214n19

Race, convent issues of, 10

Raymond, Janice, 27, 66, 175, 198n10, 207n40; on friendships, 63–64
Reading, 159–60
Real Cédula, 117–20, 200n32
Respuesta a Sor Filotea de la Cruz, 127–28, 130
Rhetoric of marginality, 134–36
Ring, symbol of, 47–48
Robertson, Karen, 142
Rodríguez, María Gertrudis, 53, 65, 67, 71, 73, 74, 80, 181, 197n6
Romance, 163–64
A Room of One's Own (Woolf), 129
Ross, Kathleen, 100, 213n6
Rubial, Antonio, 18–19, 190n13

Sabat Rivers, Georgina, 166, 220n68
Salas de Barbadillo, Alonso Jerónimo de, 148
Same-sex relationships, 55–57, 79–80, 197n3, 198n11, 198n13, 202n43; poetry of, 168
Sampson Vera Tudela, Elisa, 6, 17, 190n11
Sánchez, José, 147, 148, 216n37
Sánchez de Tagle, Esteban, 87, 204n12
Santa Inés, 120–24
Santísma Trinidad. *See* La Santísma Trinidad
Scarry, Elaine, 164
Schlau, Stacey, 128–29
Scott, Joan, 14
Secret society, 166
Segundo volumen (Juana Inés de la Cruz), 141, 147, 160
Self-censorship, 160
Self-mortification, 11, 41, 44, 128, 177, 195n43
Serafina de Cristo, 127–79, 213n7, 214n19; comparing Sor Juana with Camilla, 138; on dueling texts issues, 139; letter of, 16, 130–32; Sor Juana, nuns of Casa del Placer and, 136–43

Servants, 92, 94, 115, 118, 200n32, 201n36, 206n29, 209n53; expulsion of, 110; nuns' relationships with, 65–66, 92, 94
Sharp, Ronald, 25
Sigüenza y Góngora, Carlos de, 58, 60–64, 82, 100–101, 178
Silence, 102, 166
Simoa de Castilla, 145, 151–52
Siren, from Greek mythology, 170
Sodomy, 56–57, 198n12
Solitude, 194–95n34, 212n3; collective, 37, 52; necessary, 38; over solidarity, 175; worth of, 11
Song of Songs, 38–39
Stallybrass, Peter, 101

Tálamo, symbol of marriage bed, 46
A Tale of Two Cities (Dickens), 177
Tenorio, Lilia, 132, 137, 214n16, 215n25, 216n27
Teresa of Ávila, 9, 24, 38–39, 58–60
Trabulse, Elías, 131, 132, 215n19
Traub, Valerie, 43, 49; on women's same-sex relationships, 57
Tyranny, 103

Unworthiness theme, 163–64
Utopia, 162; convents space as, 10; death contrasting female space of, 169; female body, 151–53; female space as, 10, 162–64

Vallejo, Augusto, 132
Veil, symbol of, 47, 196n47
Ventriloquized Voices: Feminist Theory and English Renaissance Texts (Harvey), 22
Vida común (common life), 15–16, 93, 115, 203n1, 209n55, 212n84; city of ladies, 89–92; convents and bourbon reform, 85–87; fight against, 81–126, 102–4; gender and religious reform, 83–85; gendering luxury, 88–89; King enforcing, 118–19; masculine power exercised, 95–102; new novices accepting, 125–26; nuns of La Santísma Trinidad, 104–17; Santa Inés and, 120; vida particular opposite of, 96
Vida particular, 92; Santa Inés, 120; vida común opposite of, 96
Vieira, Antonio, 130, 137
Violence, 10, 85, 109–11, 119, 208n45, 208n50, 208n52, 209n57; power and, 103–4, 111, 112, 207n38
Virgil, 137, 138
Virgin Mary, 100
Virtual female literary academy, 144–45
Vows. *See* Nuns; *specific vows*

Wayne, Valerie, 133, 138–39
Weber, Allison, 59–60
Whore of Babylon, 26, 27, 31
Wilmot, Edward Sloane, 88
Women: Aguiar y Seijas on friendships of, 64–65; Amazon, 138–39, 215n25; Boniface VIII decree influencing, 5; Catholic Church attitude towards, 1, 5–6; challenging ecclesiastic authorities, 13; dangers of power of, 3; education of, in convents, 9–10; as guardians of purity, 4; love of, muses, goddesses and, 162–74; men controlling, 7–9; Núñez on inferior brainpower of, 35; prejudice against, 11; singularity of religious, 2; voice of, 104; writing of, 128–79, 161, 167. *See also* Female religious; Nuns
Woolf, Virginia, 129
Writing, 217n39, 219n66; eroticism in, 151–53; gender and, 133–34, 140, 162; nuns, patronage and, 145, 157; with patriarchy's tools, 146; patriarchy's tools for, 167; as political solidarity, 153–62; pro-female, 135–36; strategies of, 134–36; women and, 128–79, 161, 167. *See also* Poetry

Stephanie Kirk is professor of Spanish at Washington University in St. Louis and the editor of the journal *Revista de Estudios Hispánicos*. She is the author of *Sor Juana Inés de la Cruz and the Gender Politics of Knowledge in Colonial Mexico*.

www.ingramcontent.com/pod-product-compliance
Lightning Source LLC
Chambersburg PA
CBHW031434160426
43195CB00010BB/723